SOCIAL CLASS IN
AMERICAN PROTESTANTISM

Social Class
in
American Protestantism

N. J. Demerath III

**Department of Sociology
UNIVERSITY OF WISCONSIN**

**A Publication from the Research Program in
the Sociology of Religion, Survey Research
Center, University of California, Berkeley**

Rand McNally & Company · Chicago

RAND MᶜNALLY
SOCIOLOGY SERIES
Edgar F. Borgatta, Advisory Editor

ALFORD, *Party and Society*
CHRISTENSEN, ED., *Handbook of Marriage and the Family*
DEMERATH, *Social Class in American Protestantism*
FARIS, ED., *Handbook of Modern Sociology*
MARCH, ED., *Handbook of Organizations*
NYE AND HOFFMAN, *The Employed Mother in America*
WARREN, *The Community in America*

to my Father

colleague and confidant,
who can always say
he warned me

Foreword

A common element in all disciplines which are or aspire to be scientific is a commitment, virtually "sacred" in character, to theory and research. Scientific progress, it is claimed, can only be achieved on the foundation of sound and insightful theory, tested, refined, and informed by well designed and carefully executed research. Abstractly stated, such truisms receive universal acclamation and support and no one even deigns to question their validity. Consensus at this abstract level, however, masks in most disciplines considerable disagreement as to what constitutes sound theory and research. Moreover, the idea that the two ought to be effectively interrelated is open to different interpretations as well.

Speaking specifically of sociology, the achievement of consensus on these issues seems particularly distant. What is one man's meat—in the area of theory—is another's poison. Similarly, research praised by some is almost inevitably damned by others. The relative lack of consensus is a sign of sociology's youth as a discipline. There has not been the time nor the experience to develop standards on which all can agree. Youth can also be blamed perhaps for the discipline's failure so far to develop the kind of rigor in theory construction and research so necessary for the evolution of consensus about what constitutes quality.

The general point is perhaps best illustrated by weaknesses both in conceptualization and in the way that concepts are operationalized for purposes of research. It has often been commented upon that sociology faces a more difficult task than, say, chemistry because the phenomena to be investigated and understood are infinitely more variate and complex. Yet, more often than not, the conceptual formulations of sociology would suggest just the opposite. The very strong propensity for sociological conceptualizations to be unidimensional—Gemeinschaft-Gesellschaft, church-sect, upper, middle, lower class, for example—scarcely documents the complexity hypothesis. The fault, it is suspected, lies not with the hypothesis but with the continuing commitment in sociology to arm-chair theorizing, with the too frequent failure to put into practice the principle that research ought to be closely related to theory, and, most importantly perhaps, with still unsolved methodological difficulties as to how to deal effectively with dependent variables of a multi-dimensional or polytomous kind.

Different readers will find themselves informed in different ways by Professor Demerath's book. Certainly, his work significantly illuminates our understanding of the relationship between social class and religion, and, on this score alone, it represents an important contribution to the literature. In addition to its substantive worth, however, the book demonstrates what can be done when a sociologist takes seriously the need to confront theory with research and to question the acceptability of the unidimensional conceptualizations, unidimensionally operationalized, with which the discipline has long been content. The belief that people can be meaningfully distinguished as being simply more or less religious or that single indicators such as frequency of church attendance are adequate to measure the phenomenon of religiosity has been the rule rather than the exception in research on religion. Similarly, research on social class has been dominated by unidimensional conceptualizations of that phenomenon. Professor Demerath has perhaps not said the last word on how religiosity and social class ought to be conceptualized. He has, however, demonstrated the power of more sophisticated and complex conceptualizations to inform our understanding of social behavior. In so doing, he has contributed to the evolution of the kind of rigor in sociological research to which we all might profitably aspire. It seems important, therefore, that his book be read from this perspective, as well as from the perspective of what it has to say about social class and religion per se.

CHARLES Y. GLOCK
Survey Research Center
University of California, Berkeley

Acknowledgments

In more than the usual sense this study has been a profound learning experience. Originally a doctoral dissertation, it received closer and more conscientious attention than most. The bulk of this attention was from Charles Y. Glock, Director of the Survey Research Center at the University of California, Berkeley. His thorough supervision of the manuscript took long hours and resulted in a whirl of ball-point blue. A survey researcher who puts the lie to rank empiricism, he ferreted out conceptual ambiguities, methodological inadequacies, and numerous problems of prose style.

Nor was Professor Glock alone helpful among the Berkeley faculty. Hanan Selvin and Gertrude Jaeger Selznick had solutions to many editorial conundrums in the manuscript. M. Brewster Smith, S. M. Lipset, David Matza, and Alan Wilson all lent constructive advice after careful readings.

The study has also benefited from the reactions of non-Berkeleyites. Phillip Hammond, Elton Jackson, Benton Johnson, Joseph Kahl, Walter Kloetzli, Gerhard Lenski, and Kenneth Lutterman read earlier drafts and responded in detail. Reverend Kloetzli, Secretary of Urban Church Planning in the Division of American Missions of the National Lutheran Council, also provided much of the data and some important funds from his own Russell Sage grant. Other funds came from a two-year intermediate research training grant from the National Institute of Mental Health.

In the most recent stages my colleagues at the University of Wisconsin have been uncommonly cheering and helpful. Gerald Marwell has been especially obliging. He was rarely too busy to come next door and serve as a mock audience on the spur of the moment.

Finally, my family has been of inestimable value. Although I am a second-generation sociologist, my father has been a model of restraint, offering support but never prodding. Last, but by all means most, I owe deepest appreciation to my wife and son. Judy was a beguiling critic, an indefatigable editor, and a constant guard against discouragement. Loren came at precisely the right time, and his triumphs of walking and talking more than compensated for my own defeats. Where these defeats have gone unrectified, I am alone to blame.

N.J.D.

Madison, Wisconsin

December, 1963

Table of Contents

PART FOUR

List of Tables

Introduction

If consistency is the "hobgoblin of little minds," the student of American religion need not fear the bogy. Raise almost any issue, and two documented but conflicting sides jump to attention. Is there a religious revival underway? The answer may be "yes" if one looks at church membership, church attendance, and church finances; the answer may be "no" if one examines the influence of religion in everyday life and listens to clergymen deplore religion's growing compromise with society. Or how religious are we when compared to the rest of the world? Church-going figures indicate that Americans are among the world's most active religious participants; if one looks at the influence of religion on politics and everyday life, it may be that Americans are also among the world's most hypocritical. Finally, is American religion the "opiate of the masses" catering to the lower classes, or is it the lair of the middle and upper classes? Here too there is conflicting evidence. There are many ways in which a person may be involved in religion and the church. An inspection of one type of involvement suggests that the middle and upper classes are more religious; an inspection of another type of involvement suggests that the lower classes are more committed.

All of these issues are prods to research. Yet their sum is too much to handle in one limited project and one small volume. This study is concerned only with the last of the three issues: how does a person's social status affect his religion? This may have ramifications for a putative revival (revival may have occurred within one class but not within another); it should also be important for comparisons with other societies (our upper classes may be the most religious while our lower classes may be the least or *vice versa*). But the relation between social class and religion is urgent in its own right. It confronts an overarching and perhaps germinal problem in the sociology of religion, namely, the function that religion serves in society.

Theories here have differed. At one extreme, those who see religion as the opiate of the masses see its significance as an illusory escape from the troubles of the ''real'' world. At the other extreme, it is argued that religion is important in supporting the main values of society and is indispensable not as an escape but as a source of social integration. As distinct as these two approaches are, their proponents have one thing in common. Both tend to assume that religion serves one, and only one, function in society. Both view the opposing theories and contrasting functions as incompatible.

But might not religion perform both types of functions simultaneously? After all, societies are not seamless wholes with every group and member like every other. Societies are made up of different groups and different members. This makes it possible that religion will serve different functions for various segments of society, depending upon the needs of each.

All of this is especially the case in so-called complex societies like the United States. One of the major sources of differences in a complex society is its stratification system. Terms like ''upper class,'' ''middle class,'' ''working class,'' and ''lower class,'' are not idle classifications or vestiges from a bygone era. They connote different styles of life, different values, different aspirations, different associations, and, presumably, different religious needs. Those of low status may very well be discomforted by the secular society that accords their rank. Religion may indeed provide an escape through an alternative orientation that offers a more favorable self-judgment. They may be disenfranchised failures in the eyes of the workaday society; but they are redeemed in the eyes of their Lord and promised a utopia after death. On the other hand, consider those of high status. These people are adjusted to secular society. They may seek a religion that reinforces their secular values and life styles. The religion may not be otherworldly, escapist, or even traditional. Instead, it may complement a primary allegiance to this-worldly rationality, competition, and productivity.

The difference between lower-class and upper-class religion has, of course, been observed before. It is a commonplace for studies of communities to note a distinction between a town's high-status "churches" and its low-status "sects." The former may be elegant buildings on expensive lots in exclusive areas. The latter are often converted stores that are ramshackle and slum-surrounded. From this point of view, the different forms of religion occupy separate and unequal facilities. The two principal functions coexist amicably at a distance.

But the situation is not always so pat. Even a quick glance at the membership of the major American faiths reveals a surprising status heterogeneity within the "churches" themselves. Episcopalians are frequently lower class; Baptists include many from the upper classes. Different forms of religion may be unequal without being separate. The typical Protestant denomination and even its local parishes may harbor both high- and low-status parishioners and serve both types of religious needs.

This has important implications for the study of religous involvement. If different social classes do not always occupy different religious groups, one has to look more closely at how they differ within the same groups. One type of difference is a gradation in the *degree* of involvement in the church. The upper and middle classes may attend church services more frequently and belong to more parish activities. The lower classes may be less involved in both respects. But classes may also differ in the *kind* of involvement they value. If one concludes that the lower classes are irreligious on the basis of their irregular Sunday attendance and neglect of parish activities, one may sadly miss the point. It is possible that church services and activities are unimportant for the low-status parishioners who may prefer private devotion without ritual. Both kinds of involvement demand inspection before one can make any judgments on religious involvement as a whole. It is by stressing different aspects of the same church's program that different classes may share the house but derive different benefits from it.

If this is the case, what are the consequences for the church as an organization? The conventional image of the church is an institution with status homogeneity where the brethren bring common needs and find common causes. It may be, however, that the brethren are more dissimilar and effect a certain friction within the church through their competing demands, expectations, and capacities. In the short run, this friction may be an organizational liability. It can produce undercurrents of antagonism; it may even lead to dissolution, as splinter groups establish more comfortable religious niches of their own. In the long run, however, the coexisting elements may be an asset. High- and low-status parishioners may provide a division of labor where each supplies something that the other cannot, but where the contributions of both are necessary. One group may supply organizational management and an important link with the secular context to which every church must adapt. The other group may buttress the church's distinctive and traditional religious identity; its members may prevent the church from becoming altogether secularized.

In short, the problems of differential religious involvement and its relation to social class are more than empirical exercises. They bear on some of the major issues in the sociological theory of religion. They carry implications at three levels: for the individual adherent, for the church as an organization, and for religion in American society generally. If these issues are not stated throughout, they are implicit, and they will be reintroduced in the concluding chapter.

Still, the study is not exclusively concerned with religion. It is true that religion is its dominant interest and focal point. Yet there are two other areas in which the study may also be relevant. First, different kinds and degrees of individual involvement affect other organizations as well as churches. It is possible that many organizations harbor coexisting types of commitment with a distinction in short-run and long-run consequences. An analysis of Protestantism may help to raise questions for the analysis of other groups, whether universities, trade unions, the military, or even the family. The church may be theologically distinct, but it is sociologically comparable with any other organization or institution. Indeed, if one distinguishes between religion on the one hand, and the church on the other, it can be argued that the church is only one among many organizations that may serve religious functions. As these functions are sociologically defined, they involve the reinforcement of values, the interpretation of events, and an integration of the individual with his fellows. A church may provide these for some people, but a business firm may do so for others. The concluding chapter will examine this question in more detail.

A second added interest of the study is stratification. So far I have referred merely to gross distinctions between the upper-, middle-, and lower-status groups. Needless to say, the matter is more complex. It makes a difference how one measures such distinctions. The most conventional technique—and the one which will be most central in the analysis to follow—is to examine a person's *objective* rank by inspecting his income, education, and occupational prestige. But it is also possible to ask the respondent where he would rank himself. Often the objective and the *subjective* are revealingly at odds. Even factors such as age and sex carry status connotations. They may have independent relations with religion, and they may also affect or mediate the influence of status per se. Moreover, stratification may refer to collectivities as well as to individuals. Whole denominations may be ranged along a status scale; so may the separate parishes within any single denomination. Not only are our affiliations the result of our status, but our affiliations also filter the further effects of that status.

Yet a person's status may be painfully ambiguous. He may rank high on income, moderate in occupational prestige, and low in education. This poses problems: which standards should he follow? what groups should he join? which friends may he choose to keep up with? and what should his aspirations be? A technical label for this quandary is "status discrepancy." A new concept with a short research history, it has already been related to political radicalism, psychosomatic symptoms, and withdrawal from secular affiliations. Although it has not yet been related to religious involvement, the area is worth exploring and will command two chapters on its own. Just as a traditional church may offer a more rewarding orientation for those of low status, it may offer a more consistent orientation for those with high status discrepancy.

One consequence of the focus on stratification deserves comment. Stratification in its myriad dimensions is far from the only influence on a person's religious involvement. Factors such as family life, religious background, the clergyman's personality, as family life, religious background, the clergyman's personality, personal emergencies, and the attitudes of the community are also important. It is doubtful whether a complete list of influences could be enumerated, much less investigated. Rather than attempt such extensiveness, I have decided to explore the effect of only one factor in some detail. The study has no hope or pretension of accounting for all of the variance in religious involvement. However, it does seek to illumine one part of the variance and one that has a special theoretical significance extending beyond religion itself.

And now a word about the data and the methods. The kind of analysis attempted here is part of a growing tendency to apply survey research toward the understanding of organizations. Recent studies of universities, high schools, trade unions, hospitals, political groups, governmental agencies, and business firms have all sought to examine institutional characteristics through the attitudes and behaviors of participants. Here the institution is American Protestantism and the data come from members of five major denominations.

In 1957 the National Council of Churches of Christ in the U.S.A. began an analysis of the ''Effective City Church.'' Its aim was to assess the role of the church in helping its adherents adjust to urban change. To this end, the Council's affiliated denominations cooperated by sending questionnaires to the parishioners of selected congregations in strategically chosen urban areas. The present study is narrowed to the problem of social status and religious involvement. It uses the ample information collected on these topics from Congregationalists, Disciples of Christ, Presbyterians, Baptists, and Lutherans. I should note that no southern parishes are represented. The Baptists are representatives of the American Baptist Convention, a northern and western wing of the group. The Lutherans are from the National Lutheran Council and do not include members of either of the more conservative Missouri and Wisconsin synods. Finally, the Congregationalists predate the merger of the Congregational and Evangelical and Reformed churches.

In general, the methods of the study are within the accepted traditions of survey research. However, two aspects deserve brief attention. First, the study does not use statistical tests of significance for its findings. This is partly because the respondents do not comprise a completely random probability sample. It is also because a sample of this size virtually guarantees significance for even percentage differences as small as 3 per cent. Finally, it is also the result of my conviction that statistical tests are often misleading. Without impugning the test itself, its interpretations may be risky. They may lead to a hasty acceptance of possibly spurious findings, especially where the sample is as large as the present one. On the other hand, they may contribute to a premature rejection of relationships, especially when a factor is simply one among many that may have influenced the phenomenon at issue and where its influence may therefore be small in magnitude though large in theoretical import. But this is not to say that the conclusions will rest on assertions alone. Two other criteria are crucial. One is *empirical consistency:* the degree to which a hypothesis is verified by slightly different variables in slightly different contexts or with other factors "held constant." The other is *theoretical credibility:* the extent to which the findings have been predicted in advance and make sense within the suppositions of the study. This is not to rule out serendipity or the possibility of errors in the theory and the hypotheses. It is simply to guard against a patchwork of findings that are justified after the fact and often inconsistently.

A second peculiarity of the method concerns the inclusion of five denominations that differ in church history, organizational structure, theology, and over-all status composition. The primary strategy is a case-study technique of analyzing one denomination in depth and then referring to the remaining four more briefly for corroboration and elaboration. I have chosen the Lutherans for the more detailed inspection. They stand in the middle of the five denominations in the degree of liberalism of their theology and in the status composition of their membership. They offer a middle ground for developing the thesis, while the remaining denominations provide extreme tests of its applicability to Protestantism generally. The only section of the study that departs from this design is the inspection of status discrepancy. Because this analysis is more complex and demands more cases with which to work, I begin by pooling all of the denominations, though later I look at each separately as well. In all of this the reader may hold the study suspect for talking of American

Protestantism while considering only five major denominations and neglecting the fringe sects. The book's title is admittedly hyperbolic. At the same time, the study will allude to the already considerable literature on the sects at various points. In fact, the sects have commanded inordinate attention from sociology, although they account for less than 10 per cent of American religious affiliations. As religious exotics, they have seduced a good deal of interest away from the religious mainstream, and the present study can be seen ironically as an attempt to restore perspective.

Finally, then, the structure of the study divides into four major parts. *Part One* examines previous findings on social class and religious involvement. Chapter I gives detailed consideration to the inconsistency noted earlier, in the initial paragraph of the Introduction. Chapter II attempts to resolve the inconsistency and develop a theory to guide the research to follow. *Part Two* delves into the research itself. Chapter III inspects the available measures of religious involvement, places them in the theoretical framework, and emerges with two general indexes of involvement in which contrasting relations to status are hypothesized. Chapter IV builds an Index of Objective Status and tests the hypotheses with variations in terms of subjective class, age, and sex. Chapter V takes up the context of the individual's religious involvement. It examines parishes of different status among the Lutherans and looks at all four of the remaining denominations. *Part Three* turns from conventional stratification to status discrepancy. Since it is more technical than the preceding, and is a rare instance of the publication of null findings, it may appeal only to the more methodologically inclined. In any event, Chapter VI gives a brief history of the concept of discrepancy, hypothesizes its relation to religion, and performs a preliminary test of the hypothesis. Chapter VII is more skeptical and more thorough. It pursues alternative explanations of the seeming influence of discrepancy. The pursuit is more successful than the theory and hypotheses would warrant. In conclusion, *Part Four* ponders all of the empirical results of the study with an eye to broader issues and future research. It asks for the implications of the church's role in society, of the study of organizational involvement in general, and of the over-all relation between stratification and involvement in various types of organizations.

Part One

I

Social Class and Religious Involvement in Previous Research

Two hallmarks of American religion are its susceptibility to non-religious factors and its resulting variety. In the absence of any state church, religion is particularly vulnerable to influences such as social class. This has been a central theme in observations of American society since the beginning of the nineteenth century. In 1832, Alexis de Tocqueville[1] commented that the denominational competition in American religion lent it a unique vitality. Only a few years later, Harriet Martineau[2] witnessed the same competition but saw it as contributing more hypocrisy than vitality, and she pointed an especially accusing finger at an unscrupulously tyrannical clergy. Contemporary observers have also agreed on the perception of diversity while disagreeing over its effects. On the one hand, Talcott Parsons[3] has urged that denominationalism provides an adaptable religious system to meet the needs of a variegated society. On the other hand,

[1] Alexis de Tocqueville, *Democracy in America* (New York: Vintage Books, 1954), Vol. II.

[2] Harriet Martineau, *Society in America*, ed. S. M. Lipset (Garden City, N.Y.: Doubleday Anchor Books, 1962), especially pp. 332–55.

[3] Talcott Parsons, *Structure and Process in Modern Societies* (Glencoe, Ill.: The Free Press, 1960), Ch. X.

1

H. Richard Niebuhr[4] deplored denominationalism as a fragmentation of the true religious spirit.

While denominationalism is not our concern, it reflects the influence of social class, and this is very much to the point. It is no secret that class has had more than passing effect on American religion. Not only is this a theme among foreign journalists, social theorists, and theologians, but it has also commanded the attention of empirical analysts. By now, it is almost

TABLE I-1
Social Class Profiles of American Religious Groups

Denomination	Upper	Class Middle	Lower	N
Christian Scientist	24.8%	36.5%	38.7%	(137)
Episcopal	24.1	33.7	42.2	(590)
Congregational	23.9	42.6	33.5	(376)
Presbyterian	21.9	40.0	38.1	(961)
Jewish	21.8	32.0	46.2	(537)
Reformed	19.1	31.3	49.6	(131)
Methodist	12.7	35.6	51.7	(2100)
Lutheran	10.9	36.1	53.0	(723)
Christian	10.0	35.4	54.6	(370)
Protestant (small bodies)	10.0	27.3	62.7	(888)
Roman Catholic	8.7	24.7	66.6	(2390)
Baptist	8.0	24.0	68.0	(1381)
Mormon	5.1	28.6	66.3	(175)
No preference	13.3	26.0	60.7	(466)
Protestant (undesignated)	12.4	24.1	63.5	(460)
Atheist, Agnostic	33.3	46.7	20.0	(15)
No Answer or Don't Know	11.0	29.5	59.5	(319)

From Herbert Schneider, *Religion in 20th Century America* (Cambridge, Mass.: Harvard University Press, 1952), Appendix, p. 228.

de rigueur, and certainly a commonplace, to begin studies of American religious variation with a table showing the relation between social class and denominational affiliation. This study is no different, and Table I-1 is drawn from data that originally appeared in the National Council of Churches' Information Service.

Based on a national sample, the table orders the major United

[4] H. Richard Niebuhr, *The Social Sources of Denominationalism* (New York: Henry Holt & Company, 1929).

States religious groups by decreasing status. At the high-status extreme, nearly one-fourth of the Christian Scientists, Episcopalians, and Congregationalists are from the upper class; fewer than one-half are from the lower class. At the other end, fewer than one-tenth of the Roman Catholics, Baptists, and Mormons are from the upper class; roughly two-thirds are from the lower class.

Although the particulars of the relationship will vary over time and between different areas of the country,[5] Table I–1 is generally representative of myriad studies of local communities as well as of large national samples. There are, however, two important caveats which bear upon the present study. First, even though denominations can be ranked by status, there is no justification for converting relative rankings into absolute categorizations. Episcopalians may be *relatively* upper class, but more than 40 per cent are from the lower class. Baptists may be *relatively* lower class, but they claim their Rockefellers as well. Status heterogeneity within denominations is crucial in this study, for it is less concerned with gross differences among groups and more concerned with the subtler distinctions within them.

A second qualification concerns the difference between religious preference and religious involvement. These are not identical, and it is possible that their relations to social class may be dissimilar. Thus, lower-class Episcopalians may be more religiously involved than their more heralded upper-class co-members. At the same time, although the Baptists are generally lower class, the upper-class adherents may control the church organization.

---

[5] Temporal variation in status composition is a theme as old as the sociology of religion itself. Religious groups frequently begin as lower-class splinter movements, but undergo upward mobility in the quest for stability and community influence. As one example of geographical variation, note the contrast between the lower-class Methodism of Warner's Catholic-dominated Yankee City (Newburyport, Massachusetts) and the middle-class Methodism in the South. In fact, a number of southern Methodists are concerned about their "exclusiveness" as a high-status church. While they may be guilty of a bit of status up-grading, a meeting of Methodists in Richmond, Virginia, recently recommended increased attention toward the lower classes. "Methodists Told Church in Danger of 'Class' Label," *Richmond Times-Dispatch,* July 14, 1960.

But if research on actual religious involvement is more important for our purposes, it is also less common and less precise compared to studies of class and religious preference. Perhaps because of its relative sparseness, its neglect of denominational distinctions, its oversight of the differences between various kinds of involvement, and its general quality as a research "aside," research on involvement has harbored an unexposed contradiction. The majority of studies find those of high status (middle and upper class) more religiously involved. Yet an important minority report that those of low status (working and lower class) are more involved. The task of this chapter is to present a critical review of both sides of the contradiction. In the next chapter, I will present a theoretical rapprochement that will also serve as a framework for the research to follow.

The Case for High-Status Religiosity

American religion, especially Protestantism, has been widely held to be an activity of the middle and upper classes. The argument rests principally on three indicators of involvement: church membership, attendance at church services, and participation in the church's formal activities. On each of these measures, persons of high status appear to be more deeply involved than those of low status.

Before moving to the actual studies, two comments are appropriate. First, although the empirical relations are relatively unambiguous, their meaning is open to question. Throughout I will try to show that the three measures do not exhaust, nor always illuminate, the concept of religious involvement. Rather than stop short at the data themselves, I will try to probe beneath them.

A second comment concerns my use of the term "high status" to refer to the combined middle and upper classes. This is partly a reflection of the chapter's principal concern with the latent debate between those who see the greatest involvement among the middle and upper classes and those who see it among the working and lower classes. More important, however, is another conflict within the former camp alone. While all of the studies in this section agree that those of high status are more involved than those of low, they disagree on the relative involvement of the middle and upper classes themselves. Some have described a *linear* relation where involvement increases consistently with increasing status so that the lowest class is the least involved and the upper class is the most. Others, however, have reported a *curvilinear* pattern. Here there is a slight drop-off in involvement among the upper class, and the middle class is most involved, though both high-status groups are more committed than those of low status. This is a minor but persistent inconsistency that I will deal with in the conclusion of this section. Until then I will note its occurrence but stress the larger difference between the high- and low-status groups over all.

Religious identification. It was not until the 1930's that social scientists began to examine variations in religious involvement or religiosity[6] empirically. Because information on church preference and membership was easily available from questionnaire surveys and from the churches themselves, this was one of the first measures explored. Because social class had already proved a potent explanatory factor, it was one of the first correlates examined.

Hadley Cantril,[7] a pioneer of the national poll, used data similar to those in Table I–1. Pooling four surveys from the Office of Public Opinion Research and Gallup's American Institute of Public Opinion, he went beyond the question of informal religious preference and investigated the more formal issue of actual membership. Cantril was especially concerned with the class differences between Protestants and Catholics. He divided the aggregate sample into three categories: Protestant church members, Catholic church members, and non-members. Needless to say, he found that Protestant members had generally higher status, though the difference was not large in the South where Protestant fundamentalism is strong among the lower classes.

[6] The term "religiosity" is a convenient shorthand for the phrase "religious involvement." The usage here, however, should not be confused with Harold Laski's where it is used to suggest hypocritical, self-centered religion at odds with the "pure" religious motive.

[7] Hadley Cantril, "Educational and Economic Composition of Religious Groups," *American Journal of Sociology*, XLVIII (1943), 574–79. Much of the same data is taken to similar conclusions in Liston Pope, "Religion and the Class Structure," in Reinhard Bendix and S. M. Lipset (eds.), *Class, Status and Power* (Glencoe, Ill.: The Free Press, 1953), pp. 316–23.

But the more important finding for our purposes concerns the non-members. Membership per se was not Cantril's focus; hence he lumped Jews into the non-member category. Yet, despite the high status of Jews generally, the non-members were still lower in status than the Protestant and Catholic members combined. In other words there was a generally positive or direct relation between membership and social class. Although the extreme upper class had a slightly lower rate of membership than the middle class, the two high-status groups combined had a higher rate than the lower classes. The finding, while curvilinear, gave early support to the larger pattern of high-status religious involvement.

Subsequent support is available from the so-called community studies with which empirical sociology cut its teeth in the late thirties and forties. Lloyd Warner's[8] Yankee City series and Robert and Helen Lynd's[9] celebrated study of Middletown confirmed the pattern described by Cantril. Although the upper classes were slightly less frequent church members than the middle classes, both had higher rates of membership than the lower classes.

Studies of other communities give still more support. Louis Bultena's[10] analysis of Madison, Wisconsin, James West's[11] investigation of Plainville, Lee G. Burchinal's[12] examination of a small midwestern farm community, Warner's[13] analysis of the similarly midwestern Jonesville, and Hollingshead's[14] more so-

---

[8] W. Lloyd Warner and Paul S. Lunt, *The Social System of a Modern Community* (Yale University Yankee City Series, vol. 1; New Haven, Conn.: Yale University Press, 1941).

[9] Robert and Helen Lynd, *Middletown* (New York: Harcourt, Brace & Company, Inc., 1929).

[10] Louis Bultena, "Church Membership and Church Attendance in Madison, Wisconsin," *American Sociological Review*, XIV (1949), 384–89.

[11] James West, *Plainville, U.S.A.* (New York: Columbia University Press, 1945).

[12] Lee G. Burchinal, "Some Social Status Criteria and Church Membership and Church Attendance," *Journal of Social Psychology*, XLIX (1959), 53–64.

[13] W. Lloyd Warner *et al.*, *Democracy in Jonesville* (New York: Harper and Brothers, 1949).

[14] August Hollingshead, *Elmtown's Youth* (New Haven, Conn.: Yale University Press, 1949), and "Selected Characteristics of Classes in a Middle Western Community," in Bendix and Lipset (eds.), *op. cit.*, pp. 213–24.

phisticated analysis of Elmtown (Warner's Jonesville) corroborate a higher rate of religious identification among the high-status townsfolk. Unlike the findings of Cantril, the Lynds, and Warner in his work on Yankee City, however, the relations with class in these latter studies are linear. Here the upper classes have the highest rates of church membership, with the middle classes next and the lower classes last. This difference between linearity and curvilinearity will be taken up later. Meanwhile, the larger and more consistent difference between the combined high-status groups and the lower classes is of paramount concern.

Table I–2 presents Hollingshead's results for Elmtown. Although Hollingshead is better known for his focus on Elmtown's

TABLE I–2

Religious Affiliation and Social Class in Elmtown

	Social Class			
	I and II	III	IV	V
% Members	97%	94%	87%	71%
N	(35)	(158)	(312)	(230)

From August Hollingshead, "Selected Characteristics of Classes in a Middle Western Community," in Reinhard Bendix and S. M. Lipset, *Class, Status, and Power* (Glencoe, Ill.: The Free Press, 1953), p. 218.

youth, he also published material on the general population of the community which sought to refine Warner's technique of assessing social class. For each person, Warner relied upon class ratings from a select body of informants who were mostly upper-middle-class housewives. Hollingshead also used ratings but, to avoid any bias, from informants scattered throughout the class hierarchy. The table, then, is the product of a more reliable analysis. Classes I and II are the upper- and upper-middle classes, and these are combined because of the small number of cases. Class III, of course, is the solid middle class, Class IV represents the skilled and working class and Class V includes those of extremely low status, generally either unskilled laborers or unemployed. The relationship is clear and, in this case, linear. Fully 97 per cent of the topmost classes are church members; this declines consistently to only 71 per cent among the lower class.

Note that Hollingshead's percentages of identification are high for a nation in which the over-all level of formal church membership is under 65 per cent. Of course, this is largely because of Hollingshead's inclusion of informal religious preference as well as formal church membership. It is also because Hollingshead deals with a small town, and rates of religiosity and the size of the community are inversely related in our society. It is no accident that most American Protestantism has its strongest roots in a rural or frontier past.

From another view, however, these community studies raise more serious issues. It is true that each finds the lowest percentage of church members among the lower classes and the greatest proportion within the combined high-status group. But this alone does not insure an unambiguous interpretation. The studies also find social class to stand in a similar relation to every other type of voluntary association, whether social clubs, community service groups, political parties, or the PTA. In every instance the lower classes are the most withdrawn. The conclusion is reinforced by Mather,[15] Komarovsky,[16] and Wright and Hyman.[17]

The question, then, is whether church affiliation has a religious significance beyond that of organizational affiliation in general. It is possible that church membership per se is a particularly poor measure of religiosity. Membership need not connote a commitment to religion. It may stake a status claim or serve as a vehicle for mobility as the cynics suggest and as Underwood[18] observes. It may be a prerequisite for something as basic as credit or a job, as witnessed by Pope and Weber.[19] Or it may

[15] W. A. Mather, Jr., "Income and Social Participation," *American Sociological Review*, VI (1941), 380–83.

[16] Mirra Komarovsky, "The Voluntary Associations of Urban Dwellers," *American Sociological Review*, XI (1946), 686–98.

[17] Charles R. Wright and Herbert H. Hyman, "Voluntary Association Membership of American Adults: Evidence From National Sample Surveys," *American Sociological Review*, XXIII (1958), 284–94.

[18] Kenneth W. Underwood, *Protestant and Catholic: Religion and Social Interaction in an Industrial Community* (Boston: Beacon Press, 1957), especially pp. 246–50.

[19] Liston Pope, *Millhands and Preachers* (New Haven, Conn.: Yale University Press, 1942), pp. 322–25, provides a specific instance in which the churches served as clearing-houses for mill employees. Max Weber, "The Protestant Sects and the Spirit of Capitalism," in Hans Gerth and C.

simply represent a penchant for formal associations. In fact, it can be argued that the churches have sought to capitalize upon all of these motives. Warner and Lunt,[20] Robert Lee,[21] and Charles Page[22] have all noted that churches increasingly recruit members through a network of activities that are more secular than sacred. The proliferation of church recreation leagues is the referent in Page's phrase, the "basketballization" of American religion. William H. Whyte[23] describes the appeal of age-group social clubs in the churches of the middle-class organization men in Park Forest, Illinois. There, during 1955, a modern jazz concert and a folk sing were the most successful gatherings of one congregation. Finally, many persons have suggested that the churches function as ladders of social standing; memberships change in response to actual, anticipated, and illusory mobility.

But, of course, church membership is not antithetical to religious commitment. Moreover, the foregoing does not explain the low membership rates of the lower classes. One possible explanation here, however, is that the churches engage in selective recruitment. While their doors are open to all, as Table I–1 attests, they may be especially keen on the higher-status member because of his ability to staff important positions of lay responsibility and because of his contribution to the congregation's image in the community. And yet the lower classes are not simply the abject victims of neglect or discrimination. Many prefer a more spontaneous religion and pay little attention to actual membership or even to a consistent organizational allegiance. Neither of these are important to the celebrated lower-class revivals and "storefront" sects. Here there is great

---

Wright Mills (eds.), *From Max Weber: Essays in Sociology* (New York: Oxford Galaxy Books, 1958), pp. 302–22, makes a similar point after his travels through the United States in 1904, when he visited relatives who were backwoods farmers in North Carolina.

[20] Warner and Lunt, *op. cit.*

[21] Robert Lee, "The Organizational Dilemma in American Protestantism," in The Conference on Science, Philosophy and Religion, *Ethics and Bigness*, ed. Harlan Cleveland and Harold D. Lasswell (New York: Harper and Brothers, 1962), pp. 187–211.

[22] Charles H. Page, "Bureaucracy and the Liberal Church," *The Review of Religion*, XVI (1952), 137–50.

[23] William H. Whyte, *The Organization Man* (New York: Simon & Schuster, Inc., 1956), p. 372.

turnover, and, even when membership is tallied, there is little inclination (and few channels through which) to report it to the larger Protestant councils who add the summary totals.

As further evidence for religiosity among non-church members and further testimony of the gap between formal membership and informal preference, consider the aforementioned research of Bultena[24] in Madison, Wisconsin. While Bultena found a slight positive relation between membership and social class, he also inspected the non-members on their own terms. Roughly one-fifth of the Madison adult population in 1949 were not church members. But of these, fully 60 per cent expressed both a specific denominational preference and a high degree of private religious concern. Clearly membership is not coterminous with religious feeling or personal commitment, nor is it a prerequisite. It may represent only the most secular aspect of the high-status religious experience, and it may be irrelevant to much of lower-class religiosity. At best it is only one among many measures of involvement. At worst, it may harbor a systematic bias that affects the lower classes for whom religion may be important while membership is not.

Church attendance. Since the early 1940's, church membership has given way to church attendance as the most prominent measure of religiosity. The question, "How often have you attended church in the past month?" is now fully entrenched in the standard repertoire of survey items. It has been related to everything from political preference and academic success to sexual compatibility. Throughout there is the assumption that attendance is an accurate gauge of religious involvement generally; indeed, for some researchers, the two are seen as identical. And yet here again the measure is far from unassailable. Although all of the studies cited show that those of high status are more frequent attenders than those of low status, the question of meaning remains. As we shall see, a low rate of attendance is not tantamount to irreligion. Attendance, like membership, assesses only one part of the religious experience.

One of the first studies to examine the relationship between church attendance and social class was the Lynds'[25] analysis of Middletown (Muncie, Indiana). Using a dichotomous distinction

[24] Bultena, *op. cit.*
[25] Robert and Helen Lynd, *op. cit.*

between the business (white collar) and working (blue collar) classes, the Lynds found that 55 per cent of the business-class adults attended church at least three times a month, but only 25 per cent of the working class attended that frequently.

More recent community studies provide corroboration. Hollingshead's[26] work in Elmtown uses more elaborate class distinctions as in Table I–2 and finds a positive linear relationship between class and attendance that is similar to the relation between class and membership. Burchinal's[27] findings for attendance are almost identical. Finally Gerhard Lenski's[28] recent analysis of *The Religious Factor* in Detroit shows that the middle classes have a higher percentage of regular attendance than the working class, using a two-category class system similar to the Lynds'.

Further support comes from national polls. In 1951, the *Catholic Digest*[29] found that only 62 per cent of the lower class attended church but some 75 per cent of the upper class did so. A 1955 poll by the American Institute of Public Opinion[30] reports a similar if somewhat weaker relationship. Analysis of more recent data from the A.I.P.O. again supports a positive, linear relationship between class and attendance. Here the relation was even stronger than that reported by the *Catholic Digest*.

Finally, two analyses of the actual members of single denominations have also examined the relation between class and attendance. Charles Y. Glock and Benjamin B. Ringer[31] inspect several measures of religiosity in their unpublished study of Episcopalians. So does Yoshio Fukuyama[32] in his study of urban Congregationalists. Both studies are consistent with previous re-

[26] Hollingshead, "Selected Characteristics of Classes," *op. cit.*

[27] Burchinal, *op. cit.*

[28] Gerhard Lenski, *The Religious Factor: A Sociologist's Inquiry* (Garden City, N.Y.: Doubleday & Company, Inc., 1961), pp. 102–3.

[29] *Catholic Digest*, polls release, 1957.

[30] American Institute of Public Opinion, polls release, 1955.

[31] Charles Y. Glock and Benjamin B. Ringer, *Society, the Church, and Its Parishioners* (Book in preparation, Survey Research Center, University of California, Berkeley), see especially Ch. V.

[32] Yoshio Fukuyama, "The Major Dimensions of Church Membership," *Review of Religious Research*, II (1961), 154–61. Actually, Fukuyama's study closely parallels much of the present research. It appeared after the present essay was conceived, however, and provides a form of independent replication, though its brevity precludes the kind of extensive exploration intended in the following.

search in their findings that the lower classes have the lowest rate of attendance, although Glock and Ringer find a curvilinear relation in which the middle classes have the highest rate and the upper-class members suffer a relative dip. Two things are important here. First, the issue of linearity versus curvilinearity apparently confounds the research on attendance as well as the research on membership. Second, the class differences in attendance are generally smaller among those who are church members than among the general population. This last observation is a useful point from which to begin a critical assessment of the research on attendance.

I have already mentioned Burchinal's results concerning class and attendance for the community at large. But the most arresting feature of Burchinal's study is his simultaneous examination of status, attendance, and church membership. Dividing his small-town sample into two groups, church members and non-members, he finds that there is only a very slight relationship between social class and attendance within the categories of members and non-members considered separately. Thus, although I have earlier indicated that membership is not the only criterion of religious involvement and may include some bias, it seems to be an important intervening[33] factor in the relation between class and attendance. The implication is that attendance may not simply reflect personal religious need, but rather the extent to which one is subject to the pressures of the church as an organization. Certainly non-members are less exposed to these pressures. This may account for as much of their low attendance as does their low status. Here, then, is one reason for restricting the generalizability of research on attendance. Much of this research ignores the factor of membership. Attendance may also reflect

[33] Technically, the term "intervening" has temporal connotations. An intervening factor occurs before either the independent or the dependent variable and dictates the course of their relationship. In this case, it is difficult to make assertions regarding time order. Since membership is frequently inherited from one's parents, there are a number of persons for whom it is indeed an intervening influence in the strict sense. On the other hand, there will also be persons who begin by attending a given church and only later join it. Here the term is imprecise. Without getting into semantic difficulties, the over-all point is that membership has an effect on the relationship between attendance and social class. Time order is less important than the fact of multivariate interaction.

only a more formal and institutionalized aspect of religion and not the religious experience as a whole.

Church attendance is, of course, often pictured as pharisaical by those who are alienated from religion altogether. But without going to such extremes, there is evidence to suggest that not all attendance is religiously motivated and that the non-attenders are not exclusively Godless. Consider again the Lynds' research on the church-going practices of Middletown. With their customary thoroughness, they report not only the statistics but also some of the reasons for the statistics as supplied by the towns-people themselves. The business-class (high-status) attenders give several explanations of their behavior. Among them are the following:

> You can usually hear a good sermon when you go to church, and I really have more respect for myself when I do attend church. (*or*) Why, it just never occurred to me to question church-going! (*or*) I would hate to live in a community where there was no church. I must confess I am not as interested in church or in church work as a good many. Lots of the time I am just plain bored by church, but feel I ought to go. (*or, finally*) I haven't any very definite beliefs, but feel about going to church pretty much the way I do about bringing up children; I'm afraid not to go for fear my child will be missing something valuable if she is not established in habits of going to church and Sunday School.[34]

Note the major themes of unquestioned loyalty, boredom, external obligation, and the need for self-respect. By contrast, the working-class non-attenders seem less inhibited about resisting social convention. They explain their lack of attendance like this:

> I feel just awful and I'm ashamed, but we never go. The reason people don't go to church as much as they used to is lack of discipline in the home and lack of interest. Then there's other things: unless a person is prominent in the church or socially, people in the church have no interest in her. (*or*) Just never got interested in going to church, though I go to revivals and things like that. (*or*) There's too much dressing up for church these days; he used to go in his overalls just as good as anybody. But now it won't

[34] Robert and Helen Lynd, *op. cit.*, adapted from pp. 366–67.

do for people to go without being all dressed up and we just haven't got the clothes for that. (*or, finally*) People are mostly hypocrites. If they really believed the things they say in church they would do something about all the things that are wrong. If all the people who have called themselves Christians for 2,000 years had really believed in Jesus and his way of living, they'd 've made the world a mighty different place from what it is now.[35]

It is true that the Lynds had the ears of skeptics and I have picked selectively from their quotations. Nevertheless, these remarks suggest the possible independence of church attendance, on the one hand, and religious concern, on the other. Attendance may play vastly different roles in the religious experience of different classes—or, indeed, no role at all. For some of the high-status attenders, actual religious feeling is strikingly absent. At the same time, all of these lower-class non-attenders can hardly be classified as irreligious. There is one who enjoys revivals and another who is agitated over religious hypocrisy.

Actually most of the authors cited in this section make similar qualifications of the meaning of the relation between class and attendance. In addition to Burchinal and the Lynds, Hollingshead reports that social class bears no relation whatsoever to belief in God. Attendance and belief are both important facets of religiosity, however, and if social class is not consistently related to both, one must probe deeper for a more complicated relation between class and religiosity as a whole. As we shall see later, Glock and Ringer, and Fukuyama also report that class stands in different relation to other facets of involvement. Clearly attendance does not exhaust the domain. It is possible that it, like membership before and like parish activities to follow, reflects only the "doing" dimension of religiosity and not the important aspect of religious "feeling." The relation with class seems dependent upon the distinction.

Parish activities. In moving from church attendance to activities within the organization, we are moving in a secular direction. I have already noted that the churches sponsor many groups which compete with the attractions of the non-church community. In addition to such common activities as the choir,

[35] *Ibid.*, adapted from pp. 362–66.

the Sunday School staff, and the ladies' aid, a parish will frequently sponsor a basketball team, a bowling league, a great-books discussion group, and possibly a circle or two of group therapy. Moreover, every congregation relies upon its laymen to staff important positions of responsibility which keep the organizations going. These might include positions on the finance committee and the building committee, and the representatives to the denominational lay councils on a national level. Among these activities, one might distinguish between recreational activities and responsibilities. However, persons of high status appear to dominate both.

Some of the earliest speculation on the relation between class and religion centers in this area. Max Weber's[36] comparative analysis of Confucianism, Hinduism, Judaism, and emerging Protestantism makes the point that religious movements carry the near indelible stamp of the status group that founded them. For example, some Protestant groups such as the Episcopalians, Presbyterians, and Congregationalists have their roots in a bourgeois reaction to Catholicism and seem to have retained this high-status trademark Extending Weber's argument, a corollary applies to more recent denominations that began as lower-class sects in the wake of the Reformation. Thus, within any religious movement, the highest-ranking status group will assume lay leadership and dictate the religious mood. This would apply to the Baptists, the Methodists, and the Lutherans, for example.

Weber's argument rests on the premise that parish activities are more than incidental to the religious spirit of the congregation. For one thing, they provide more intimate contact with the religious leadership and, thereby, an avenue of influence. For another, many of these activities are instrumental in getting things done. Laymen are often ascribed a knowledge of finance and secular concerns that extends beyond the pastor's. They often have the opportunity to turn the church as an organization to their own designs.

Qualitative evidence that this has occurred is available in several historical analyses of developing churches and denomi-

---

[36] For a useful summary of Weber's work in this area, as well as a detailed bibliography, see Reinhard Bendix, *Max Weber: An Intellectual Portrait* (Garden City, N.Y.: Doubleday & Company, Inc., 1960), pp. 71–265.

nations. S. D. Clark's[37] study of Canadian Methodism reveals the growing pressures of the high-status laity and the growing disaffection of the lower classes. Paul Harrison's[38] more recent analysis of the American Baptist Convention affords another instance of this. Although it began as a lower-class sect, the Baptist movement has taken on higher-status members who have exerted increasing influence towards modernization. According to Harrison, not only has much of Baptist fundamentalism been subdued, but its principle of local autonomy for each parish has been subverted. Bureaucratization has quietly gained sway at the national level.

But apart from qualitative evidence of influence in strategic spots, there is also quantitative evidence of greater high-status participation in activities generally. Glock and Ringer[39] find that the association between class and parish activity is no different than that between class and membership or church attendance. While women are typically more active than men, and the upper class is less involved than the middle class, it remains true that those of generally high status participate more than those of low status.

Although parish activity does not have the currency of attendance as a measure of religiosity, Glock and Ringer are not alone in their general findings. Fukuyama[40] reports a generally similar relation between class and activity among Congregationalists. Hollingshead's[41] aforementioned study of adult religion in Elmtown confirms the lower classes as the least active in church organizations. Harold Kaufman[42] has found both participation and lay leadership positively related to class in a rural farm community in upper New York state. It might be noted, however, that these latter three studies differ from Glock and Ringer's work with urban Episcopalians in two respects. First, neither

[37] S. D. Clark, *Church and Sect in Canada* (Toronto: University of Toronto Press, 1948).

[38] Paul M. Harrison, *Authority and Power in the Free Church Tradition: A Social Case Study of the American Baptist Convention* (Princeton, N.J.: Princeton University Press, 1959).

[39] Glock and Ringer, *op. cit.*

[40] Fukuyama, *op. cit.*

[41] Hollingshead, "Selected Characteristics of Classes," *op. cit.*

[42] Harold Kaufman, "Prestige Classes in a New York Rural Community," in Bendix and Lipset, *op. cit.*, pp. 190–203.

Fukuyama, Hollingshead, nor Kaufman reports a curvilinear relation as do Glock and Ringer; in each case, the extreme upper class is the most active and the association is consistently linear. Second, because Glock and Ringer as well as Fukuyama, are dealing with church members alone, the relation between class and activity is weaker than those reported in Hollingshead's and Kaufman's studies of whole communities. Once more, membership seems to be an important factor in the relation between class and involvement.

But there is a more important qualification of the association. Like membership and attendance, the meaning of parish activities is unclear. I have already mentioned the secular quality of most activities. This alone creates suspicion of attempts to use them as measures of religious involvement as a whole. A more empirical caveat can be inferred from Glock and Ringer's study. Their concern is not solely with religious involvement in itself, but also with involvement in the church versus involvement in other aspects of the community. Now it is true that class is positively related to parish activity when other commitments are not considered. But if one compares high- and low-status adherents on the *proportion* of sacred to secular activities, the differences reverse. Thus, the low-status parishioner spends a larger amount of his organizational investment on the church than does the high-status member. Kenneth Lutterman provides similar evidence for investment of a more literal sort in his study of financial giving to churches.[43] Although the low-status church member may give less money to the church on absolute grounds, he gives a higher percentage of his income. In short, even a small donation or a single activity may be more salient for the lower-class member because it is less rivalled by commitments of other sorts. Again, then, there are reasons for doubting the case for high-status religiosity.

Linearity versus curvilinearity. Although all of the studies cited agree that the higher classes generally are the most active, several dispute the linearity of the association. Warner and Lunt,

---

[43] Kenneth J. Lutterman, "Giving to Churches: A Sociological Study of the Contributions to Eight Catholic and Lutheran Churches," unpublished Ph.D. dissertation, University of Wisconsin, 1962, see especially Ch. VIII, pp. 37–38.

Cantril, Bultena, and Glock and Ringer have all found that involvement is highest among the middle classes. This is at odds with the studies of Fukuyama, Hollingshead, West, Kaufman, Burchinal, the *Catholic Digest,* and later reports of the American Institute of Public Opinion that find religiosity at its peak among the extreme upper classes.

Now survey research is subject to myriad idiosyncracies which make comparisons among studies risky. It is possible, for example, that the discrepancy between Cantril, Warner, and Glock and Ringer, on the one hand, and Fukuyama, the *Catholic Digest,* and the American Institute of Public Opinion, on the other, is adducible to different definitions of social class. The latter studies use a broader definition of upper class, and, thus, include many of the highly involved middle-class types as well.

But the disparity in the remaining studies may reflect something else. All of the studies reporting the upper class most involved deal with predominantly farming communities of less than 6,000 persons. By contrast, all of the studies that find the middle classes most involved deal with samples drawn largely from urban areas with populations in excess of 50,000. There are, of course, considerable differences between America's Elmtowns and Middletowns. One particular difference seems crucial here. Most small towns do not observe a sharp demarcation between the middle and upper classes. Not only are rural upper classes "less upper" than their urban counterparts, but they are also more visible and better integrated into the community as a whole. In fact, the small-town upper classes are the community leaders, and this is necessarily manifest in such key community institutions as the churches.

On the other hand, urban areas are better able to sustain a distinction. The upper class is more socially distant through pronounced educational and power advantages. It is also less visible since its members are usually ensconced in retreats such as the board of directors of a business firm, foreign travel, exclusive country clubs, and a self-sustaining social world that is frequently endogamous. The urban upper class may rule the productive community, but it tends to withdraw from the community's voluntary activities. As if filling a vacuum, the middle classes provide the leadership here and, again, this is manifested in the churches.

Sinclair Lewis supplies a biting distinction between the upper- and middle-class religious styles in his stereotyped city of Zenith. The speaker is advising the Reverend Mr. Gantry on the local social clubs:

> Yeh, but the owner of the Advocate, and the banker that's letting Win Grant run on till he bankrupts, and the corporation counsel that keeps 'em all out of jail, you don't find *those* malefactors going to no lunch club and yipping about Service! You find 'em sitting at small tables at the old Union Club, and laughing themselves sick about Service. . . . I couldn't get you into the Union Club. They wouldn't have any preacher that talks about vice—the kind of preacher that belongs to the Union talks about the new model Cadillac and how hard it is to get genuwine Eyetalian vermouth. But the Tonawanda—They might let you in. For respectability. To prove that they couldn't have the gin they've got in their lockers in their lockers.[44]

This distinction between the populations of the discrepant studies is only speculative, but it does provide one possible reconciliation.

Of course, the problem of the relative involvement of the upper and middle classes pales beside the larger issue of the religiosity of the lower classes versus the higher classes generally. Here, as we have seen, the statistics are clear enough, yet they are qualified by three major considerations. First, church membership, attendance, and parish activity all relate to formal participation in the church as an organization and not necessarily to private religious feelings. Second, the relation of class to attendance (and possibly parish activity) is partially an artifact of differential exposure to organizational pressures rather than a simple reflection of personal religious needs. Finally, the same type of religiosity may mean one thing to high-status parishioners and quite another to those of low status. Thus, church membership may be irrelevant to the more spontaneous religion of the lower classes. Here revivals may supplant formal church attendance, and even a small amount of parish activity may be more meaningful since these people are less active in secular groups.

[44] Sinclair Lewis, *Elmer Gantry* (New York: Dell Publishing Co., 1960), p. 373. By permission of Harcourt, Brace & World, Inc., original publishers.

The Case for Low-Status Religiosity

All of the qualifications of high-status involvement would seem hollow indeed if there were no empirical support in the opposite direction. The present section suggests, however, that this has not been mere cavilling. Although studies reporting the lower classes most involved are in the minority, their sparseness is no measure of their significance. Accuracy rather than bulk is the final arbiter.

Actually, some of the studies already mentioned include side-remarks on low-status religiosity—remarks that are overwhelmed in the final tally. The Lynds, for example, divide their treatment of Middletown religion into four chapters: Dominant Religious Beliefs, Where and When Religious Beliefs Are Carried On, Leaders and Participants in Religious Rites, and, last, Religious Observances. The fourth of these is by far the most elaborate. It was cited in the last section for its description of the business class as the most frequent church-attenders and most likely church members. But the first chapter offers a contrast in dealing with religious beliefs. The Lynds summarize as follows:

> First, members of the working class show a disposition to believe their religion more ardently and to accumulate more emotionally charged values around their beliefs. Religion appears to operate more prominently as an active agency of support and encouragement among this section of the city. A second point is the shift in the status of certain religious beliefs during the past generation—notably the decline, *particularly among the business class*, in the emphasis upon Heaven, and still more upon Hell [italics added].[45]

The Lynds observe further that the secularization of Middletown religion has occurred at different rates for the two classes. When asked if "it is wrong to go to the movies on Sunday," roughly a third of the working-class high schoolers replied "yes," as compared with only a sixth of the business-class students.

A second research that finds both positive and negative relations between status and religiosity is Gerhard Lenski's[46] recent analysis of a small sample of Detroiters. The study is concerned

---

[45] Robert and Helen Lynd, *op. cit.*, p. 329.
[46] Lenski, *op. cit.*

more with the effect of religiosity on status than vice versa, yet it reports not only that attendance is directly related to class but also that other forms of involvement are inversely related to class. Persons of middle-class occupations and college educations are slightly less likely to be doctrinally orthodox and devotionally active than those with working-class occupations and without college educations.

Another study that harbors a discrepancy between high- and low-status religiosity is Glock and Ringer's research with Episcopalians. In addition to church attendance and organizational activity, they used a third measure of involvement pertaining to the "intellectual dimension." This refers to the parishioner's knowledge of traditional doctrine and the extent to which he reads religious literature. Whereas church attendance and parish activity are at their lowest ebb among the lower classes, the situation is reversed for intellectual involvement. Among women, the lower class scores highest with 51 per cent intellectually involved, and this decreases to 41 per cent among the lower-middle, 34 per cent among the upper-middle, and 28 per cent among the upper class. Among men, the percentages run in the same order from a peak of 32 per cent for those of low status to a depression of 17 per cent for those of extremely high status.

Conflicting relations with status also occur in Fukuyama's analysis of Congregationalists. Fukuyama delineates four types of religiosity which he labels the cultic, cognitive, creedal, and devotional. The cultic is an amalgam of church attendance and organizational activity and its positive relation with class has already been reported. The cognitive represents the parishioner's knowledge of religious doctrine and the affairs of his congregation. The creedal signifies personal allegiance to traditional doctrine, regardless of one's detailed knowledge. Finally, the devotional connotes personal prayer and reliance upon religion beyond the church itself.

Table I–3 presents the relation between each of these facets and social class. As we learned previously, the *cultic* is positively related to class, and gives a range from 53 per cent involved among those of generally high status to only 35 per cent among those of low status. The relation is also positive for the *cognitive* dimension, although it is important to note that, unlike Glock and

TABLE I–3

Social Class and Four Types of Religiosity among Congregationalists

Four Dimensions % Highly Involved	Socioeconomic Status		
	High	Moderate	Low
Cultic	53%	43%	35%
Cognitive	28	24	15
Creedal	27	28	31
Devotional	16	23	32

Abstracted from Yoshio Fukuyama, "The Major Dimensions of Church Membership," *Review of Religious Research*, II (1961), 159 (Table 4).

Ringer's "intellectual commitment" above, this dimension refers only to knowledge itself and not to involvement in it. Moreover, it refers to knowledge of the congregation as well as to knowledge of the doctrine. That one *knows* the financial state of his parish does not mean that he will develop a deep-rooted attachment to it. As with knowledge of most things, religious knowledge should increase with familiarity and with education. Since the high-status parishioners are apt to be active in parish administration and well educated, this helps to account for their high score. However, the other two dimensions of religiosity offer contrasting relations with class. Both *creedal* and *devotional* religiosity increase among progressively lower-status groups, although this is only pronounced for the latter. Both refer to a more inward religiosity that is concerned less with the formal church and more with personal feelings. Fukuyama concludes that "different social classes differ not so much in the degree to which they are religiously oriented but in the manner in which they give expression to their religious propensities."[47]

A last study that finds the lower classes more religiously involved is my own survey in Winchester, Massachusetts.[48] Actually, in this area the individual's own status has less bearing upon his religiosity than does his parents' status—succor to the argument that one's religion is a product of one's rearing and changes little in substance thereafter. Nevertheless, both forms

[47] Fukuyama, *op. cit.*, p. 159. This insight will be explored in more detail in Ch. II.

[48] N. J. Demerath III, "Religious Participation, Attitudes and Beliefs in an Adult Sample," unpublished A.B. honors thesis, Harvard College, 1958.

of status are negatively related to fundamentalism in religious beliefs,[49] and, in both cases, the lower classes are less tolerant of religious relativism. Roughly one-third of the high-status group believe in either or both heaven and hell; this increases to more than two-thirds among the low-status respondents. When asked their hypothetical reaction to their child's desire to change his religious affiliation, a similar pattern obtains. The lower class is apt to be reproachful, while the middle and upper classes are more permissive.[50] Finally, those of low status have a higher frequency of personal prayer and even perceive prayer differently. They see it as a spiritual duologue and divine source of guidance. The higher-status respondents interpret it more as self-administered therapy in the secular psychiatric sense.[51]

And yet here, as with high-status religiosity, there are grounds for dispute. Although the Lynds, Lenski, Glock and Ringer, Fukuyama, and my own previous research suggest that the lower classes are more religious when religiosity is measured by personal belief and private practice, two final studies provide some doubt. One of these is Gerhard Lenski's[52] early analysis of social class and ''religious interest'' in a representative sample of the Indianapolis area. Certainly interest alone is more personal and less institutionalized than formal membership, attendance, and parish activities. But when Lenski related interest to four sepa-

[49] The doctrine of predestination provides an interesting exception among Catholics. High-status Catholics are more frequent believers on this item alone when compared to low-status Catholics. But, of course, predestination is antithetical to traditional Catholic theology and the absence of belief among the lower classes reflects orthodoxy rather than apathy.

[50] In this connection, see Clyde Z. Nunn, "Child-Control through a 'Coalition with God,'" *Child Development*, XXXV (1964), 417–32. Nunn finds that the coalition is most common among lower-class parents. This is one of several unique measures of religiosity that might be added to the support for the argument that lower-class religious involvement is greater than middle- or upper-class involvement. I am indebted to Warren O. Hagstrom for this reference.

[51] Cf. Gerald Gurin, Joseph Veroff, and Sheila Feld, *Americans View Their Mental Health* (New York: Basic Books, Inc., 1960), pp. 372–76. Here it is reported that those of low status are more apt to resort to prayer in periods of emotional stress. Hence we have still another measure of religious involvement that indicates that the lower-class are far from alienated from religion altogether.

[52] Gerhard Lenski, "Social Correlates of Religious Interest," *American Sociological Review*, XVIII (1953), 533–44.

rate measures of status, he found more ambiguity than consistency. When class is measured by occupational prestige, the family's total financial worth, and the respondent's education, the lower classes are slightly more interested than the middle and upper classes. When class is measured by the household's yearly income, the high-status respondents show more interest. Although one can argue that the differences are generally in the predicted inverse direction and are no smaller than the differences that Lenski later accepted in Detroit, here he rejects all of the findings as statistically insignificant.

The second study which provides grounds for suspicion is Rodney Stark's[53] recent analysis of national polls in Great Britain and the United States. Surprisingly, Stark finds that *both* participation and belief are positively related to social class in each country. Thus, the higher one's status, the more one is likely to attend church regularly and the more one is likely to claim belief in God. The latter finding is, of course, the puzzle since its positive relationship is a blatant contradiction of the negative association described by others.

How can we explain these discrepancies? One tack is to point out the considerable difference between such nebulous items as "belief in God" and "religious interest," on the one hand, and more precise questions such as religious reading and the interpretation and extent of personal prayer, on the other. The former questions will elicit positive answers from all but the most confirmed atheists, and atheism has never been the vogue in American upper-class circles. The latter questions, however, provide more range. They allow the researcher to discriminate between the more traditional and the more secularized positions. It may be that the essential difference between classes lies at this more delicate level.

Another explanation for the disparity concerns the populations studied. Both Lenski and Stark examined samples that were designed to represent whole metropolitan areas and whole nations. By contrast, my own research in Winchester focused

---

[53] Rodney W. Stark, Class, Radicalism, and Church Attendance in Great Britain, a paper delivered at the meetings of the American Sociological Association, Washington, D.C., September, 1962. This paper includes only part of the results mentioned. The remainder were communicated in a personal conversation and are intended for later publication.

on a small town in New England where the Catholic church sets much of the religious tone for the lower classes. The Lynds looked at only a single small city where church membership was the norm in the 1920's. And Glock and Ringer and Fukuyama were concerned only with affiliated Episcopalians and Congregationalists. The difference here points to an important hypothesis concerning lower-class religion in general. If a lower-class individual is committed to religion at all, his internal involvement is likely to be higher than that of his higher-status churchfellows. On the other hand, there is a large segment of the lower class that has no religious commitment whatsoever. Perhaps because these people have found functional alternatives to religion in political extremism,[54] trade unions, or the extended family, they are markedly different and must be held apart in any assessment of the church's importance to its members. Neither Stark nor Lenski compartmentalized the two lower-class groups, and this resulted in a low over-all rate of religiosity. My research in Winchester dealt with an anomalous town where the distinction may not have been so important. Glock and Ringer and Fukuyama focused only on those who had some religious commitment in the first place. The latter strategy will characterize the study to follow. This is not a study of social class and the religion of Americans generally. Instead, it is an analysis of self-defined American Protestants in particular.

Summary

In reviewing the previous literature on social class and religious involvement, we have seen a major knot and several loose strings. The knot is, of course, the contradiction between those studies which find those of high status most religiously involved and

[54] It is important to note that some of the most militant anti-clerical and, indeed, anti-religious movements are both lower-class and politically to the left. The American Rationalist Federation, for example, has deep roots in European socialism. Many of its branches comprise lower-class European ethnics who rally around rationalism for an identity that is distinct from the persecuting state churches of their native countries. In Europe itself, the ties between organized free thought and left-wing politics are even stronger. For example, the West German "freie Gemeinde" are particularly powerful but also particularly communistic in political coloration. The author is currently beginning research on this end of the religious spectrum.

those studies that find religiosity at its peak among the lower classes. The strings involve issues such as church members versus non-members, rural versus urban populations, religious versus organizational motivations, sacred versus secular affiliations, and, above all, the different forms of religiosity examined. Pulling any of these strings should be fruitful. The present study will pay particular attention to the last. Religiosity is apparently not a single dimension. It has various facets which are given various emphases by various social classes. The problem is to find a theoretical framework within which to elaborate the issue and from which to draw hypotheses for the research to follow. This is the problem to which we turn next.

II

Types of Religious Involvement: A Rapprochement and Framework for Analysis

If one were hurling brickbats, he might characterize previous research on class and religiosity as an instance of the synecdochal fallacy. There seems to be a profound confusion of the whole with its parts. While focusing on only one aspect of involvement such as attendance, parish activity, belief, or prayer, studies have made assumptions about the whole. But, like the fabled blind men of India, different studies may describe different parts of the same religious elephant. While relating social class to the *degree* of involvement, research has generally ignored differences in the *kind* of involvement at issue.

To emphasize these distinctions in kind, consider two hypothetical individuals with contrasting religious styles. The first has inherited his church membership as a family legacy. Although the congregation is across town from his present home and none of his closest friends are members, he remains loyal to the church and reserves Sundays for dispensing his obligations to it. His attendance record is virtually unblemished. As a banker, he is chairman of the parish's financial committee. But

27

while a sincere participant in the congregation's weekly prayers of thanks, he is not given to spontaneous devotion. A modernist, religious doctrine is neither very urgent nor very clear to him. The church provides a point of stability and reinforces his views on business ethics, yet his religious experience is rarely emotional. For all of this, he is esteemed within the church and within the community as an eminently religious man with unassailable integrity and a sense of Christian service.

By contrast, the second person is not a formal church member at all. However, he does have a denominational preference and feels nominally affiliated with the denomination's neighborhood parish. While he attends church infrequently and participates in no responsibilities, the congregation provides a local symbol of the traditional doctrine that he accepts and applies. Further, most of his close friends are also affiliated with the parish. This affords a religious fellowship that is more meaningful than his contacts on the job, and independent of the church's formal structure. Peaks and depressions in his everyday affairs often lead to private prayer. He and his wife are mindful of an afterlife and have fostered in their children a similar regard. In general, religion transcends and uplifts his life, although it is the source of no prestige and is more a feeling than an activity.

Now who is to say which of these is the more religious? Both are involved in different kinds of religion; neither is hypocritical. The first is a mainstay of the church as an institution. Without him, the parish would founder, and, in return, the church offers him support for his position in society. This is not only a matter of social standing. It is also justification for his values and way of life. It was this type that Alexis de Tocqueville had in mind when he commented of an earlier day that:

> Not only do Americans follow religion from interest but they place in this world the interest which makes them follow it. In the middle ages the clergy spoke of nothing but the future state. They hardly cared to prove that Christians may be happy here below. But American preachers are constantly referring to the earth. . . . To touch their congregations they always show them how favorable religious opinion is to freedom and public tranquility; and it is often difficult to ascertain from their discourses whether

the principal object of religion is to obtain eternal felicity
or prosperity in this world.[1]

De Tocqueville, of course, spoke from the skeptical perspective
of a European Catholic among American Protestants. Nevertheless, his description is apt, if not his denigration.

The second person is equally important to religion, and, indeed, religion is equally important to him. Yet, his is a less
formal, more internal religiosity. It may be that he retreats
from the organized church precisely because of its effort to relate
to the religious needs of the first type. It is as if he were responding to the advice of a contemporary of De Tocqueville's, Søren
Kierkegaard.

> Thou plain man! . . . one thing I adjure thee, for the sake
> of God in heaven and all that is holy, shun the priests, shun
> them, those abominable men whose livelihood it is to prevent
> thee from so much as becoming aware of what Christianity
> is, and who thereby would transform thee, befuddled by
> galimatias and optical illusion, into what they understand
> by a true Christian, a paid member of the State Church, or
> the National Church, or whatever they prefer to call it.
> Shun them. But take heed to pay them willingly and
> promptly what money they should have. . . . No, pay them
> double, in order that thy disagreement with them does not
> concern thee at all, namely, money; and, on the contrary,
> that what does not concern them concerns thee infinitely,
> namely, Christianity.[2]

Kierkegaard's distinction between religion and the church remains relevant. Hyperbole and the clergy aside, it seems that
the plain men have, in fact, withdrawn from the church as a
formal institution. And yet this is not to equate withdrawal with
total alienation. The second type is also involved in the organized
church but to a lesser degree and in a different way.

The point of all of this is that one cannot assess the degree
of religiosity without also evaluating the different kinds of involvement that are possible. If one were to measure only mem-

[1] Alexis de Tocqueville, *Democracy in America* (New York: Vintage
Books, 1954), II, 127.

[2] Søren Kierkegaard, *Attack upon "Christendom,"* trans. by Walter
Lowrie (Boston: Beacon Press, 1960), p. 288. Copyright 1944 by Princeton
University Press.

bership, attendance, and parish activity, the first individual would put the second to statistical shame. If one looked only at personal devotion, traditional beliefs, and the quality of the church as an informal community, the first would pale beside the second. Both errors can be found in previous research, and the present study seeks a rapprochement.

But, of course, caricatures are no substitute for theory. Since the aim of this chapter is to seek out the several dimensions of religious involvement, we must go further than our two hypothetical, somewhat exaggerated individuals can take us. In what follows, therefore, we will consider several more theoretical perspectives from which to view religiosity and social class. The first of these is Charles Glock's dimensionalization of religious behavior.

Four Dimensions of the Religious Experience

Perhaps the dominant issue in current scholarly debate over religion is whether or not there has occurred a religious revival in the United States.[3] There is evidence on both sides. But much of the contradiction lies in the same misconception that one finds in the previous studies on the relationship between class and religiosity. In both cases, there is a tendency to treat religion as a seamless whole. In both cases, this has led to confusion. Yet

---

[3] Much of this debate is concerned with the credibility of church-collected statistics. For example, the proportion of the population that are church members can be shown to have risen steadily and somewhat spectacularly since the middle of the nineteenth century. And yet critics point out that this may be attributed not to any rise in membership per se but rather to an increasingly reliable and exhaustive counting procedure, coupled with the tendency of the churches to inflate the numbers by counting increasing numbers of children and by multiple-counting the same individual who has moved between parishes. At least one person has argued that the level of religiosity is about the same today as it was in 1850. S. M. Lipset points out that standardized per capita church contributions are less now than they were during the depression and that this offsets any gain in sheer membership and attendance. On the other hand, there are at least two arguments that both revival and decline have occurred. First, Charles Glock points out that the two trends may affect different forms of religious involvement. Second, Talcott Parsons has intimated that secularization may be a precondition for revival in that religion must change to fit the temper of the times in order to flourish and the temper of *these* times is secular indeed.

there is one person in the revival debate who has spotted this difficulty and sought to obviate it. Charles Y. Glock suggests that the religious experience has several distinct dimensions[4] and that revival may have occurred along some, while decline may have characterized others. Now the question of long-term religious trends is beyond the province of this study. The data are not directly relevant and any conclusion would only add a guess to an area already awash with speculation. But Glock's dimensions are helpful for other issues as well. After a brief introduction, I shall apply them to the question of class and religious involvement.

Essentially, the dimensions elaborate Durkheim's now traditional distinction between *beliefs* and *rites*.[5] The latter concept is closely akin to Glock's *behavioral* religiosity, which refers to one's participation in the church as an organization. Its concerns are, for example, church attendance and parish activities. Durkheim's concept of beliefs is similar to Glock's *ideological* sphere, which is concerned with one's religious convictions and commitment to doctrine. Glock's final two dimensions, however, refer to the impact and intensity of the first two. Thus, the *experiential* concerns one's emotional response to religion. The *consequential* is the extent to which religion influences one's everyday activities and attitudes.

The beauty and utility of this scheme lies in its property of independence. Theoretically, it is possible to be highly involved on one dimension but not on another. One may be a believer but not a participant. One may both believe and participate, but with little emotion and with little effect on his activity outside of church. Instead of assuming that the four dimensions are intimately tied, the researcher is forced to consider their relations problematic.

Let us examine the dimensions with respect to the studies in

---

[4] Charles Y. Glock, "The Religious Revival in America?" in Jane C. Zahn (ed.), *Religion and the Face of America* (Berkeley: University of California Press, 1959), pp. 25–42. In recent revision of this paper, Glock has spoken of five dimensions instead of four. Rather than using the *ideological* to refer to both belief *and* knowledge, he restricts it to the former and gives the latter an *intellectual* dimension all to itself.

[5] See Emile Durkheim, *The Elementary Forms of the Religious Life* (Glencoe, Ill.: The Free Press, 1957).

Chapter I. Clearly, those studies that find greatest involvement among those of high status are working within the behavioral dimension. On the other hand, those studies that find the lower classes most involved concentrate on the ideological and experiential facets where the measures are not attendance and parish activity but rather religious belief, personal concern, and private devotion. Although the consequential dimension is not especially addressed by this research, this too could be hypothetically labeled a lower-class province since we noted that those of low status share their church affiliation with fewer secular allegiances, thus giving religion less competition in its direction of their workaday rounds. Certainly the paradigm is apt. Its central postulate of independence gains support from the literature on social class and religious involvement, and indeed, it is a major conclusion of Fukuyama's study of Congregationalists.

But, at the same time, the scheme is overly simple for deriving more specific hypotheses concerning religiosity. It would be inaccurate to assert that the middle and upper classes have no religious beliefs or ideological commitment at all. It is misleading to conclude that the lower classes are wholly non-involved in the behavioral dimension. To be sure, one can make *relative* statements of degrees in each case. However, each of these dimensions requires another distinction of kind as well. Glock does not intend his scheme to answer the questions, ''what *kind* of beliefs distinguish those of high and low status?'' or ''what *kind* of participation marks distinctions in status?'' The introduction to his discussion of the ideological factor makes this clear:

> The ideological dimension is constituted, in turn, by what people believe along religious lines rather than what they feel. It includes all of those items which represent what is believed about the nature of the divine or ultimate reality and its purpose. The designation of beliefs as religious may be made by an individual, by a religious group, by a society, or if you will, by a social scientist. The designations of one, to be sure, may not and probably will not always jibe with the designations of another. While these differences cannot be ignored, they need not concern us here. Our present interest is to indicate that belief is a dimension of religion, not to establish what makes a belief religious.[6]

[6] Glock, *op. cit.*, p. 27.

In short, Glock makes no predictions as to actual beliefs or the meaningful differences between them. The ideological dimension has room for Zoroastrian dualism, the Hindu doctrine of Kharma, Calvinist predestination, and even a thoroughgoing atheism which, according to Paul Tillich, may be quite validly religious. While it is hospitable to both high- and low-status beliefs, another perspective is necessary to distinguish them.

All of this applies to the other dimensions as well. Most studies, of course, have stressed church attendance and formal activities as examples of the behavioral dimension. But there are less institutionalized behaviors too. These might include participation in personal friendships within the parish, Bible reading, personal prayer, and even confessionals within some branches of Protestantism. All of these require ''doing'' rather than simply ''feeling.'' Turning to the experiential dimension, religion may trigger not only different degrees of emotion but also different types. For one person, religion may involve thanksgiving; for another, supplication. And, finally, even the consequential facet of religion may be qualitatively different from person to person. It may involve any of the several responses to the world that are developed in Weber's writings[7]; for example, worldly asceticism or otherworldly mysticism.

Thus, each of Glock's dimensions embraces further differences of a more than random sort. I am suggesting that social classes can be qualitatively as well as quantitatively distinguished within all four. Hence a more complete analysis of social class and religiosity will need a further distinction in kind as well.

Some Eligible Supplementary Distinctions

In seeking a supplement to Glock's dimensions, two criteria are pertinent. First, the distinction must fit each of the previous dimensions in a manner that illuminates social class differences in religiosity. Second, the distinction should take us beyond the specific area of class and religiosity by evoking meaningful linkages with other problems in the sociology of religion. This, after

---

[7] See Hans Gerth and C. Wright Mills (eds.), *From Max Weber: Essays in Sociology* (New York: Oxford Galaxy Books, 1958), especially Chs. XI and XIII.

all, is a prime advantage of a theory that is broader than the data and issues at hand. It leads beyond these to new areas and wider ramifications.

Now the study of religion fairly wallows in conceptualizations and distinctions. While not all of these are related to the problem at hand, there are several candidates that require consideration. A brief inspection may anticipate any charge of arbitrariness in the final selection. It will also provide a bird's-eye view of various theories in the area of the individual and his religion. Each of the following distinctions has had a wide hearing. But, without implying an indictment of the theories themselves, each is deficient in some way or another as a capstone to a theory of social class and religious involvement.

I have already mentioned Emile Durkheim's distinction between beliefs and rites. Another of his classic dichotomies concerns the *sacred* and the *profane*.[8] The distinction was originally designed to illumine the cycle of work and religion among the Arunta, a primitive tribe in Australia. But, as Kingsley Davis[9] points out, it has a limited use in the analysis of contemporary society. Davis suggests that the sacred-profane distinction is a false alternative. There is a third choice, the *ordinary*, that is irreducible to either of the previous two. Moreover, this third choice is especially popular in contemporary life. Apart from Davis' insightful critique, the distinction is inapplicable to religious involvement for another reason. I am not suggesting that one type of religiosity is more profane than another since the colloquial term "profane" connotes a strict opposition to the sacred and a sense of contamination. Instead, I am arguing that different types of involvement represent different orientations to the sacred, all of which are within the range of acceptable religious expression. One may be more secular than another, but the concepts secular and profane are not at all synonymous.

A second possibility is Henri Bergson's[10] distinction between *static* and *dynamic* religion. I have noted throughout that the lower classes manifest a more inward religion, less connected with

[8] Durkheim, *op. cit.*

[9] Kingsley Davis, *The Human Society* (New York: The Macmillan Company, 1949), p. 520.

[10] Henri Bergson, *The Two Sources of Morality and Religion* (Garden City, N.Y.: Doubleday Anchor Books, 1956).

the church as a formal organization, and the middle and upper classes evidence the reverse. In Bergson's terms, then, the former could be seen as dynamic, while the latter approximates the static. But this does both involvement and the Bergsonian terminology an injustice. While it is true that dynamic religion refers to a more personal type, this is really the outbursting of religious creativity and the transcendence of traditional religion altogether. While it is true that static religion centers upon the church as an institution, it really embraces all of conventional religion. At close inspection, then, neither of Bergson's extremes is apt. I am concerned with types of involvement within conventional religion, not without. This also rules out a distinction that is similar to Bergson's: Max Weber's delineation of *mass* religiosity as opposed to *heroic* or *virtuoso* religiosity.[11]

William James's classic portrait of the *sick* versus the *healthy* soul, however, does apply to the normal rounds of religion. James distinguishes them this way:

> Now in contrast with such healthy-minded views as these, if we treat them as a way of deliberately minimizing evil, stands a radically opposite view, a way of maximizing evil, if you please so to call it, based on the persuasion that the evil aspects of our life are of its very essence, and that the world's meaning most comes home to us when we lay them most to heart.[12]

Although James makes no reference to such sociological factors as social class, there is a sense in which the distinction is applicable to class differences in religion. Because the middle and upper classes are more successful according to society's standards of prestige, they should be less aware of life's perversities. It follows, then, that this should result in a "healthier" religion than that of the lower classes. But this distinction too has its disadvantages. It concerns only two of Glock's four dimensions: the ideological and the experiential. What would be the behavioral evidence of a healthy orientation? How is the consequential dimension related? Finally, James's psychological interests are

---

[11] Gerth and Mills (eds.), *op. cit.*, pp. 267–301, especially pp. 287–90.

[12] William James, *The Varieties of Religious Experience* (New York: The Modern Library, 1936), p. 128. Reprinted by permission of Paul R. Reynolds, Inc., 599 Fifth Avenue, New York 17, N.Y.

also a liability. Rather than seek sociological explanations of individual behavior, James looks more at the inner world of inveterate mood and temperament. Rather than explore the consequences of religious differences for social organization, James's theory examines linkages within the individual's world alone.

The same disadvantages accrue to Gordon Allport's distinction between *extrinsic* and *intrinsic* religion. In the former, "the person does not serve his religion; its function is to serve him. The master motive is always self-interest."[13] By contrast, the intrinsic orientation is motivated by altruism. Here religion is not a talisman but a quieter, more humble faith. Once again, the distinction does not extend readily to all of Glock's dimensions of the religious experience, and it is related to personality factors rather than social influences.

In contrast with these psychological frameworks, Joseph H. Fichter, S. J.[14] offers one that is more sociological. His description of the Catholic *Southern Parish* suggests strong competition from the parishioners' secular commitments. The Catholic church may seem dysfunctional in the light of the contrasting values of other institutions and their conflicting demands. Fichter goes on, then, to delineate four degrees of involvement within the Catholic church: the *nuclear*, the *modal*, the *marginal*, and the *dormant*. He suggests that the types are differentially exposed to competing pressures and that this accounts for the variation in the degree of their Catholicism.

While this approach returns us to more sociological concerns, it has weaknesses of another sort. Fichter's types are only quantitatively differentiated and his measures are exclusively behavioral in Glock's terms. That is, they include attendance at Mass, the observance of the sacraments of Communion and Penance, and the parochial education of children. No linkages emerge for religious beliefs, or the experiential and consequential facets of religion. And yet Protestants, at least, may be nuclear on one dimension and dormant on another. This is precisely the insight contributed by Glock.

[13] Gordon W. Allport, "Religion and Prejudice," *Crane Review*, II (1959), as cited in John Photiadis and Jeanne Biggar, "Religiosity, Education, and Ethnic Distance," *American Journal of Sociology*, LXVII (1962), 667.

[14] Joseph H. Fichter, S. J., "The Marginal Catholic: An Institutional Approach," in Milton J. Yinger (ed.), *Religion, Society and the Individual* (New York: The Macmillan Company, 1957), pp. 423–33.

So far, then, all of the candidates have had disqualifying shortcomings. Some do not apply to the individual; some are too psychological. Several focus on virtuoso rather than conventional religion. Another is too quantitative. Some are too general to apply to Glock's specific dimensions; others refer only to one or two of these dimensions. The discussion has not been fruitless, however, if it has emphasized the criteria that must be met, given a brief sketch of some major theoretical formulations, and indicated that the final choice is not fortuitous. Let us turn to that choice now in the church-sect distinction of previous literature.

Church-Sect Theory in General Review

No field is more indebted to its predecessors than the sociology of religion, and none of its legacies is more enduring than the church-sect dichotomy. The dichotomy has cut a wide swath through religious scholarship. Its various facets should illuminate the problem of social class and individual religiosity, while relating this to other areas. Before applying the distinction to individual involvement, it is worth reviewing the theory as it has been traditionally applied to religious organizations.

The concepts of ''church'' and ''sect'' are not wholly anchored in reality. Intended as ideal types, no actual religious group is expected to satisfy all of the criteria for one type or the other. Rather groups can be compared on the extent to which they approximate either of the ideal extremes. The extremes differ along two principal axes; first, their internal characteristics, and second, their relation to the external world at large.

Internally, the church has a professional leadership, a relatively impersonal fellowship, and lax criteria for membership. It stresses the sacraments and ritualistic religion. In sharp contrast, the sect's leadership is charismatic and non-professional. Its founder is typically a religious eccentric in the eyes of the church, and his successors in authority are drawn from the ranks of the congregation. Further, the sect's membership standards are stringent and include conversion and signs of salvation. The fellowship is an exclusive moral community and charged with intimacy. Spontaneity replaces ritual; personal testimony is valued more highly than any sacrament.

Externally, the church accommodates the secular order. Its posture is one of adaptive compromise, and this leads to organizational stability and a large following. But a compromise carries its own imperatives. Traditional doctrine is deemphasized if it is apt to breed conflict with secular values. The church must be willing to share its adherents with a number of secular institutions. Again in contrast, the sect is either aloof or antagonistic toward the secular society. Animated by a distinctive doctrine, the sect is unwilling and unable to capitulate. Its members have only secondary allegiances to secular groups and their contaminating ideologies.

In all of this, Max Weber[15] is credited with the original formulation, although the distinction was applied more extensively by his student, Ernst Troeltsch.[16] The latter's *The Social Teachings of the Christian Churches* is a compendium of examples of both churches and sects. It is a lengthy account of their historical antagonisms, with the church emerging as the ultimate winner in a pyrrhic victory that sacrificed many of the original Christian ideals. It is important to note, however, that Troeltsch does not force all of religion into the dichotomy. He sees "mysticism" as a third type of religion that is independent of either church or sect. An individualized expression, somewhat akin to Bergson's dynamic religion, this has been largely overlooked in the subsequent rush to elaborate the church-sect distinction alone. However, Troeltsch felt that mysticism would be the dominant religious type among the educated classes of the twentieth century, and there is evidence that it has gained a foothold.[17]

[15] Max Weber, *The Protestant Ethic and the Spirit of Capitalism* (New York: Charles Scribner's Sons, 1958), especially pp. 145–54.

[16] Ernst Troeltsch, *The Social Teachings of the Christian Churches* (New York: The Macmillan Company, 1932), especially I, 331–82. In contemporary usage, "sects" are generally thought of as splinter movements that retreat to a more conservative and more extreme religious position when compared to the "church" that spawned them. This, however, is not necessarily the case. Troeltsch points out that many of the early Catholic sects were movements of liberalization. Subsequent theorists have suggested that the terms "church" and "sect" are independent of theology and should be restricted to purely organizational matters. Others argue the reverse and seek to relate church and sect primarily to theology. The debate persists and may outlive the distinction itself.

[17] *Ibid.,* I, 376, and II, 993. Note that Troeltsch's usage of "mysticism" is broader than the traditional reference to a striving for higher spirituality

Unlike the previous concepts, "church" and "sect" were related to social class differences from the start. Weber comments upon the low status of American sects compared with the "genteel" constituency of the churches. Troeltsch makes the point more generally:

> The fully developed Church, however, utilizes the State and the ruling classes, and weaves these elements into her own life; she then becomes an integral part of the existing social order; from this standpoint, then, the Church both stabilizes and determines the social order; in so doing, however, she becomes dependent upon the upper classes, and upon their development. The sects, on the other hand, are connected with the lower classes, or at least with those elements in Society which are opposed to the State and to Society; they work upwards from below, and not downwards from above.[18]

Theoretically, then, church and sect form a division of labor among religious organizations. This is reflected in the status of their members as well as in their programs.

More recent research has supported this relationship with class. S. D. Clark,[19] Liston Pope,[20] and Thomas O'Dea[21] are but

---

by eschewing the conventional and contemplating the obscure. The important thing to Troeltsch is an individuation of the religious experience so that it lacks the fetters of an organizational allegiance. To be sure, this may include the spiritualist, but it is meant to embrace the atheist as well, since Troeltsch discusses mysticism's affinity for humanism and "autonomous science." Actually, it is possible to trace the history of Christianity in terms of the progressive development of mysticism, as is suggested by J. M. Guyau, *The Non-Religion of the Future* (New York: Schocken Books, 1962; first published in 1897). Distinct spurts are marked by the Protestant Reformation, the rise of Unitarianism, and the emergence of even more liberal movements such as Freethought and Ethical Culture. Indeed, the latter two have been seriously affected by this individualism. A founding principle of both groups, it has returned to haunt any kind of organizational program. Not only has this inhibited the achievement of ideological consensus and social action, but it has seriously hampered the recruitment process since it is difficult to proselytize unless there is agreement as to what is being offered.

[18] *Ibid.*, I, 331.

[19] S. D. Clark, *Church and Sect in Canada* (Toronto: University of Toronto Press, 1948).

[20] Liston Pope, *Millhands and Preachers* (New Haven, Conn.: Yale University Press, 1942).

[21] Thomas O'Dea, *The Mormons* (Chicago: University of Chicago Press, 1957).

a few who have found churches to have a higher-status composition than sects. Moreover, their studies elaborate Troeltsch's
conception of a church-sect dynamic in relation to class. Sects
generally begin as lower-class splinter movements of the established but compromised churches. The lower classes have an
affinity for a movement of the elect, one that promises ultimate
salvation despite present secular failure. Yet most sects are unstable. A fully converted membership is increasingly hard to
come by; non-professional leaders do not always have the necessary charisma; and an ethic at odds with secular values is difficult to sustain. In order to maintain itself, the sect gradually
takes on the qualities of a church. The initial blush of enthusiasm
gives way to relaxed membership standards, a less aggressive doctrine, training of lay leaders, and a groping for secular recognition. All of these qualities can be traced in the development of
Quakerism, the Jehovah's Witnesses, the Mormons, and even the
Baptists and the Methodists.

An important correlate of this change from sect to church is a
change in status composition. As the sect becomes more churchlike, its status level rises accordingly.[22] This may occur in two
ways. On the one hand, there may be a wholesale turnover of
membership of the kind described by Pope and Clark among
southern Baptists and Canadian Methodists respectively. On the
other hand, the original members of the sect may undergo upward mobility. Here O'Dea's study of the Mormons and Benton
Johnson's[23] work with the Holiness sects provide illustrations.
Indeed, Johnson argues that some sects have a salutary rather
than regressive effect on the mobility of their parishioners. They
encourage an asceticism that is conducive to economic success as
the seventeenth-century Puritans and the nineteenth-century
American Quakers illustrate.

Apart from these organizational analyses, however, there is

[22] In Ch. VIII I will argue that increased stability is as much the result
of status heterogeneity as it is the result of upward status mobility. Actually no sect undergoes complete upward mobility. While many take on higher-
status members, this generally effects a heterogeneous parish rather than
a purely aristocratic one.

[23] Benton Johnson, "Do Holiness Sects Socialize in Dominant Values?"
Social Forces, XXXIX (1961), 309–16. Note that Johnson does not extend
his argument to all sects. In fact, he explicitly recognizes that the Holiness
groups may be an exception and not the rule.

another group of studies that comment on class differences between churches and sects from a more social-psychological perspective. Walter Goldschmidt,[24] Anton Boisen,[25] John B. Holt,[26] and Richard Niebuhr[27] have all discussed the special religious needs of different social classes and the distinct fulfillments each requires. For example, Goldschmidt relates the sect to the social deprivations of the lower classes as follows:

> In a society which makes overt expression of the hierarchy of its members in terms of traditional and invidious social values, the individual seeks the companionship of those who reinforce his own position. . . .
> [The sect] denies the existence of this world with its woes; it denies the values in terms of which they are the underprivileged and sets up in their stead a putative society in the Kingdom of God, where because of their endowments (which we will call emotionalism), they are the elite.[28]

Goldschmidt emphasizes two qualities that appeared in Weber's and Troeltsch's original models of the sect. The first is the intimate moral community: a kind of fraternity under duress. The second is a withdrawal from the secular world and its canons of success.

The literature on sects is a repository for the sociologically exotic, and it provides numerous illustrations of both of these qualities. Arthur Fauset[29] reports an instance of almost literal fraternalism in the Negro cult of the Moorish Science Temple. It is common for sect members to refer to each other as "brother" or "sister," but here the prefixes "el" or "bey" are added to each name to emphasize the sense of kinship. Anton Boisen provides a poignant example of cultivated withdrawal at a convention of the Church of God in Chattanooga, Tennessee. One of

[24] Walter R. Goldschmidt, "Class Denominationalism in Rural California Churches," *American Journal of Sociology* XLIX (1944), 348–55.

[25] Anton Boisen, *Religion in Crisis and Custom* (New York: Harper and Brothers, 1945).

[26] John B. Holt, "Holiness Religion: Cultural Shock and Social Reorganization," *American Sociological Review*, V (1940), 740–47.

[27] H. Richard Niebuhr, *The Social Sources of Denominationalism* (New York: Henry Holt & Company, Inc., 1929).

[28] Goldschmidt, *op. cit.*, p. 354. By permission of The University of Chicago Press.

[29] Arthur Fauset, "Moorish Science Temple of America," in Yinger (ed.), *op. cit.*, pp. 498–507.

the featured entertainments was a seven-year-old girl singing, "I'll never feel at home in this world anymore."[30] Finally, there is even evidence that these latent purposes of the sect are more important than their manifest doctrinal mission. An early nine-teenth-century apocalyptic sect, the Millerites, persisted long after their original prediction of the end of the world had failed to materialize. After several recalculations of the date, the apocalypse was ignored, and even so the sect continued for a short time. Festinger, Riecken, and Schachter[31] provide a contemporary example in the Seekers, a group that retreated in advance of an interplanetary attack. Again, it seems that the retreat was more salient than the expectations of doom.

In contrast with the sect's fulfillment of lower-class needs, consider Richard Niebuhr's description of the church's response to the middle classes:

> As in the case of the poor, the sanction of religion is invoked upon the peculiar virtues of the group itself; honesty, industry, sobriety, thrift, and prudence, on which the economic structure of business as well as the economic and social status of the individual depend, receive his veneration while the virtues of solidarity, sympathy, and fraternity are correspondingly ignored. . . . The religious ethics of the middle class is marked throughout by this characteristic of individualism.[32]

Unlike the sect, then, the church is more individualistic than fraternal and works within, rather than outside of, secular society and its values. This echoes Max Weber's earlier description of the religious propensities of the "civic strata." Weber[33] noted their "elective affinity (for) technological or economic rationalism" and observed that this intruded into their religion as well. Harold Laski makes the point with less reserve in his remark that American churches

---

[30] Anton Boisen, "Religion in Hard Times: A Study of the Holy Rollers," *Social Action* (1939).

[31] Leon Festinger, Henry W. Riecken, Jr., and Stanley Schachter, *When Prophecy Fails* (Minneapolis: University of Minnesota Press, 1956).

[32] Niebuhr, *op. cit.*, pp. 86–87. By permission of Mrs. H. Richard Niebuhr.

[33] Max Weber, "The Social Psychology of the World Religions," in Gerth and Mills (eds.), *op. cit.*, p. 284.

make peace with convention as a condition of survival in a
world in which material success is the value which permits
no rival to challenge its authority.[34]

In sum, the church-sect dichotomy finds a parallel in the distinction between the religious needs of the higher- and lower-
status groups. So far, however, the dichotomy has been restricted
to religious organizations. To what extent is it helpful in de-
lineating types of religious involvement within the same organization?

The Church-Sect Dichotomy and Individual Religiosity

There is, of course, a reason why the church-sect distinction has
not been applied to individuals within the same denomination
or congregation. One of the criteria of the ideal church and the
ideal sect is that the members of each will be similar. But there
is an important sense in which any ideal type is intended for
contamination. As a methodological device, it is meant to provide
a model against which the departures of reality can be charted
systematically. This is hardly possible if the ideal becomes so
unreal as to be irrelevant. Hence there must be continual refine-
ments, and this is part of the goal in using it as a framework for
individual religiosity. Not only may the distinction aid the research, but the research may further clarify the distinction.

Actually there are already grounds for speculating that sectlike religiosity extends beyond the sects themselves. Conversely,
it is possible that churchlike religiosity is present even within
some sects. Thus, Walter Goldschmidt's comments imply that
lower-class religious needs are common to the class as a whole
and not just to those who are members of sects. The same is
true of Richard Niebuhr's comments on the middle and upper
classes, since church members may not be alone in their emphasis
on religious individualism.

Now we have already seen in Table I–1 that even the most
churchly and aristocratic denominations have more members
from the lower class than from any other status group. On the

[34] Harold Laski, *The American Democracy* (New York: Harper and
Brothers, 1948), p. 321.

other hand, established sects such as the Mormons, the Quakers, and especially the Christian Scientists have a considerable following among the middle and upper classes. These are all "cross-pressured" situations, to borrow a metaphor from students of voting. Both the lower-class church member and the high-status sect member have status influences at odds with their religious affiliation. It would seem that their religious needs are inevitably frustrated. But one release from this frustration is the individual's control over his mode of involvement. The higher-status sect member may have a churchlike orientation to the sect. The low-status church member may have a sectlike orientation to the church. Actually the latter may have the best of both worlds. His style of religiosity fits his current illness. Yet, in belonging to a church, he is not insulated from the community at large, and church contacts may make upward mobility more likely than would be the case if he belonged to a sect.

The first step in providing empirical trappings for these suppositions is to specify what churchlike and sectlike modes of individual involvement might be. In general, the two can be distinguished quantitatively and qualitatively along each of Charles Glock's four dimensions of religious behavior. Although my own data will not cover all four dimensions, it is helpful to consider each, if only hypothetically.

Consider first Glock's *ideological* dimension. It is not simply that the sect type believes in religious doctrine and the church type does not. Nevertheless, a quantitative distinction is meaningful. Every individual has a range of beliefs and values and the church-type parishioner apportions his differently than the sect type. Specifically, the church type will be more influenced by non-religious ideologies. He will derive more of his basic orientation from secular values and strive more to achieve secular goals than the sect type. But in addition to this quantitative distinction in degree, there should also be a qualitative distinction in kind. The church type's religious beliefs will be more modern in the sense that they are more dictated by his everyday concerns. The sect type, on the other hand, will reverse the priority. Traditional beliefs will determine his concerns and the secular values to which he can subscribe.

There are numerous illustrations of this polarity in beliefs.

Indeed, Christian doctrine offers salve to both the higher-status church type and the lower-class sectarian. Childs and Cater note two conflicting messages in Christ's parables:

> In the Parable of the Talents Christ taught that each man should be rewarded according to his "good and faithful" services; here lay solid foundations for [Cotton] Mather's emphasis on hard work and wealth-amassing. In the Parable of the Vineyard Christ taught that each worker would be rewarded equally no matter what part of the day he labored; here was a message that goes beyond socialistic equality.[35]

As a further example, churchlike and sectlike ideology can be distinguished within early Calvinism. The original doctrine of predestination chafed the bourgeoisie who demanded greater meaning for their secular pursuits. The notion of an immutable destiny made life on this earth a marking of time rather than an adventure. Partly in response to this pressure, Calvinist theology took a more secular turn as Calvinism in general became more a church than a sect. In doing so, however, many lower-class parishioners were betrayed in their support for a rigid conception of predestination. Since salvation could not be earned through worldly success, their present impoverishment was happily irrelevant to their ultimate existence.

Turning next to the *experiential* dimension, Glock describes it as

> all of those feelings, perceptions and sensations which are experienced by an actor or defined by a religious group or a society as involving some communication, however slight, with a divine essence, i.e., with God, with ultimate reality, with transcendental authority. It is, in effect, spirituality— emotional experience defined as religious which in its extreme forms would be represented by conversion, the visitation of the Holy Spirit, and mysticism.[36]

Again one would expect the sectarian to be quantitatively more affected than the churchlike parishioner. The perfervid revival is nearly synonomous with the sect, and, of course, I am simply

---

[35] Marquis Childs and Douglas Cater, *Ethics in a Business Society* (New York: Harper and Brothers, 1954), p. 85.

[36] Glock, *op. cit.*, pp. 26–27.

translating organizational characteristics into individual terms. At the same time, even the church-type individual will have an experiential streak to his religion, since few organizational involvements are unaccompanied by emotion. Thus, a qualitative distinction in kind is required here as well. William James's[37] distinction between the religion of "healthy-mindedness" and that of the "sick soul" is relevant. Both types are experiential; the emotions of one are primarily optimistic, while the emotions of the other are more pessimistic. The first would be the more churchlike, the second more sectlike.

Schneider and Dornbusch[38] illustrate the distinction with regard to American inspirational religious literature. They note two strands, one that fosters a withdrawal from secular society and another that encourages adaptation of the personality to secular life. They use Erich Fromm's labels of "soul therapy" and "adjustment therapy," and note that both use experiential religion as a therapeutic technique.

Glock's third dimension, the *consequential*, refers to

> what people do and . . . what attitudes they hold as a consequence of their religious beliefs, practices, and experiences. The notion of "works" in the theological meaning of the term is connoted here. The consequential dimension deals with how man relates himself to man rather than how he relates himself to God.[39]

Glock admits that this dimension is the most difficult to assess empirically. On conceptual grounds, however, it too yields both churchlike and sectlike extremes.

Quantitatively, of course, the consequences of religion should be more pervasive for the sectlike parishioner. Religion should extend deeper into his everyday affairs and fare better in the competition with secularism for his general orientation. Qualitatively, the consequences of sectarian religiosity should lead away rather than toward the secular world. In contrast with the church type, the sectarian will place less importance on the

---

[37] James, *op. cit.*

[38] Louis Schneider and Sanford M. Dornbusch, *Popular Religion: Inspirational Books in America* (Chicago: University of Chicago Press, 1958).

[39] Glock, *op. cit.*, p. 27.

secular tasks in which he is judged a failure by his social class position. For the sectarian God is a savior; for the church type He is more of a divine help-mate.[40]

Actually the consequential dimension is the source of some revealing paradoxes in the study of religion. I have already mentioned the virtue of independence in Glock's formulation: a person may be highly involved in one respect but considerably less so in others. One example can be taken from southern fundamentalism as seen through the eyes of a barbed cynic. The alleged high point of that fundamentalism occurred during the famous Scopes Trial in Dayton, Tennessee in the 1920's. But while the citizens were sectlike in their defense of traditional doctrine, H. L. Mencken raises some doubts as to any sectlike consequences of their ostensible religion:

> Even in Dayton, I found, though the mob was up to do execution upon Scopes, that there was a strong smell of antinomianism. The nine churches of the village were all half empty on Sunday, and weeds choked their yards. Only two or three of the resident pastors managed to sustain themselves by their ghostly science; the rest had to take orders for mail-order pantaloons or work in the adjacent strawberry fields; one, I heard was a barber. On the courthouse green a score of sweating theologians debated the darker passages of the Holy Writ day and night, but I soon found they were all volunteers, and that the local faithful, while interested in their exegesis as an intellectual exercise, did not permit it to impede the indigenous debaucheries. Exactly twelve minutes after I reached the village, I was taken in tow by a Christian man and introduced to the favorite tipple of the Cumberland range. . . . They were all hot for Genesis, but their faces were far too florid to be-

[40] The consequential dimension affords a key example of the usefulness of Glock's framework when applied to the church-sect distinction in religious organizations. Normally, the Catholic church is held to be a model of church-type religion. Its stability, emphasis on ritual, impersonal fellowship, and professional priesthood are all solid qualifications. Yet, on other grounds, Catholicism resembles a sect, and this is nowhere more obvious than in the consequential sphere. Thus, Catholicism may sanction a withdrawal from secular pursuits; it certainly presents an image of God as offering salvation and forgiveness as well as an all-embracing escape from one's worldly woes. In similar terms, the Protestant Reformation can also be seen as both a churchlike and a sectlike reaction to Catholicism. The Reformation was churchlike in its injunction to secular perseverance; it was sectlike in its organizational characteristics as a splinter movement.

long to teetotalers, and when a pretty girl came tripping
down the main street which was very often, they reached
for the places where their neckties should have been with
all the amorous enterprise of movie actors. It seemed some-
how strange. . . . Dayton was having a roaring time. It was
better than the circus. But the note of devotion was simply
not there.[41]

Turning last to Glock's *behavioral* dimension, the distinction
between churchlike and sectlike involvement is obvious in its
quantitative sense. Just as the church places far greater emphasis on the ritual and formal organization of religion, so will the
church-type parishioner be more involved in these aspects. As
we have seen, the high-status parishioners are indeed the more
frequent church-attenders and belong to more parish activities.
It bears repeating, however, that the low-status sect types are
not totally alienated from religious organizations. They too may
have a form of behavioral involvement within the church, though
of a qualitatively different sort.

I mentioned earlier that the typical sect stresses spontaneous
participation and an intimate moral community.[42] The sectlike
parishioner should share these proclivities, whether he is a member of a sect or a church. Many will be apathetic toward the
formal ritual of a Sunday service. Church activities may seem
too task-oriented; the normal round of parish gatherings may
appear coldly impersonal. Instead, the sectarian may develop a
group of close friends within the parish. He may attend weekday
services, thus disqualifying himself from the count of Sunday
morning attenders. He may read the Bible at home and have
private prayer and devotion. All of this is participation and
behavioral religiosity, but of a less conventional, less emphasized
variety.

[41] H. L. Mencken, "The Hills of Zion," in Alistair Cooke (ed.), *The Vintage Mencken* (New York: Vintage Books, 1955), pp. 154, 161.

[42] The so-called gnostic sects are atypical in this respect, however. Indeed
these groups are generally more intellectually inclined and are also more
middle and upper class in composition as the example of the Christian Scientists suggests. For further elaboration on various types of sects, see
Bryan R. Wilson's excellent article, "An Analysis of Sect Development,"
American Sociological Review, XXIV (1959), 3–15, and his book, *Sects and
Society* (Berkeley: University of California Press, 1961).

Some Prior Corroborations

The hypothesis that religious organizations host two divergent forms of involvement in the sectlike and the churchlike may seem radical and without justification. Actually it is neither. There is already evidence on the point, ranging from the historical to the statistical. Troeltsch himself discussed the co-existence of churchlike and sectlike tendencies within the typical Christian church. While much of his argument concerned organizational and ideological characteristics, he also makes the point with reference to heterogeneity in class composition. Thus, his remarks on the "primitive church" of the first century were meant to rebut the Marxian view of Christianity as a proletarian movement. It included a substantial number of upper-class members who saw to the financial and organizational exigencies, while the more sectarian lower-class members attended to doctrine and the purities of spirit.[43] The Marxists may reply that this is all part of the proletariat model. Nevertheless, Troeltsch gives succor to the present argument.

Nor was he alone. Moving from the primitive to the monolithic, a number of authors have noted a similar co-existence in the Catholicism of the Middle Ages and the Renaissance. Huizinga[44] contrasts the skeptical ecclesiasticism of the upper and middle classes with the gullible devotionalism and anti-clericalism of the peasantry. Burckhardt sees the gulf widening during the Renaissance as a pre-condition for the Reformation.[45] He de-

---

[43] Troeltsch, *op. cit.*, I, 42–43.

[44] J. Huizinga, *The Waning of the Middle Ages* (Garden City, N.Y.: Doubleday Anchor Books, n.d.), especially pp. 165–81. It is fair to point out, however, that my own interpretation violates much of the spirit of Huizinga's analysis. Although he mentions such distinctions he prefers to explain the variety in styles of religiosity in terms of the "marvelous complexity of the human soul" rather than any similar complexity of the social structure. Huizinga is primarily concerned with the deterioration and excesses in religious symbolism, however, and this leads him to a more psychological analysis.

[45] Jacob Burckhardt, *The Civilization of the Renaissance in Italy* (New York: The Modern Library, 1954), pp. 341–69. Burckhardt suggests paradoxically that it was the Reformation that came to the ultimate rescue of Catholicism. In order to combat the new force and prevent any further fragmentation, Catholicism regrouped its forces and sought to provide more of a home for all classes rather than restrict its organizational appeal to the middle and upper classes. Without the Reformation, Catholicism might

scribes the churchlike religiosity of the upper classes as "compounded of a deep and contemptuous aversion" to spirituality and doctrinal disputes but an "acquiescence in the outward ecclesiastical customs" and "a sense of dependence on ceremonies and sacraments."[46] By contrast, the lower classes were more fervent and, in some senses, less obedient. They were played upon by itinerant preachers and given to intense emotionalism. Yet this was more revivalistic than ecclesiastical and their allegiance was to a different aspect of Catholicism. Alfred von Martin's *Sociology of the Renaissance* makes a similar point.[47] He goes further, however, to contrast lower-class Catholicism as an end in itself with middle class Catholicism as a means to more political and economic goals.

Moving on to the Reformation and the first flowering of Protestantism, we again find coexisting religious styles within the same religious house. It is true that Max Weber's celebrated but controversial treatment[48] has a way of assuming equal and total involvement among all Protestants. But R. H. Tawney goes to some pains to indicate the error.[49] He suggests that much of the development of Calvinism and Puritanism was due to a warring of social doctrines within the movement itself. He contrasts the religious, political and economic views of several groups within the early Protestant folds. It is true, of course, that lower-class movements like the Levellers and the Diggers give clear indication that Protestantism was dominated by the middle classes who pushed their inferiors to rebellion. And yet part of the problem was that the middle-class religiosity was more churchlike than Weber indicates. According to Tawney, and more recently to Kurt Samuelson,[50] we again find the middle classes using the church as a means to an end rather than an end

have deteriorated to the point where it was beyond recovery as a religious, rather than specifically political, institution.

[46] *Ibid.*, pp. 342–43.

[47] Alfred von Martin, *Sociology of the Renaissance* (New York: Harper Torchbooks, 1963), p. 90.

[48] Weber, *The Protestant Ethic and the Spirit of Capitalism, op. cit.*

[49] R. H. Tawney, *Religion and the Rise of Capitalism* (Baltimore, Md.: Penguin Books, Inc., 1947), especially p. 262, fn.

[50] Kurt Samuelson, *Religion and Economic Action: A Critique of Max Weber* (New York: Harper Torchbooks, 1961), especially pp. 27–79.

in itself. Tawney describes middle-class religious involvement as secondary to economic pursuits and conditional upon a favorable ruling for those pursuits.

Or consider Protestantism in nineteenth-century America. Here too there was a co-existence of social classes and religious styles. Here too the middle-class churchlike religiosity dominated. In fact, many of the lower-class sectlike congregants were forced into a marginal position in the church as their cause was spurned by a middle-class leadership. Issues like the right to strike, socialism, and, indeed, poverty itself, were divisive influences that made class distinctions especially salient. Who can wonder that the lower classes should have retreated from Protestant services when the prominent minister Henry Ward Beecher advised workers to rest content on a dollar a day for a family of eight since "water costs nothing; and a man who cannot live on bread is not fit to live."[51] At the same time, the *Congregationalist* of 1878 described the migrant workers of the day as "profane, licentious, filthy, vermin-swarming thieves" and suggested that "the long obsolete whipping-post" might be brought back into use for discipline. Yet even so there remained a substantial proportion of lower-class members in these denominations. These people did not leave the church, but they did leave churchlike involvement for a more private, more traditional, and more comforting sectarian allegiance. It is true that the Social Gospel helped to stem a total alienation, though its policies were hardly radical and it was a disappointment to many and a sop to others. But the important thing about the Social Gospel was the groundwork it laid for Protestantism in the 1930's and the change in tone that finally took root after the Great Depression.

More recently, two authors have dealt with contemporary instances of coexistence, using the same terminology and framework that I have adopted above. After observing the membership of several Protestant churches in southwestern Germany, Peter Berger[52] distinguishes between a congregation's "elite" and the mass of its parishioners. He urges that the former are more

[51] Henry F. May, *Protestant Churches in Industrial America* (New York: Harper and Brothers, 1949), p. 96. See also Martin E. Marty, *The Infidel: Freethought and American Religion* (New York: Meridian Books, 1961).

[52] Peter L. Berger, "Sectarianism and Religious Sociation," *American Journal of Sociology*, LXIV (1958), 41–44.

sectarian because of their greater devotion to the congregation and their greater influence within it. He labels the latter as more churchlike because of their less intense allegiances to the organization. Although I would reverse the labels and call the elite more churchlike precisely because of their greater involvement in the organizational and administrative aspects of the parish, the semantic differences are less important than the common perception.

Finally, Russell Dynes[53] has not only used the same terms but applied them as they are used in this study. Dynes provides the first statistical support, although his study deals with hypothetical religious preferences rather than actual religious involvement. To study the preferences of an adult sample in Columbus, Ohio, Dynes's questionnaire included twenty-four items for which there were five possible responses ranging from "strongly agree" to "strongly disagree." The items were largely based upon Liston Pope's list of characteristics that distinguish the ideal sect from the ideal church.[54] They include statements such as "I think a minister should preach without expecting to get paid for it," "I feel that a congregation should encourage the minister during his sermon by saying 'amen,'" "I think success in one's job is one mark of a good Christian," and "I think it is more important to live a good life now than to bother about life after death." The first two of these examples are clearly more sectlike; the last two are more churchlike.

Dynes assigned the respondents scores on a church-sect scale. A high mean score on all the items represents an over-all churchlike preference. A low mean score signifies an over-all propensity for sectlike religiosity. Table II–1 presents the relation between these scores and social class. In this case, class is measured by the North-Hatt scale of occupational prestige in which a high

---

[53] Russell R. Dynes, "The Church-Sect Typology and Socio-Economic Status," *American Sociological Review*, XX (1955), 555–60. Note that the term "typology" is technically inappropriate, however common here. It implies that all of the distinguishing dimensions are made explicit and that all of their combinations have been taken into account. Lamentably, this is not yet the case with church-sect theory. In fact, the failure to isolate its dimensions and their multiple combinations has been a considerable disadvantage in its use and development.

[54] Pope, *op. cit.*

score represents high prestige. The prestige ranks run down the left-hand column. For each prestige level, the respondent's church-sect scores were averaged, and there is a strong relationship. In general, the mean score decreases with declining occu-

TABLE II–1

Church-Sect Scale of Religious Preferences by Occupational Prestige

Occupational Prestige	Mean Church-Sect Scale Score
80 and above	80.5
75–79	77.0
70–74	78.2
65–69	69.9
60–64	62.2
Under 60	56.8

From Russell R. Dynes, "The Church-Sect Typology and Socio-Economic Status," *American Sociological Review*, XX (1955), 559. By permission of the author and The American Sociological Association.

pational prestige or class standing. Thus, sectlike preferences wax, while churchlike propensities wane.

Dynes found in addition that this relationship obtains even among those who gave verbal allegiance to the same denomination. Among Methodists, for example, the high-status score was 78.0 on the church-sect scale compared with a low-status score of 67.1. Among Presbyterians, the comparable scores are 78.4 and 71.1. Apparently, then, churchlike and sectlike orientations do coexist within the same religious institution. The problem now is to discover whether this finding for abstract religious preferences extends to actual religious involvement.

Summary

This chapter has sought a reconciliation for the conflicting research in Chapter I and a theory of social class and religious involvement generally. The task required two separate distinctions in kind, both of which were intended for quite different purposes. First, Charles Glock's four dimensions of the religious experience provide an over-all scheme that abandons the fallacious nicety of generalizing from one aspect of religiosity to all others. Second, the church-sect dichotomy applies to each of Glock's dimensions to provide hypotheses for social class and a link to other problems in the sociology of religion. Whether one is concerned with behavioral, ideological, experiential, or consequential religiosity, one can expect both churchlike and sectlike patterns. These are distinct both quantitatively and qualitatively.

Any study that begins with a theory risks embarrassment of two sorts. First, the theory may simply be wrong. Second, the theory is apt to be far more comprehensive than the data which test it. In the next part, these embarrassments will begin to emerge, especially the latter one. Because this is a secondary analysis of information collected for another purpose, the data do not cover all of the specific hypotheses I have advanced. Nevertheless, the data that are available should supply a first evaluation of the theory by examining some of its key elements.

Part Two

III

Tools for Testing:
The Available Measures of Religiosity

The principle of maximizing resources is nowhere more compelling than in the secondary analysis of questionnaires. Unlike the researcher who designs his own instrument and collects his own data, the secondary analyst must use information originally intended for quite different purposes. The disadvantages here are obvious and well known. But there are also two important advantages. For one, the secondary analyst is sometimes forced to be unorthodox, and, in exploring new items, techniques, and conceptualizations, he may make a contribution. A second virtue is related. The offbeat requires justification in research circles. While the innovations may not be spectacular in themselves, accounts of them may involve more open consideration of a study's difficulties and more precise explication of its premises and theory.

The church membership surveys of Baptists, Congregationalists, Disciples of Christ, Lutherans, and Presbyterians included six common measures of religiosity or religious involvement. Unhappily these items do not exhaust the measures possible. There are several conspicuous omissions such as a sophisticated indicator of religious belief, and an accurate gauge of emotional response. Then, too, there is a decidedly proreligious bias in any questionnaire that asks cooperation as part of "God's work."

But these difficulties are not insuperable. While the study will not be exhaustive, the items do range beyond the now conventional use of church attendance alone. Matters of belief and emotional response are undeniably important, and the available items do allow some cautious inferences about each. Although there is a bias, it applies throughout the sample and should not grossly distort a search for relative differences instead of absolute levels of involvement. Finally, the theory of the previous chapter should be an ally. By placing the items within the theory, their connotations should be broader and their interrelations clearer. If there are gaps in the items themselves, the theory should supply some provisional filling.

Two further remarks by way of introduction. First, throughout this chapter and the next, the focus will be on Lutheranism, for an initial and rather intensive case study. In Chapter V, the analysis will turn to the remaining denominations to allow a wider test that applies to Protestantism generally. A second comment concerns the research procedure. Matters of research history are far from scholarly trivia. Every schoolboy knows that the proper scientific method moves from hypotheses to testing. This study is an instance where the actual departs from the preferred. It is true that the hypotheses concerning three of the items—outside commitments, religious reward, and the reaction to ministerial participation in community controversy— were spawned before the actual tests, as was the notion that the Lutheran case could be generalized to other denominations. But the remaining three measures of involvement have less proper pedigrees. Two of these—church attendance and parish activities —are closely explored by previous research. For this reason alone, a hypothesis may seem to be a certainty masquerading as a gamble. But, in addition, I was aware of some of my own findings before the conceptualization. A major stimulus to the study was my puzzlement over the peculiarly low relation between attendance and activities on the one hand, and close friendships in the parish on the other, among the Lutherans. Despite these compromises with the scientific model, my own feeling is that the results should not be ignored. Whether a finding is predicted in advance or explained *post hoc,* some body of theory is necessary. The crucial matter is whether a set of findings are consistent and consistently sensible when judged from a broader perspective. By now, the reader has that perspective and, hopefully, he will be a better critic as a result.

The plan of the chapter is as follows. First, I will consider the six items singly, pointing out their position within Glock's dimensions, defining churchlike and sectlike responses, and hypothesizing their relations with social class. Next I will convert the six measures into two summary indexes, one of churchlike and one of sectlike religiosity. Last, I will present the indexes' sample distributions and interrelations as a prelude to their actual associations with status in Chapter IV.

Attendance at Sunday Services

By now church attendance is an old friend. As Chapter I suggested, it is a *sine qua non* of surveys in the sociology of religion. This has presented difficulties, yet these are not with attendance itself but rather with reliance upon it as the sole measure of religiosity. Since it represents only one part of religious involvement, the problem is to ascertain which part.

In Glock's terms, church attendance is the prototype of behavioral religiosity. It involves active participation in prescribed ritual. It need have no relation to doctrinal belief, emotionality, or the consequences of religion in everyday life, although, in practice, the four dimensions will likely be associated to some degree.

But this is only a first step in the conceptualization of church attendance as a measure of religious involvement. The next step involves the church-sect distinction. Earlier I described the ideal-typical church both internally and externally. Internally, it is professionally led, highly formalized, impersonal, and non-exclusive. Externally, it invokes a two-way compromise with secular society; secular concerns penetrate the church, and the church supports the secular order. The Sunday services of all five Protestant denominations fulfill these two criteria of the ideal church. The Lutherans are a case in point.

Originally, of course, Lutheranism was the pioneer of Protestantism. As first formulated by its namesake, it was a counter movement to Catholicism, designed to put men in closer touch with God and each other. In the later sixteenth century, then, its services were sectlike. But both Troeltsch[1] and Weber[2] indicate that Lutheranism was never as radical or as alienated as its Calvinist successor. Moreover, Lutheranism soon abandoned many features of its reformation protest and began to ape Catholicism itself. It took on a professional clergy and developed a high regard for sacraments and ritual despite its early protests against the Catholic middleman between God and the parishioner. It also supported the traditional secular order and resisted the radical innovations of encroaching capitalism.

Still, if this was true of European Lutheranism, the nineteenth-century American transplant revived at least a few of the early sectlike characteristics. An ethnic enclave, it catered to unassimilated Germans and Scandinavians. Its function was to provide camaraderie, an Old World afterglow, and solace to those who found little secular success. The services were conducted in the native tongue. The clergy were frequently nonprofessional wisemen of the ethnic community.

This phase, however, was short-lived and American Lutheranism began to change in the early twentieth century, regaining many of the churchlike characteristics of its European counterpart. Marcus Hansen[3] attributes a signal influence to rebellious youth who insisted on an English-speaking Lutheranism and doctrinal concessions from the traditional Augsberg Confession. As acculturation took root, the church was no longer an island of comfort for the ethnically unadjusted. As its members became better able to compete for success in the wider society, the church began to share them with other institutions. Camaraderie lessened with decreasing duress. Exclusiveness declined as the church became more liberal and more Americanized. In all of this, the services no longer provided balm for the dispossessed;

---

[1] Ernst Troeltsch, *The Social Teachings of the Christian Churches* (New York: The Macmillan Company, 1932), especially Vol. II.

[2] Max Weber, *The Protestant Ethic and the Spirit of Capitalism* (New York: Charles Scribner's Sons, 1958).

[3] Marcus Hansen, *The Immigrant and American History,* quoted in Robert Lee, *The Social Sources of Church Unity* (Nashville, Tenn.: Abingdon Press, 1960), p. 45.

they became spurs for the ambitious. Note the growing church-like quality suggested in Walter Kloetzli's description of services in one of the Lutheran congregations studied here:

> [The Master Plan for Immanuel Church] reveals a genuine turning *from a closely bound fellowship to a body aware of its responsibility to the community.* . . . Accompanying the recent changes in the church's program has been a new "tone" in church life, manifested chiefly in changes in the worship service. "The whole worship service is *far more liturgical* than before," noted the pastor, and added, "It must be *business like and professional.*" The new service book of the Lutheran church and other departures from the old familiar practices symbolizes Immanuel's efforts to raise the tone of its services *in keeping with the urbanity of its environment* [italics added].[4]

The italicized phrases signify a compromise with secular standards that no sect would tolerate. Worship in the sects differs radically from the services of the major Protestant denominations in general, and the contemporary Lutherans in particular. The sects feature extensive audience participation ranging from spontaneous "amens" to perfervid gospel singing. Members testify to their conversion. The gathering is intimate rather than impersonal. The service leads away from the secular world instead of towards it. The Bible is an inspiration and not a liturgical text. Sermons are expressive and emotional, lacking the cool exegesis of a churchlike minister's discourse.

In short, high church attendance within our five Protestant denominations can be seen as a churchlike form of involvement. While it is misleading to categorize non-attendance as sectlike, it is plausible to predict that those with sectlike predilections will shy away from services through boredom and even alienation. Not only do the services invoke a quite different religious style; they also address themselves to secular issues that are either burdensome or simply irrelevant. Sinclair Lewis puts these words in the mouth of one character, and a number of sectarians might agree:

[4] Walter Kloetzli, *The City Church: Death or Renewal* (Philadelphia: The Muhlenberg Press, 1961), pp. 24–25. Kloetzli worked with the same Lutheran data to somewhat different ends. His book is a description of each of the twelve congregations, the problems they faced, and their attempted solutions.

My objection to the church isn't that preachers are cruel, hypocritical, actually wicked, though some of them are that too. . . . And it isn't that the church is in bondage to Big Business and doctrines as laid down by millionaires—though a lot of churches are that too. My chief objection is that ninety-nine per cent of sermons and Sunday School Teachings are so agonizingly *dull*![5]

Now given the findings of previous research, it may seem to be anticlimactic and even dishonest to "hypothesize" a positive relationship with status. It is true that, among Lutherans, attendance is generally greater among those of high status. But Appendix A injects surprise into an apparently pat subject by showing that the relationship is slight indeed for the total sample of Protestants.[6] There are peculiar methodological circumstances, to be sure. Nevertheless this underlines the warning that there are few findings in sociology which are impervious to flux under repeated replication. There are clearly a number of factors in addition to vertical social status that may affect church attendance. For example, one status dimension which this study does not consider is that of "situs" or horizontal differentiation on the rung of the vertical scale. Joel E. Gerstl provides a revealing illustration by contrasting dentists and college professors, both of whom would score high on the current scale. After reporting that dentists had much higher rates of church attendance, Gerstl notes that "the dentists apologized for not attending more, the professors for attending as much as they did."[7]

[5] Sinclair Lewis, *Elmer Gantry* (New York: Dell Publishing Co., 1960), p. 392 By permission of Harcourt, Brace & World, Inc., original publisher.

[6] For an analysis that bears directly on this finding, see Harry C. Dillingham, "Protestant Religion and Social Status," unpublished paper, Central Michigan University, 1964. After re-examining some of the same studies cited in Ch. I of the present study, Dillingham finds that "a moderate *negative* relationship existed when the units of analysis were the denominational averages of social status and church attendance. Further evidence . . . showed that within each denomination a moderate *positive* relationship existed, or was deducible. These two opposing relationships tended to cancel one another, producing a net or over-all relationship approaching zero" (p. 8).

[7] Joel E. Gerstl, "Leisure, Taste and Occupational Milieu," in Erwin O. Smigel (ed.), *Work and Leisure* (New Haven, Conn.: College and University Press, 1963), p. 68.

Parish Activities

Like church attendance, parish activity is not new to research in the sociology of religion. Also like attendance, it falls along Glock's behavioral dimension of religion. Thus, it involves active "doing" within the church organization, and it has no necessary relation to ideological, experiential, or consequential religiosity.

Actually two types of activities are distinguishable. The first are primarily social functions and provide structured fellowship. These may range from age-group discussion circles to recreation leagues and philanthropic organizations. The second type of activity is more instrumental than expressive and bears much of the burden for maintaining the church as an institution. Here the tasks are supervising the congregation's finances, house and grounds, Sunday School program, choir, and sometimes the allocation of cemetery lots. Both forms of activitiy are churchlike, though for slightly different reasons.

Robert Lee has commented on the first type of activity, suggesting that major Protestant denominations have purged themselves of much of their traditional religious content:

> Nowadays rarely does a denomination convince a person to join on the grounds that it alone bears the true doctrine; the claim to be the True Church is relegated to the limbo of arrogancy. *Organized activities in churches tend to follow along interest-group lines; they are underdeveloped in areas of theological discipline and discussion* [italics added].[8]

Others have made similar observations in pointing to the church's competition with secular associations. Meetings of the young adults, the women's auxiliary, and the high schoolers are designed to provide secular attractions within the church itself. The common weekly businessmen's lunch is a counter to such groups as the Rotary, Lions, and Kiwanis clubs. In all of this, then, there is a tendency to dilute the traditional doctrine and to accommodate the outside world in a decidedly churchlike fashion.

Another churchlike characteristic is related to this secular competition. Activities are not restricted to the fully converted

[8] Lee, *op. cit.*, p. 86.

or spiritually committed. Instead they are used as beacons and are often the prospective member's first contacts with the church. Because membership is not selective on religious grounds, there is a less than optimum sense of an intimate community of the religious elite. On this score too the activities are far from sectlike. It is true that the sectarian seeks fellowship within his religion, but he prefers fellowship of a closer, more exclusive, and more traditionally religious sort.

If anything, activities of the instrumental type are even more churchlike. Here discussion and fellowship give way to less leisurely functions. The goal of camaraderie is replaced by efficiency, and practicality takes precedence. All of this smacks of the secular world of business. Moreover, the responsibilities involve grappling with eminently secular problems. Matters such as finances, building care, and new construction require this-worldly talent and interest. The sectarian should have neither interest in nor ability for these concerns because of his inclination to turn away from the world and treat religion as a haven rather than an enterprise.

Again, the hypothesis for social class is not surprising. Activities of both sorts should appeal more to high-status than to low-status parishioners. It does not follow that total inactivity is the quintessence of lower-class participation. Nevertheless, those of low status should be considerably less involved. Actually, the hypothesis gains support from still another consideration. Not only should those of low status have a lesser penchant for activities, but the activities should have less need for them. This is especially true of the instrumental tasks where those of low status have few business or administrative skills to contribute. While the activities may not be exclusive on religious grounds, some are selective on criteria of status and worldly competence to insure a productive membership. As one church leader in the sample put it:

> All of the men of the council should know a considerable amount about business. We are not interested in getting any Tom, Dick, or Harry on the council.[9]

A pastor discussed his lay committees similarly, while hinting

[9] Kloetzli, *op. cit.*, p. 23.

that membership is both a reward and a goad for monetary generosity:

> They're the biggest givers to the church, that is, financially, they're the right men for the job.[10]

Of course, it is easy to overstate the case for selective recruitment. But while most church councils include some low-status members, it is not surprising that the councils and activities tend to disenchant the majority of lower-class parishioners. Without reinforcing this disenchantment, the churchlike leaders may simply ignore rather than counteract it. In any event, discrimination is not a major theme in this discussion. The primary point is that if parish activities are churchlike one can explain their lesser popularity among the more sectarian lower classes.

Organizational Involvements Outside the Church

Although church attendance and parish activities are "old hat" in the sociology of religion, the next four items are less conventional. Here conceptualization is more important, for hypotheses are no longer buttressed by previous research. In fact, the first measure here is not of church involvement at all, but rather of affiliations outside the church in activities such as the Rotary Club, the PTA, political groups, and volunteer community agencies. Though far-ranging, the item is far from irrelevant.

One of the basic criteria of the church is its accommodation to the secular world. Certainly there was a time when American Protestants sought to overpower secularism instead of adjusting to it. This, however, is now an anachronism of the nineteenth century. The contemporary denomination not only emulates the secular in its own activities; it also recognizes outside groups as legitimate and sees itself as one among many organizations which serve meaningful purposes. The recognition may be begrudging, but it is dictated by the demands of realism. The denomination needs the support of outside groups. Moreover, it can ill afford to alienate its members by demanding an exclusive allegiance in a society which is built upon multiple associations. Since the churchlike parishioner is one who is of the world and not beyond

[10] *Ibid.*, p. 13.

it, the church must reinforce his secular life and neither dominate nor supplant it.

The sect and the sectlike parishioner stand in sharp contrast.
Just as the church is defined by accommodation, the sect is distinguished by alienation. Whether aggressive or simply withdrawn, it suffers two points of friction with secular society.
First, its self-consciously distinctive doctrine and values allow
for no recognition of competing claims. As Bryan Wilson[11] has
indicated, the small sect is an ideological monolith that requires
total control. Second, the sect is designed as a refuge from the
secular concerns and judgments that pervade the remainder of
society, including its voluntary associations. Apart from the
dangers of competition, the sect and the sectlike should have
little interest in the topics that occupy Elks, Rotarians, political
groups, and even the trade unions. All make status judgments
in which the sectarian suffers a critical lack of esteem. While
trade unions and some political parties offer an exception, they
differ from the sect in their strategy of coping. The union and
the party have an active, almost aggressive posture that combats
the secular on its own terms. The sect is either passively withdrawn or seeks changes from a wholly different, otherworldly
perspective that is invulnerable to secular evaluations.

In short, the churchlike parishioner should be *segmentally*
involved in his religion, while sectlike parishioners are *organically* involved. As Philip Selznick[12] uses the terms, a segmental
commitment claims only part of the individual and shares his
allegiance with other groups. Organic commitment is enveloping.
If one assumes that every individual has a limited resource of
affiliational energies and a limited portfolio of commitments,
then the one who concentrates these most heavily on the church
is most involved. Most involved, that is, in this one particular
facet of religiosity, another that occurs along Glock's behavioral
dimension. As for the status hypothesis, high-status parishioners
will be more churchlike, and, hence, more apt to belong to outside
secular organizations. Low-status parishioners, who are more
sectlike, will be less involved in these groups.

---

[11] Bryan R. Wilson, *Sects and Society* (Berkeley: University of California
Press, 1961).
[12] Philip Selznick, lectures, University of California, Berkeley.

Close Friendships or Communal Involvement

So far I have sketched at best a paradox and at worst a contradiction. On the one hand, the sectlike parishioner is organically involved in religion, giving it the major portion of his allegiance. On the other hand, he is apt to be bored or alienated by church services and many parish activities. If the sectarian is so involved in religion, how is it manifested?

Plainly, Sunday services and formal activities do not exhaust the commitment alternatives. These, along with outside involvements, give an adequate coverage to churchlike religiosity but leave the sectlike untapped. Two likely areas for sectarian involvement are Glock's ideological and experiential dimensions. The sectlike parishioner should be especially tied to traditional doctrine. He should also have a greater emotional response to his religion. Unfortunately, the data are inadequate here, as was mentioned earlier. There is no item whatsoever that pertains to the experiential dimension. Insofar as the questionnaires concern belief, they ask for agreement about doctrinal placebos with which all church members are likely to agree. Questions about whether one "believes in God" and accepts the general notion of an afterlife are not very revealing. According to the depth interviews of Richard McCann,[13] these are the last outposts in the individual's resistance to secularization, and Emily Dickinson provides a sardonic explanation:

> The abdication of belief
> Makes the Behavior small—
> Better an ignis fatuus
> Then no illume at all—[14]

Some 95 per cent of Americans[15] echo Christian doctrine on

[13] Richard Vincent McCann, "The Nature and Variety of Religious Change," unpublished doctoral dissertation, Harvard University, 1955.

[14] Emily Dickinson, "Those—Dying Then," stanza 2. Reprinted by permission of the publishers and the Trustees of Amherst College from Thomas H. Johnson, editor, *The Poems of Emily Dickinson*, Cambridge, Mass.: The Belknap Press of Harvard University Press, Copyright 1951, 1955, by The President and Fellows of Harvard College.

[15] Will Herberg, *Protestant, Catholic, Jew* (rev. ed.; Garden City, N.Y.: Doubleday Anchor Books, 1960), pp. 72–73. The figures vary slightly, of course, with question wordings and sample characteristics. Herberg relies here on polls from the *Catholic Digest*, the Public Opinion News Service, and even *The Ladies Home Journal* (November, 1948). My own suspicion

these broad points, yet less than 65 per cent are church members and less than 40 per cent allow their beliefs to enter meaningfully into their everyday lives and decisions. Clearly, one must delve deeper into actual conceptions of the nature of God and the specifics of an afterlife to detect real differences. Then too, the same belief may be felt and called upon to varying degrees.

Nevertheless, it is useful to make some assumptions about the ideological before going on to the better measures of sectarian commitment that are available. The Sunday services and parish activities of many Protestant denominations have liberalized their doctrine since the nineteenth century to make it more compatible with secular values. But note that the pastor and the church authorities offer only one interpretation of a scripture whose meaning is continually debated. In one sense, doctrine is a *tabula rasa* which the parishioner can turn to his own liking. The most sectlike elements of belief cannot be wholly purged. The church depends upon these for its traditional flavor and institutional identity, although it may invoke them explicitly on only rare occasions. All of this suggests, then, that the sectarian can indeed find a home in the church. This may entail interpretation at odds with that of the churchlike members and even the

is that considerably more than 5 per cent of Americans are dissidents on matters of religious belief, whether atheists, agnostics, or whatever. Part of the problem is methodological. Most estimates are based on questionnaires or doorstep interviews in which the respondent is simply asked whether or not he "believes in God." Since disbelief is allegedly deviant in our society and since the question often assumes a believing response by providing, say, four categories of belief but only one for disbelief (always disreputably at the bottom), it is no wonder that the number openly confessing disbelief is small. Another factor, however, concerns the wording of more complicated and more probing questions. One difficulty here is to phrase a question and its response categories with sophistication and yet maintain their clarity for relatively non-educated respondents. Another difficulty, however, is that ministerial consultants will often argue that they themselves would be considered atheists if they were asked to place themselves in some sets of categories. Thus, they argue that the categories must be made far more liberal. Here, however, it is possible that some ministers are indeed atheists in traditional terms. Given their background, training, and exposure to theological criticism, ministers as a group will probably have a higher percentage of atheism and agnosticism than either their parishioners or the nation at large. In trying to include them among the believers, the category of disbelief is very nearly dissipated altogether.

minister, but the differences need not be blatant or even fully conscious.

Let us assume then that our sectarians have found an ideological position that serves their needs—a set of beliefs that is otherworldly oriented and provides a sanctioned withdrawal from secular woes. What other forms of commitment to the church should follow?

The first of these differs radically from attendance or organizational involvement. It has no currency in previous research and it is seemingly far removed from actual religious involvement. Nevertheless, the question "how many of your five closest friends are members of your congregation?" is far from idle. While it has no link to theology, or to the religionists' own criteria of commitment, it is sociologically insightful as a more direct measure of the sectarian's organic involvement as cited above. If church services and parish activities represent the formal aspect of behavioral religion, close friends or communal involvement represents the informal. If services and activities connote an *effective* form of involvement, communality suggests an *affective* one. Close friends make the difference between the church as a locus of obligations and the church as a community.

In this connection, the item reflects an important quality of the ideal-typical sect. The sect puts inordinate emphasis on an intimate fellowship of the morally elect. Troeltsch stresses this quality in his original formulation of the church-sect distinction:

> In all things the ideal of the sects is essentially not one which aims at the destruction of the sense life and of natural self-feeling, but a union in love which is not affected by the social inequalities of the world. . . . [This] makes the sects incapable of forming large mass organizations, and limits their development to small groups, unities on the basis of personal intimacy. . . .[16]

Max Weber makes a similar point and relates it to the peculiar development of New England communities:

> Internally, among the sect members, the spirit of early Christian brotherliness prevailed. . . . Among some sects it was considered taboo to call on the law courts. In case of need, mutual aid was obligatory. Naturally, business deal-

[16] Troeltsch, *op. cit.*, I, 337.

ings with non-members were not interdicted (except occasionally among wholly radical communities). Yet it was self-understood that one preferred the brethren. . . . The cohesiveness of the congregations was so great that, with good reason, it is said to be one of the factors determining New England settlements. In contrast to the South, New England settlements were generally compact and, from the beginning, strongly urban in character.[17]

Chapter II cited several recent corroborations of communalism within the sects. Walter Goldschmidt argues that sectarians seek interpersonal relations that are set apart from the secular world and its invidious class distinctions. These people "seek the companionship of those who reinforce [their] own position."[18] Arthur Fauset describes a case where Weber's term "brethren" has a near literal application.[19] H. Richard Niebuhr notes that the contrasting religion of the churches is stamped by an individualism that militates against a sense of community.[20]

Russell Dynes[21] gives even more direct support. Earlier, I reviewed Dynes's delineation of churchlike and sectlike religious preferences and their relations to social class. In an extension of that study, Dynes found that close friendships within the parish are a correlate of a sectarian predilection. Those who prefer a sectlike religious style are more likely to have close friends in the congregation than those who prefer a more churchlike religiosity.

But in all of this, my use of the term "communal involvement" is subject to two confusions. First, it should be distinguished from the superficially similar phrase "social involvement." American religion has been vilified for its social quality.

---

[17] Max Weber, "The Protestant Sects and the Spirit of Capitalism," in Hans Gerth and C. Wright Mills (eds.), *From Max Weber: Essays in Sociology* (New York: Oxford Galaxy Books, 1958), pp. 318–19.

[18] Walter R. Goldschmidt, "Class Denominationalism in Rural California Churches," *American Journal of Sociology*, XLIX (1944), 354. By permission of The University of Chicago Press.

[19] Arthur Fauset, "Moorish Science Temple of America," in Milton J. Yinger (ed.), *Religion, Society, and the Individual* (New York: The Macmillan Company, 1951), pp. 498–507.

[20] H. Richard Niebuhr, *The Social Sources of Denominationalism* (New York: Henry Holt & Company, Inc., 1929).

[21] Russell R. Dynes, "The Consequences of Sectarianism for Social Participation," *Social Forces*, XXXV (1957), 331–34.

Its critics suggest a growing disparity between religion as spiritual sustenance and religion as an act of conformity. The church has become a vehicle of upward status mobility.[22] The Easter Parade is a far cry from a symbolic witness of the resurrection. Finally, if church attendance is little cause for kudos, non-attendance is a costly break with convention.

None of these charges is entirely libelous. Indeed, from a sociological point of view, they point out that American religion is no different from any other. If religion is to function as a point of community integration, then such extrareligious pressures are expected, even necessary. At the same time, this bears little relation to communal involvement. The social pressures suggest an impetus to religion that lies outside the church; it is said to make no difference which church is attended so long as it is in the mainstream, with a status ranking at least as high as the individual's. Communal involvement, on the other hand, suggests an attraction within the church itself. It matters greatly which congregation is chosen. Religion is less a symbol than a primary allegiance. In sum, *social* involvement is churchlike, but *communal* involvement is sectlike.

A second possible confusion concerns Gerhard Lenski's recent use of "communal" in *The Religious Factor*.[23] Lenski uses "religious involvement" to refer to participation in organized churches. By "communal involvement" he refers to participation in the broad religious subcommunity, whether it be white Protestant, Negro Protestant, Catholic, or Jewish. For Lenski, a

[22] Some may be chagrined that I have neglected the essence of middle-class religion by failing to stress the hypocrisy of playing musical church to a status-striving tune. It is not simply that I have no data on mobility. It is also that it is difficult to make judgments of this sort, since one man's hypocrisy may be another's secondary or segmental involvement. While there is evidence that upwardly mobile people change their religious affiliations accordingly and that others make the change to anticipate and aid the mobility itself, their actions need not stem from the crass motivations that are often imputed to them. Moreover, there is evidence that downward as well as upward mobility produces an increase in religious participation. This suggests that mobility in either direction requires an anchorage that is somewhat off the status ladder and that the church offers this in its distinctive identity as an otherworldly institution. For further discussion and data, see Richard F. Curtis, "Occupational Mobility and Church Participation," *Social Forces*, XXXVIII (1960), 315–19.

[23] Gerhard Lenski, *The Religious Factor* (Garden City, N.Y.: Doubleday & Company, Inc., 1961).

person may be communally involved but wholly unaffiliated with the church. Thus, a non-practicing Catholic may have married a Catholic and may belong to dominantly Catholic social circles. Conversely, it is possible to be religiously but not communally involved. A practicing Catholic (perhaps a convert) may have a Protestant wife and a majority of Protestant friends and business associates. Lenski's is an insightful distinction, but it is not what I have in mind. Instead, my own use of "communality" refers to one type of commitment within the organized church per se. Here the low-status parishioners should score high in keeping with their over-all sectlike proclivity.

Religious Aid and Reward

Each of the four preceding items has referred to Glock's behavioral dimension. Church attendance, parish activities, outside commitments, and communality all refer to involvement in the church as an organization and have no direct ties with the ideological, experiential, or consequential facets of religion. At this point, however, the consequential takes over. The questionnaire included the following item:

> How much help is your church membership to you in the following areas of your life? (Please check "much," "some," or "little" for each area.)
>
> 1) In helping me to know of God's love and care for me.
> 2) In meeting the right kind of people.
> 3) In bringing my family closer together.
> 4) In making right decisions in my business.
> 5) In making me aware of the needs of others in my community.
> 6) In helping me to understand people of different cultures and races.
> 7) In strengthening my faith.
> 8) In broadening my understanding of the meaning of life.

Clearly the question probes the import of religion rather than the type of participation, or even the particular beliefs and emotions that accompany it. The next step is to distinguish between churchlike and sectlike responses.

In Chapter II, I stressed that the church-sect distinction could be applied both quantitatively and qualitatively to each of Glock's dimensions. Here, the former is relevant. One of the characteristics of the sect is that its influence is inordinately pervasive for its members. Unlike the church which either supports secular values with a liberal theology or ignores the "remaining six days of the week," the sect demands that secular life proceed on the sect's own terms. As Troeltsch put it, the church applies a "relative Natural Law" in which two standards operate: one for the ideal world of the parish and another for the real world of the on-going society. By contrast, the sect uses an "absolute Natural Law" in which ideal standards brook neither opposition nor compromise. Hence:

> . . . all secular interests are drawn into the narrow framework of the sect and tested by its standards, in so far as the sect is able to assimilate these interests at all. Whatever cannot be related to the group of interests controlled by the sects, and by the Scriptural ideal, is rejected and avoided.[24]

In a recent study of British sects, Bryan Wilson likens this to totalitarianism:

> Whether the modern sect dominates its members socially or not, its essential totalitarianism consists in the re-orientation of the ideals, values and sentiments of its members; the dictation of just what are accepted as "facts"; and in the insistence on an ethic divergent from that of wider society— a totalitarianism at the ideological level.[25]

Of course, both Troeltsch and Wilson are talking of the sect as an organizational type. But with a minor amendment, it is relevant to sectlike individual religiosity within the churches. I have already noted that the sectarian and the church type may emphasize different aspects of Christian doctrine and put them to different use. Every parish has a basic legacy which includes both churchlike and sectlike tenets, as Troeltsch himself indicated. Again, then, let us assume that a parishioner has interpreted his church doctrine and experience in a sectlike fashion. One result should be that the experience offers him succor in

---

[24] Troeltsch, op. cit., I, 339.
[25] Bryan R. Wilson, Sects and Society, op. cit., p. 4.

more of the eight areas asked about than it will for the churchlike adherents. This is the basis for a quantitative distinction.

The respondent checked "much," "some," or "little" help
for each listed area. To simplify, I have focused exclusively on
the "much help" responses. It is possible to construct a scale
by counting the number of these responses made by each person.
If he checks eight areas of "much help," he is clearly more
rewarded than if he were to check none. He is also more sectlike.

Actually, the optimum number of positive responses is reduced for the scale. One item—"In making right decisions in
my business"—excludes most women and so was dropped from
consideration. Another peculiarity of the scale is that all of its
items are not equally appealing. Three are nearly assured positive responses because of the earlier discussion of doctrinal placebos and their inclusion in what Herberg[26] calls "the American
creed." Thus, the sample was nearly unanimous in finding that
their churches offered aid "in helping me to know of God's love
and care for me," "in strengthening my faith," and "in broad-
ening my understanding of the meaning of life." As bland gen-
eralities, these required little deliberation.

The more revealing items concerned the influence of religion in
nominally secular areas. Religion is only one among many institutions that color our thinking on "the right kind of people,"
our methods of "bringing the family closer together," our
solutions to problems of "people of different cultures and races,"
and our response to "the needs of others in [the] community."
In fact, the churches have increasingly bemoaned their lack of
influence in these spheres. And yet it is precisely the sectarian
who provides the exception. It is true that the sectarian seeks
to avoid the world wherever possible; it is also true that his
interpretation of the influence of religion should differ from the
interpretation of the churchlike parishioner. Nevertheless, where
the sectarian must grapple with secular issues, he is likely to
grapple with them on religious terms as he understands them.[27]

---

[26] Herberg, *op. cit.*

[27] The phrase "as he understands them" is an important one. For example,
many liberals both in and out of religion wonder at the segregationist sen-
timents of the lower-class, fundamentalist "rednecks" in the South. The
position on civil rights is thought to be badly out of kilter with the religious doctrine of equality before God. And yet the disparity may be a

In any event, these areas are crucial to the scale. Later I will divide the scale into three categories ranging from high to moderate to low reward. It will be possible for a respondent to rank "low" even if he reports "much help" in two of three assumed areas. It will not be possible for him to rank "high" without responding to all of the placebos and three of the more problematic items as well. The hypothesis is, of course, that those of low status (the more sectlike) will evidence higher reward than those of high status (the more churchlike).

The Role of the Minister in Public Affairs

The last measure of commitment is also consequential but in a markedly different way. It pertains to the formal role of the church in society rather than the informal influence of religion for the individual. The issue is not personal piety, but whether or not the church itself should be an active agent in the secular world. Thus, Lutherans were asked: "Do you think your minister should be active in community affairs?" The question to the remaining four denominations was: "Do you feel that a minister has the right to preach on controversial subjects from the pulpit?" While the items are not identical, they do have a common referent. They should be similarly aligned with both status and the church-sect distinction.

---

fiction of the northern mind and the northern church-goer. As Pettigrew and Campbell point out in their study of Little Rock, many southern churches are avowedly segregationist and foster this interpretation of doctrine. Thus, the lower-class sectarian is permitted to believe that his segregationism is indeed in the spirit of his Lord. To take another example, some of the same liberals are surprised by a Republican vote from a lower-class Baptist. The liberal sees Christianity as a balm for the dispossessed and sees the lower-class sectarian as betraying his religion by spurning the more compatible Democratic Party. Here again, however, the religious position is misunderstood. Benton Johnson has shown that fundamentalist religious doctrine is much closer to Republican ideology than it is to Democratic. He has demonstrated that, among highly involved parishioners only, Episcopalians are more likely to be Democrats in keeping with their social-gospel roots, and Baptists are more likely to be Republicans in keeping with their more traditional dogmas. Religion may mean all things to all people. This is one more illustration that an interpretation based on only one perspective may miss the point widely. See Benton Johnson, "Ascetic Protestantism and Political Preference," *Public Opinion Quarterly*, XXVI (1962).

At first glance, it appears that a sectlike response to either question would be an unequivocal "yes." I have already suggested that the informal, personal influence of religion is more pervasive for sectarians. Seemingly, this should also obtain for the formal role of the church as enacted through the minister. Unhappily, the issue is more complex. The distinction between formal and informal is not jargonized hair-splitting. In fact, there are several reasons why the sectarian may be *averse* to ministerial participation in the community and to preaching on controversial subjects.

One reason concerns the posture of the sects themselves. It is true that the sect influences its members to an almost totalitarian degree and that its influence is keenly felt on issues that are forced to the member's attentions. This was the logic in the conceptualization of religious reward just above. At the same time, there is also a tendency to avoid these secular issues wherever possible and to keep them from intruding upon the traditionally otherworldly and spiritualized services. It is one thing to handle issues as they emerge *per force*. It is quite another to exacerbate these issues and involve the church itself within them. Actually the religious sect and the Communist Party are similar in this respect as well. Both use the strategy of insulating their members periodically to protect the intimacy of the elect community, to bar contaminations of ideological purity, and to emphasize the organization's distinctiveness. As Selznick[28] points out, insulation is crucial to the Party's girding before taking on its political enemies. Among sects, worship meetings provide moments of this, and some groups have gone beyond it to actual isolation. Examples are the Amish, the Hutterites, the Mormons, and even the early Puritans in their escape to America. If the sectarian parishioner is parallel, he too will withdraw from the community and its controversies, and he will encourage his minister to follow.

But a second reason for sectarian disfavor concerns the minister himself. For several reasons the Protestant ministry tends to be churchlike. For one, seminaries are increasingly tied to universities and this fosters a liberalization of theology and a

---

[28] Philip Selznick, *The Organizational Weapon: A Study of Bolshevik Strategy and Tactics* (New York: McGraw-Hill Book Company, Inc., 1952).

coming to grips with broader social issues from an academic perspective. For another, most ministers have more in common with high-status, churchlike parishioners and are more influenced by them. Thus, where there is conflict, the sectarian can expect little ministerial sympathy. Liston Pope[29] provides an illustration in his study of *Millhands and Preachers*. The Gastonia pastors shunned both the theological and the economic needs of the low-status adherent. In fact, the ministers sided with management in the mill strike and left only the fringe sects as an antidote to Communism among the workers. Another study that corroborates the bond between the ministry and the high-status laity is Glock and Ringer's[30] analysis of the Episcopalian polity. Although the ministry had some sectlike inclinations, these were generally repressed under the pressure of prominent churchlike parishioners. In short, the sectarian is likely to view pastoral participation in these issues as a breach of privacy and support for the opposition. Instead, he should prefer to make his own religious bed and to sleep more privately within it.

Two Contrasting Indexes of Religious Commitment

At this point, we have reviewed six measures of religiosity. Three reflect a churchlike commitment: Sunday service attendance, parish activities, and outside organizations. Three connote a sectlike involvement: the number of close friends in the congregation, religious aid, and disapproval of the minister's participation in community affairs and controversy. Of course, all of these items should confirm the hypotheses separately. But, at the same time, a parallel analysis of each is uneconomical. The introduction of additional factors such as age, sex, subjective class, congregational status, and denomination will add considerably to the confusion as it is. Moreover, no single measure of involvement is all powerful. A better picture of, say, over-all churchlike religiosity is given by pooling all three of its measures into a summary index. For this reason, I have tried to compromise. The

[29] Liston Pope, *Millhands and Preachers* (New Haven, Conn.: Yale University Press, 1942).

[30] Charles Y. Glock and Benjamin B. Ringer, "Church Policy and the Attitudes of Ministers and Parishioners on Social Issues," *American Sociological Review*, XXI (1956), 148–56.

bulk of the text will concern such summary indices. The separate items are related to status for the total sample in Appendix A.

Consider first, then, an *Index of Churchlike Religiosity*. Its construction is simple enough. Each of the three churchlike indicators yields three categories that are clearly delineated by the actual distribution of respondents. Church attendance, for example, is considered high among those who attended Sunday services at least three times a month, moderate among those who attended twice a month, and low for those who attended only once a month or less. Parish organizational involvement was high for those with two or more activities,[31] moderate for those with one, and obviously low for those who participated in no church organizations whatsoever. Finally, those who belonged to two or more outside organizations scored high, while those with only one scored moderate, and those with none scored low. Of course, the terms ''high,'' ''moderate,'' and ''low'' refer only to rankings along a hypothetical church-sect continuum and measure the respondent's approximation of the churchlike ideal.

The next step is to translate the labels into numerical weights. There is no way to calculate and quantify whether one item is more churchlike than any other.[32] In the absence of precise estimates of differential importance, it seems reasonable simply to assign equal weights to each. Hence, in all three cases, scores

[31] Later in Chapter VI, I will pull the indexes apart and consider each item separately in the analysis of status discrepancy. There the term "high parish activities" will include both the "high" and the "moderate" in the current delineation. A dichotomy is more convenient for the analysis of separate items, and this provides a dichotomous distribution that is more evenly divided. The same is true, by the way, for outside affiliations which will receive similar treatment.

[32] Actually, one might speculate that church attendance is the least churchlike while outside activities are the most. Later Chapter VII will provide some theoretical support for this contention, and Appendix A offers an empirical buttress in the separate relations with status in the over-all sample. Note, however, that the relationship with status is not a dependable arbiter of churchliness. Not only is its deployment tautological here, but the relationship itself can be affected by a great many considerations in addition to whether or not an item is churchlike or sectlike. Thus, the number of outside activities reflects the different opportunity structure of the middle class as well as a difference in preference. It is possible that the person is not only led to the well but forced to drink, despite his lack of thirst. To weight outside activities any more heavily may prejudice the argument with *ex cathedra* factors.

of 2–1–0 were assigned to correspond to high-moderate-low. The index represents the combinations of these scores and ranges from an aggregate low of 0 to an aggregate high of 6. That is, a person who is low in all three respects has a total score of 0, as the sum of three 0's. At the other extreme, a person who ranks high on each measure has an over-all score of 6, the sum of three 2's.

Table III–1 presents the absolute and percentaged distributions of the Index of Churchlike Religiosity among Lutherans. This is the first introduction of the data, and it is worth noting that the table's total falls short of the actual total of Lutheran respondents. Of 2727 questionnaires, some 356 did not include

TABLE III–1

The Actual and Percentaged Distributions of the Index of Churchlike Religiosity among Lutherans

	High			*Index Scores* *Moderate*		*Low*		*Total N*
	6	5	4	3	2	1	0	
%	6	12	18	19	21	12	12	100
N	140	280	434	445	507	278	287	2371

answers to one or more of the religiosity items at issue and are not included in the index. But in turning to the distributions of the vast majority who answered all the questions, one finds a gratifying symmetry. If the distribution were concentrated at the extremes or even at the middle, the index would be a poor tool for analysis. This would have suggested that it is undiscriminating and that the items are unimportant. Happily, this is not the case. No category claims more than 21 per cent of the sample; only the extreme score of 6 includes less than 12 per cent.

The *Index of Sectlike Religiosity* has only one difference in construction. For the churchlike index, all of the items had scores of 2–1–0. For the sectlike index, this is true of two but not the third. Thus, those with four or five of their closest friends in the parish scored high on communality, while those with one, two, or three scored moderate, and those with none were ranked low. For religious rewards, those who checked "much help" to seven or six of the eligible areas ranked high, to five, four, or three ranked moderate, and to two, one, or none ranked low. But instead of three categories, the question on ministerial participation provided only two. All of those who opposed participation or answered ''don't know'' scored high on the sectarian scale; all of those who approved participation scored low. The ''don't knows'' implied an uncertainty that is plausibly attributed to sectarian inclinations under the church-like pressures that dominate the congregation. For this reason, they were grouped with the opposition since inclinations are a primary concern.

Despite the restriction to two categories for one of its components, the Index of Sectlike Religiosity is also a scale that ranges from 6 to 0. At one extreme, the score of 6 represents a 2–2–2 combination and identifies almost a caricature of the sectarian parishioner. At the other extreme, the 0 signifies a 0–0–0 combination on the sectlike indicators, though the respondent may have scored high on the churchlike measures.

Table III–2 does for sectlike religiosity what Table III–1 did for the churchlike. Again the total does not exhaust the sample, for there are some 393 respondents who failed to answer one or more of the questions involved. Of those who did reply, the distribution is again symmetrical and roughly approximates the classic ''normal'' or bell-shaped model. Note, however, that there are some interesting differences between the distributions of the two indexes. In the churchlike index, the three highest scores account for 36 per cent of the distribution; in the sectlike index, the same three positions account for only 24 per cent. Adding the percentages for the three low scores on each, the converse

TABLE III–2

The Actual and Percentaged Distributions of the Index of Sectlike Religiosity among Lutherans

	High		Index Scores Moderate			Low		Total N
	6	5	4	3	2	1	0	
%	2	4	18	21	26	19	9	99[a]
N	43	103	418	498	615	446	211	2334

[a] The percentage total does not reach 100 per cent because of rounding to avoid decimals. This will occur in other places in the study.

appears. Categories 2, 1, and 0 account for only 45 per cent in the churchlike distribution but 54 per cent in the sectlike. Now it is tempting to see this as further validation of the indexes, since there should be fewer sectarians than church types within all major Protestant denominations, including the Lutheran. Unhappily, however, the inference is methodologically illegitimate. Because the two scales are not fully standardized as to the distribution of respondents on the component indicators, they are, in effect, incomparable. While it is at least comforting to note that the proportions of church types and sect types are not reversed, the assurance is not rigorous.

Another possible criticism of the two indexes arises out of their independence. Because each index rates respondents independently of the other, their mutual relationship is still unclear. It is possible that all of those who score high on the sectlike measure also score high on the churchlike measure. In this case, the indexes would overlap and the assumption of two distinct tendencies would be refuted.

Table III–3 checks this with a simple typology. After dichotomizing each index, four combinations result. The first could be called *total involvement* as it includes those who score high or moderate on both the churchlike and the sectlike indexes. The

TABLE III–3

The Actual and Percentaged Distribution of
A Typology of Religious Orientation among Lutherans

	Totally Involved	Pure Church Type	Pure Sect Type	Dormant Parishioner	Total
%	29	28	16	27	100
N	599	584	345	567	2095

second combination represents the *pure church type* since it combines a high or moderate churchlike score with a low sectlike rating. The third is the *pure sect type* who scores high or moderate on the sectlike measure but low on the churchlike. Finally, the fourth category scores low on both indexes and is close to what Joseph Fichter has called the *dormant parishioner.*

Now clearly there is some overlap. The two extreme categories where the indexes agree are hardly empty. Some 29 per cent are totally involved with a substantial commitment in both church-like and sectlike areas. Some 27 per cent are dormant—probably the Christmas and Easter attenders so distantly familiar to most Protestant ministers. At the same time, the two intermediate categories are also solidly represented. There are again more church types (28 per cent) than sect types (16 per cent), but the number of pure church types is as great as either the totally involved or the dormant. The number of sect types is less but still sufficient to justify and sustain analysis. In short, all four categories are important. While the church-sect distinction does not divide the Lutherans into two, wholly separate camps, there is evidence of its empirical existence beyond the theorizing that has occupied us so far. Of course, even the totally involved may include some who score higher on one index than on the other Moreover, the crucial test of the theory lies not so much in the mere existence of these categories, but rather in their relations to status. As a final hypothesis, status should be more highly related to the two middle categories than either of the extremes. The reasoning is, of course, that different social classes and status groups are more different in *kind* of religious involvement than in *degree*.

Summary

Using six items from the Effective City Church questionnaires, I have tried to conceptualize a bridge between the empirical and the theoretical. Each item had a hypothetical relation to one of Glock's dimensions of religiosity and to the church-sect distinction. Frequent Sunday service attendance, participation in parish activities, and membership in non-church organizations suggest a churchlike commitment to religion. On the other hand, high communal involvement or a number of close friends in the congregation, high religious reward extending into secular areas, and disapproval of the minister's participation in community affairs and controversy are all more sectlike. I then combined these items into two summary indexes. Their distributions and interrelationship provide evidence of their fruitfulness. Still more evidence will be sought in Chapter IV, where status makes its first empirical entrance.

IV

Religiosity and Individual Status:
A First Inspection

At this point we leave the abstractions of theory for the abrasions of data. The easiest portion of any study is its critique of past research and its speculations for the future. The greatest difficulty is to give substance to these assertions by feeding them results. After constructing an index of status to relate to our twin measures of religiosity, the chapter will provide a first test of the theory and then introduce several other facets of stratification that could alter or dissipate the initial findings.

An Index of Socioeconomic Status

All of the questionnaires included three items pertaining to the respondent's objective status position. *Education, income,* and *occupational prestige* are not peculiar to this study. They occur in most surveys as a matter of course, and they do not require an elaborate defense as status indicators. Nevertheless, a brief review of their special significance for religion may be helpful.

If rationality[1] is a criterion of high status, then the importance

[1] The concept of rationality has long plagued the social scientist. Without tracing its history and debate, I should make my own usage clear. In

of education is obvious. Presumably, education breeds a certain analytic facility, and this is a prerequisite to success, as we define it. Yet education as success does not exhaust its import for religion. Not all educated persons are successful. But most are exposed to training that is formally incompatible with arational values that rest on faith alone. In other words, a high level of education is at odds with sectarian ideologies and with sectlike religion generally. This does not mean, however, that high education leads to irreligion. Instead of ignoring religion, the highly educated may choose to rationalize it. They may opt for a churchlike interpretation that demands less faith and more credibility.[2]

Occupational prestige yields a similar hypothesis but for slightly different reasons. By itself, education offers no real substitute to religious values. Its opposition is one of analytic principle. But high-status occupations are intimately bound to a set of this-worldly, non-religious values which frame their own kingdom. Here sectlike religiosity is a rival to an almost sectlike commitment to secular values. Only a more secondary churchlike commitment to religion will be compatible.

Finally, income is the reward dimension of individual status.

---

noting that rationality is a prominent criterion of status in our society, I am talking only of the rational pursuit of ends and not the choice of the ends. Of course, the ends themselves may be arational or even irrational; a commitment to rational pursuit may be uncalculated in any strict sense; and the important point is an *attempt* to be rational, quite apart from the degree to which the attempt is successful.

[2] For evidence on the friction between high education and high religious orthodoxy, see Rodney W. Stark, "On the Incompatibility of Religion and Science: A Survey of American Graduate Students," *Journal for the Scientific Study of Religion*, III (1963), 3–20. But note that there are some important caveats in interpreting data of this sort. First it is tempting to conclude that results for the college population of today presage results for the adult generation of tomorrow. And yet this is an unwarranted leap, since the college graduate who moves into the community and the workaday world is resocialized in many respects, not the least of which concern the church. This helps to account for the seeming paradox that college students have inordinately high rates of religious dissidence but adults with college education have inordinately high rates of church participation. The paradox is further resolved, however, when it is realized that this participation is churchlike and need not rest on a groundwork of traditional doctrine and devotionalism. While part of the collegian's dissidence may be altered, another part may remain and find reconciliation with a particular type of religiosity.

The academy aside, income is an important measure of the return on our investment. If income is high, then our secular commitment is reinforced. If it is low, we are faced with a critical problem of self-esteem and are apt to turn to non-secular alternatives for gratification. Religion is only one of these alternatives, but it has the advantages of institutional stability and a distinctively different system of rewards.

In sum, education, occupational prestige, and income have the same hypothetical relation to religiosity, but each adds something different to an aggregate measure of individual status. For both of these reasons, we can combine them into an over-all status index. The construction is similar to the Indexes of Churchlike and Sectlike Religiosity except that the status indicators have five categories[3] instead of three and the index ranges from 12 to 0 instead of from 6 to 0. Thus, income, education, and occupational prestige are scored 4–3–2–1–0, and the maximum index rank is the sum of three 4's or 12, while the minimum is the sum of three 0's or 0.

[3] The three status indicators were categorized as follows: *Education—4,* college graduate; *3,* some college; *2,* high school graduate; *1,* some high school; *0,* grade school or less; *Income—4,* $9,000 or more; *3,* $6,000 to $8,999; *2,* $4,000 to $5,999; *1,* $2,000 to $3,999; and *0,* less than $2,000 per year; *Occupational prestige—4,* professionals; *3,* proprietors, managers, officials, and salesworkers; *2,* clerical workers, foremen, and skilled craftsmen; *1,* semi-skilled laborers and service workers; *0,* unskilled workers and private household servants. The occupational categories follow the listing of the United States Bureau of the Census. The question on occupational prestige included, in addition to these response categories, the category "other." Here the respondent was to write in his occupation. Since these answers were not available to me, I gave all "others" a score of *2* on occupation and relied upon education and income to push them higher or lower on the aggregate index. Finally, it should be remarked that the status breakdown for education did not avail itself of a correction for age. In several studies that I have seen since these data were tabulated, there is an adjustment made so that, say, a person of 60 can score high on education with only a high school diploma whereas a person of 30 needs several years of college to qualify. This reflects the increasing availability of higher education and avoids a bias against previous generations. In this connection, however, there may be a reverse bias operating for income. Thus, younger people make less money than older people in the same occupations. Here age should also be taken into account but in the opposite direction. Since the present study makes age corrections for neither education nor income, perhaps the two cancel each other in the aggregate index and diminish any over-all distortion. This is, however, a *post hoc* rationalization and not a recommendation to future researchers.

Table IV–1 presents the actual and percentaged distribution of the index among Lutherans. Note, however, that the twelve-point scale has given way to four categories: upper, middle, working, and low status. This is largely a convenience, and the categorization follows the natural breaking points in the distribution rather than any *a priori* guide. To some, the label ''working status'' may seem out of sorts with the ordinal terms ''upper,'' ''middle,'' and ''lower.'' Nevertheless, semantic consistency is less important than sociological relevance and the distinction between working- and lower-status persons is now an

TABLE IV–1

The Actual and Percentaged Distribution of the Index of Socioeconomic Status among Lutherans

	Index Scores				
	12–10	9–7	6–4	3–0	
	Upper	Middle	Working	Lower	Total
%	11	25	43	21	100
N	241	522	910	436	2109

important one in the literature on stratification. Because the working class stands closer to the middle class, it is more sanguine in its hopes for mobility, more apt to take on middle-class characteristics prematurely, and more vulnerable to status anxieties and their effects.

Turning to the distribution, there are twice as many rejects on the status items as there were on the religiosity questions, suggesting that status may be a more jealously guarded secret than religion in our society. Of the 2727 Lutherans, 618 shied away from status interrogation. These status rejects are examined in Appendix B where it is concluded that their absence does not affect the general results of the study. As for the distribution of those who did respond, note the happy and validating similarity between Table IV–1 and the Lutheran row of Table I–1. There the Lutherans were divided into only three groups. But in both cases the upper class accounts for roughly one-tenth, the middle class comprises approximately one-third, and the combined lower classes include more than half of the total. Actually the comparison with Table I–1 is almost as snug for the other denominations as well. Hence, the same index will be used for all five groups in the present study.[4]

A Test of the Basic Hypotheses

Table IV-2 is the first test of the hypothesis that churchlike religiosity should be positively related to social status. I have divided the churchlike index into three categories: high (6–4), moderate (3), and low (2–0). Their relation to status is con-

TABLE IV–2

Churchlike Religiosity and the Index of Socioeconomic Status

Churchlike Commitment	Index of Socioeconomic Status			
	Upper	Middle	Working	Lower
High (6–4)	51%	45%	32%	24%
Moderate (3)	20	20	19	19
Low (2–0)	29	35	48	57
Total N's	(218)	(470)	(828)	(379)

sistently supportive. More than half of the upper-status Lutherans are highly involved in a churchlike manner. The proportion falls in each decreasing status level from 45 per cent to 32 per cent to 24 per cent among the lower-status group. As could be expected, there are no status differences in the percentage moderately involved. The percentages who score low on churchlike religiosity are inversely parallel to the percentages for those of high commitment. Only 29 per cent of the upper-status group

[4] This is not to say that there are no differences whatsoever between the status distributions of the denominations here and their distributions in Table I–1. It is true that their rank ordering is the same in both cases. Nevertheless, it is also true that there is a tendency to status inflation among the present respondents. Insofar as there is a departure here, it is reflected in the generally *higher* status estimates of the denominations in question. This may very well be due to a crucial difference in data collection. Whereas Table I–1 relies upon actual personal interviews with the respondent, the present study uses impersonal questionnaires. It is easier to inflate one's status in a questionnaire than in an actual interview situation. In the latter, the interviewer himself applies pressure to be honest and is free to probe inconsistencies.

score low, and this increases to fully 57 per cent of the low-status parishioners. The positive association conforms to most of the research that Chapter II reviewed. This, of course, is no accident since churchlike religiosity includes two measures that are prominent in that research: Sunday service attendance and parish organizational activity.

Table IV–3 presents a striking contrast. Using the same Lutheran sample, it pits status against a different mode of religiosity. Sectlike involvement also supports its hypothesis, but through a negative rather than a positive association with status. Only 10 per cent of the upper-status Lutherans are highly in-

TABLE IV–3

Sectlike Religiosity and the Index of Socioeconomic Status

Sectlike Commitment	Index of Socioeconomic Status			
	Upper	Middle	Working	Lower
High (6–4)	10%	15%	25%	35%
Moderate (3)	20	19	21	22
Low (2–0)	70	65	54	43
Total N's	(231)	(486)	(810)	(365)

volved in a sectlike fashion. The percentage increases to 15 per cent among the middle class, to 25 per cent among the working class, and to 35 per cent among the lower-status parishioners. As before, there are no meaningful differences in moderate involvement. Once again, the percentages for low involvement are inversely parallel to those for high. Thus, 70 per cent of the upper-status group score low on sectlike religiosity, and this decreases to only 43 per cent of the lower-status Lutherans.

While vindicating the hypotheses,[5] Tables IV–2 and IV–3 still leave loose ends to be tied. I mentioned in Chapter III that the Indexes of Churchlike and Sectlike Religiosity overlap, and it is

[5] Another sort of vindication would run each of the separate religiosity indicators against status to insure that no single component of the churchlike or sectlike indexes is providing all the difference. Appendix A presents these tabulations. Here it should suffice to note that all of the results are in the predicted directions. The only notable peculiarity is that status seems to have a very small impact on church attendance when this is computed for the total sample rather than for Lutherans alone.

important to know something of their interaction. It is possible, for example, that the pure church and sect types bear different relations to status than the separate indexes indicate. As a more rigorous test of the hypotheses, then, Table IV–4 presents social status and the typology of religious orientation.

The categories of the typology were explained in Chapter III. But the present methodology requires some comment, particularly the departure from percentages. In conventional tables, the percentages for any single horizontal row are computed over the sums of all the categories in the vertical column. If one category

TABLE IV–4

The Typology of Religiosity by the Index of Socioeconomic Status: The Cases of Total Involvement and Dormancy

| Typology | Index of Socioeconomic Status | | | | |
	Upper	Middle	Working	Low	Total %
Totally Involved	.81	.89	1.21	1.11	28
Dormant Parishioners	.78	.93	1.04	1.03	28
Total N	(210)	(442)	(762)	(322)	

has a relationship, its contribution to the totals will be uneven, thus affecting the relation of every other category. This is appropriate when the vertical categories form a scale where the top is supposed to mirror the bottom and vice versa. Yet a typology is not a scale. Since the "types" are presumably independent, it would be illegitimate to have the results for one affect the results for any other.[6] To avoid this, Table IV–4 uses a ratio between the actual incidence and the expected incidence for each cell. For example, the upper left corner (upper class, totally involved) represents 48/59, or the actual number divided by the number that should occur judging by the marginal percentage totally involved among all respondents. A score of 1.00 indicates there is no difference between the actual and the expected; a score of less than one means that the actual underrepresents the expected;

[6] I am indebted to Charles Y. Glock for this point.

and a score of more than one means that the actual exceeds the expected.

Turning to the results themselves, consider the totally involved first. Here the relation to status is small, but there is a negative association in that the working- and lower-status Lutherans are more apt to be involved in both churchlike and sectlike respects. Of course, it is too much to expect that *all* high-status parishioners will be exclusively churchlike or that all lower-status adherents will be exclusively sectlike. For the former, close friendships in the church and a modicum of religious reward are frequent exceptions, if not the rule. For the latter, there are congregational pressures to Sunday service attendance, and their friends may lead them into a few activities. At a deeper level of analysis, however, it is possible that the same form of involvement may have different meanings for different groups. Robert and Helen Lynd, for example, compare the Sunday church-going of the business and working classes of Middletown this way:

> One has only to compare the way a working class population leaves its church services . . . lingering to talk on the aisles and on the steps, and the brisk dignity with which the business class leave their Presbyterian Church, with their heads full of plans for the afternoon, to sense some of the differential need for places and occasions of social meeting.[7]

It is true that the Lynds are looking at different congregations here and that the working class still has lower rates of attendance in their study. Nevertheless, among those who do attend, the business class tends to be brisk and ritualized, while the working class lags to quench a more sectlike thirst. In general, then, it is likely that even the totally involved give a consistent churchlike or sectlike twist to their over-all commitment. Unfortunately the data are too crude to provide a more detailed check.

Moving to the dormant parishioners at the other extreme, Table IV–4 seems contradictory. Not only are the lower-status Lutherans more totally involved; they are also more often dormant. Technically, the table is non-isotropic. Substantively, it suggests a pattern uncovered in Chapter I. Some studies have

---

[7] Robert Lynd and Helen Lynd, *Middletown* (New York: Harcourt, Brace & Company, Inc., 1929), pp. 275–76.

found that, among Americans generally, the lower class is less apt to be religiously affiliated, but, among church members in particular, the lower class is apt to be highly involved. Thus, the lower class is more flexible in its stance towards religion. Certainly churches are not the only succor for low status; it is one among many, and more a palliative than an active attempt to change the system. Apparently some members of the lower class prefer the palliative, while others prefer the more active response of trade unions and radical politics. These latter people either have no contact at all with the churches or let their involvement subside into dormancy.

Of course, it would be useful to have data in depth on participation in politics and trade unions to test this speculation. While here again the secondary analysis is frustrating, it does lend crude support to the speculation. Although the Lutherans yield no data whatsoever on political participation and have no information on the *kind* of involvement in any non-church sphere, they were asked simply if they were union members. Table IV–5 compares the religiosity typology among members and non-members. The non-members clearly have a lower incidence of total involvement, a lower incidence of pure sectlike commitment, and a higher rate of dormancy. In fact, the only form of religiosity which is not affected is the pure churchlike. This, however, fits with the theory, since churchlike involvement should be the most compatible with secular pursuits and allegiances. Actually it is remarkable that the table is as successful as it is, since membership in unions is no better a predictor of involvement than membership in churches. Less than 20 per cent

TABLE IV–5

A Comparison of Low-Status Union Members and Non-Members on the Typology of Religiosity

Religiosity	Union Members	Non-Members
Totally Involved	28%	32%
Pure Church Type	15	16
Pure Sect Type	19	28
Dormant Parishioner	37	25
N	(98)	(213)

of union members attend with any regularity and here we have
pooled the attenders with the non-attenders indiscriminately.[8]

Look now at Table IV–6 which presents the relationship between status and the two middle categories of the typology, the
most interesting from the standpoint of our theory. Apart from
their direction, the sheer magnitude of the relationships is important when compared to total involvement and dormancy.

TABLE IV–6

The Typology of Religiosity by the Index of Socioeconomic Status: The Cases of Pure Churchlike and Pure Sectlike Involvement

| Typology | Index of Socioeconomic Status | | | | |
	Upper	Middle	Working	Low	Total %
Pure Church Types	1.72	1.38	.93	.52	29
Pure Sect Types	.32	.56	1.06	1.56	16
Total N	(210)	(442)	(762)	(322)	

Status has an effect for all four categories, but the effect is
almost five times as great for the pure church types and the pure
sect types. The difference between the highest and lowest decimals
is only .28 and .25 for the totally involved and dormant; it is
fully 1.20 and 1.24 for the churchlike and sectlike. It appears

[8] Of course, one does not have to resort to statistics to detect a friction
between trade unionism and religion on the American scene. Not only was
the relationship strained by the alliance between the churches and the
business community in the later nineteenth and early twentieth centuries—
see, e.g., Henry F. May, *Protestant Churches in Industrial America* (New
York: Harper and Brothers, 1949), and Liston Pope, *Millhands and
Preachers* (New Haven, Conn.: Yale University Press, 1942)—but both
organizations tend to compete for the worker's commitment and seek to put
it toward quite different goals, the one active, the other passive. Trade
union literature and folk material are full of denigrations of organized religion. As a reaction, consider a frequent religious interpretation of C.I.O. to
mean "Christ Is Out"! (I am indebted to Richard A. Peterson for this illustration.) And yet the larger point here is that friction exists between various types of organizations. The friction is particularly exacerbated where
voluntary groups compete for voluntary commitment. All of this demands
inspection not merely of the individual's involvement in a single organization but rather of his combined involvements in several. Chapter VIII will
address the latter issue at greater length.

that a church-sect distinction is indeed instructive in the association between status and religiosity. While there are a number of parishioners at the extremes, the heaviest effects of status are concentrated in the polarized middle groups.

But what are the effects? In both cases they are firmly in the predicted direction. The decimal figures are clear enough, but it might be helpful to supplement them with percentages not in the table. Fully 50 per cent of the upper-status Lutherans sustain a churchlike commitment with low sectlike involvement. The percentage falls to 40 per cent among the middle class, 23 per cent among the working class, and only 15 per cent among the extreme lower-class parishioners. On the other hand, status bears an opposite relation to pure sectarianism. Even within a major Protestant denomination, a full quarter of the lower class is *only* sectlike in its commitment, but this falls to 18 per cent of the working class, 9 per cent of the middle class, and only 5 per cent of the upper class. Looking at the extreme status groups, many more of the upper class are pure church types than pure sect types; more of the lower class are pure sect types than pure church types.

Table IV–7 puts these comparisons more concisely. For each status group, it gives the absolute ratio of pure sect types to pure church types. Where the ratio is low, the church type is dominant. Where the ratio is high, the sect type prevails. For any group, a ratio larger than one signifies that an exclusive sectarianism is more popular than a solely churchlike mode of religiosity. The problem of percentaging typologies is again obviated, since the totals represent only the sum of those who

TABLE IV–7

The Ratio of Pure Sect Types to Pure Church Types within Each Status Category

| | Index of Socioeconomic Status | | | |
	Upper	Middle	Working	Lower
$S\bar{C}/C\bar{S}$[a]	.11	.22	.77	1.63
	(116)	(216)	(312)	(129)

[a] This notation will occur throughout the next several chapters. Thus, $S\bar{C}$ indicates high sectlike but low churchlike involvement. Conversely $C\bar{S}$ signifies high churchlike but low sectlike religiosity.

are either pure church types or pure sect types. This ratio will replace the typology in the remainder of the analysis in order to focus on the more theoretically interesting pure types. Here, of course, the results of Table IV–7 parallel those of Table IV–6; the ratio plainly increases among categories of decreasing status.

To summarize, these first tests of the hypotheses have been consistently successful. Every table and every comparison within them support the thesis that religiosity has churchlike and sectlike components which have opposite associations with social status. Before seeking further evidence and exploring for possible spuriousness, however, one point should be emphasized. Although the percentage differences are consistent and clearcut, status hardly accounts for all of the variance in religiosity. Not *all* upper-class parishioners are churchlike; not *all* lower-class members are sectlike in their commitment. If the object were to account for differences in religiosity in their entirety, the tables would surely be inadequate. But such is not the goal. The impact of stratification alone is at issue and it is perhaps remarkable that its impact is as great as it has seemed so far. Certainly there are other factors that influence individual religiosity such as parental religion, family composition, ministerial personality, local community norms, and so on. Some of these factors may even counteract status by producing conflicting predispositions. The important finding is that status seems to produce a meaningful effect despite any cross pressures.

Subjective Class: Elaboration in the Search for Spuriousness

To many, the foregoing may suffer from a glaring omission. It uses no statistical tests of significance; the argument rests on percentage differences with no Chi-square support. I mentioned in the Introduction, however, that statistical tests are often inapplicable in sociological research and that they are especially unwarranted here because of sampling imprecision. Rather than use statistical canons,[9] the study relies on two other criteria:

[9] Actually most of the relationships which occur in this analysis are statistically significant at far better than the conventional .05 level. This is partly due to the strength of the relationships themselves. But it is also due to the size of the sample—a factor that should not intrude in any assessment of the analytic factors involved.

theoretical credibility and empirical consistency within different subgroups and within categories of strategic third variables. The theoretical criterion has already been confronted. This section begins the examination of third variables. Of course, the object is to pick those variables which would most reasonably affect or obliterate the original relationship. In this case, they can be relevant either through their association with status or through their association with religiosity. Beginning with the former, consider the respondent's subjective class identification.

So far we have been exclusively concerned with status factors such as income, education, and occupational prestige. Because the individual is ranked anonymously and empirically, these facets of stratification are objective. However, another item in the questionnaires asked the respondent to evaluate his *own* class position. The question was borrowed from Richard Centers'[10] research. The respondent was to place himself in one of four categories listed in the following order: working, upper, lower, and middle. As with Centers' own sample, more than 90 per cent chose the working- and middle-class labels, and fewer than 10 per cent were bold enough to place themselves at the upper or lower extremes.

Table IV–8 relates subjective class to objective status. To simplify the analysis, I have combined upper and middle as well as

TABLE IV–8

Objective Status and Subjective Class

Class	Status	
	Upper and Middle	*Working and Lower*
Upper and Middle Class	71%	30%
Working and Lower Class	29	70
N	(710)	(1191)

[10] Richard Centers, *The Psychology of Social Class* (Princeton, N.J.: Princeton University Press, 1949). Centers found that both class and objective status were related to political and ideological predispositions. He argued—somewhat dubiously—that class was actually the more influential determinant. Of course, the concept of subjective class has firm historical roots in the work of Karl Marx, with its premium on class consciousness. So far as I know, however, it has not been previously related to religiosity.

working and lower categories of both class and status. Clearly, the two measures of stratification are highly associated. Some 71 per cent of those who rank in the upper or middle brackets of the status index rank themselves at the upper or middle ends of the subjective class scale. Nevertheless the association is far from perfect, and the data can be summarized from another point of view. Fully 29 per cent of the objectively higher-status respondents are subjectively working or lower class. Some 30 per cent of the objectively lower-status parishioners think of themselves as middle or upper class. The former group might be called the ''self-deprecators,'' the latter the ''self-aggrandizers.''

It is at least conceivable that the effect of objective status seen in the previous section is an artifact of uncontrolled subjective class. One could argue that the respondent's self-estimate is the crux of stratification and that objective status is simply a convenient approximation. My own hypothesis is different. Previous research, such as Centers', has shown that objective and subjective stratification are partially independent of each other, although their influences are similar. Thus, both objective status and subjective class should produce effects on religiosity that are irreducible to each other.

The interesting aspect of the analysis, however, concerns the deviant cases, i.e., the self-aggrandizers and the self-deprecators. In general, it seems reasonable to predict that their subjective evaluations will set them apart from their status peers where religiosity is concerned. Thus, the self-aggrandized should have a greater churchlike predilection than those working- and lower-status persons who also think of themselves as working or lower class. Conversely, the self-deprecated should be more sectlike than the upper- and middle-status respondents who also think of themselves as upper and middle class.

Table IV–9 provides a first test of these more complicated expectations. It presents the relation between churchlike commitment and objective status within categories of subjective class. Only the percentage highly involved in a churchlike manner is listed. Once again, the results confirm the hypotheses. Clearly, the effect of status is not simply an artifact of the effect of class, since the two coexist. As before, the high-status respondents are more frequently involved in a churchlike fashion,

TABLE IV-9

Churchlike Religiosity and Objective Status within Categories of Subjective Class

	U and M Status	W and L Status	
% High Churchlike	48 (493)	35 (347)	U and M Class
% High Churchlike	44 (189)	28 (835)	W and L Class

and this is true regardless of subjective class. The difference is between 48 per cent and 35 per cent among those who see themselves as upper or middle class. It is between 44 per cent and 28 per cent among those who see themselves as working or lower class.

The table also confirms the hypothesis regarding the deviant cases. Note that the self-aggrandizers in the upper right-hand corner are 35 per cent highly involved in churchlike religiosity as compared with only 28 per cent among the rest of the working- and lower-status group. On the other, lower left-hand side of the table, only 44 per cent of the self-deprecators are involved whereas 48 per cent of their objective status peers are involved. In short, class and status have cumulative effects, though they also exert independent influences of their own.

Table IV-10 puts this to a further test concerning sectlike religiosity. Again the original effect of objective status persists. Again class and status interact, at least among those of high

TABLE IV-10

Sectlike Religiosity and Objective Status within Categories of Subjective Class

	U and M Status	W and L Status	
% High Sectlike	12 (516)	27 (356)	U and M Class
% High Sectlike	19 (194)	28 (809)	W and L Class

objective status. Here 12 per cent have sectarian commitments among those who think of themselves as middle or upper class, but this rises to 19 per cent among the self-deprecators. Apparently, class estimates have no influence on the level of sectlike involvement among those of working and lower status. It may be that the American's alleged hyperconsciousness of status is only true of the middle class where mobility-striving is a way of life.

Finally, Table IV–11 puts the hypotheses to an even clearer test by inspecting the relation between status and the ratio of pure churchlike to pure sectlike religiosity within categories of subjective class. Here too, the hypotheses are vindicated. Within both class categories, the ratio increases with decreasing status. Moreover, within both status groups, the ratio increases with decreasing class. The self-aggrandizers score only .72 as compared

TABLE IV–11
Ratio of Pure Sectlike to Pure Churchlike Religiosity and Status within Categories of Class

	U and M Status	W and L Status	
$S\bar{C}/C\bar{S}$	.12	.72	U and M Class
	(242)	(124)	
$S\bar{C}/C\bar{S}$	.38	.98	W and L Class
	(87)	(303)	

with a score of .98 for the working- and lower-status respondents who see themselves the same way. The self-deprecators, however, score .38 as compared with a score of only .12 for the upper- and middle-status respondents who evaluate themselves as upper and middle class. Clearly, then, the lower one's class *or* status, the more likely he is to be purely sectarian in his religious commitment.

Of course, subjective class is not the only factor that could alter the effect of objective status. Knowing that the influence of objective status persists here is hardly proof of its effect generally. Yet proof is impossible in the complex domain of sociological explanation. Instead, a goal of confidence is more reasonable, and the next section pursues that goal further by examining two other factors that could affect the findings and the thesis.

Age and Sex as Test Factors

Age and sex may seem strange items to include in a study of stratification, but two considerations recommend them. First, they have been demonstrated to exert powerful influences of their own on religiosity: women are more involved than men, and older persons are more involved than younger.[11] Second, age and sex do have an indirect relation to stratification. Certainly our society places a premium on qualities that accrue more to the young male than to the older female. In fact, this reasoning has been applied to their religious differences in a manner that smacks of the study's theory of status per se. Presumably, women are more religious in the United States because their social roles get little reinforcement from secular values; hence, they must turn to the church for reinforcement. The male has more of a place in the secular fabric and, therefore, he needs less non-secular support. Although Thorstein Veblen may be overstating the point, he puts it this way:

> The logic, and the logical processes, of her everyday life are carried over into the realm of the supernatural, and the woman finds herself at home and content in a range of ideas which to the man are in great measure alien and imbecile.[12]

Much of the same explanation applies to age differences in religiosity. Increasing age often involves decreasing involvement in secular pursuits. For males, aging means ultimate withdrawal from the upstage drama of productive life; retirement is often compulsory. For females, aging means that the children mature and leave home. The church takes on increasing significance, then, as a compensation for occupational life and the bustling family.

Although these are only brief interpretations, their general

[11] See, for example, Joseph H. Fichter, S. J., "The Profile of Catholic Religious Life," *American Journal of Sociology*, LVIII (1952), 145–49. For a more recent and extended analysis of age and sex among Protestants, see also Charles Y. Glock and Benjamin B. Ringer, *Society, the Church and Its Parishioners* (Book in preparation, Survey Research Center, University of California, Berkeley).

[12] Thorstein Veblen, *The Theory of the Leisure Class* (New York: Mentor Books, 1953), p. 211. By permission of The Viking Press, Inc.

theme is similar to the prior interpretation of socioeconomic status differences. This makes it all the more possible that status may have different effects depending on a person's age and sex. Indeed, it is conceivable that age and sex could account for the effects of status altogether. As before, however, the hypothesis is that this is not the case. Age and sex should influence religiosity, but this should be largely independent of status (and, implicitly, of subjective class).

Table IV–12 provides a first test for churchlike religiosity. Instead of elaborating for age and sex separately, I have combined them into four categories: young men, young women, old men, and old women. "Young"[13] refers to respondents under fifty; "old" refers to those fifty or over whose families are

TABLE IV–12

Churchlike Religiosity and Objective Status within Categories of Age and Sex

	Upper	Middle	Working	Lower	
% High Churchlike	47	43	33	27	Young Men (37%)
	(74)	(139)	(186)	(73)	
% High Churchlike	55	47	28	23	Young Women (35%)
	(85)	(221)	(385)	(107)	
% High Churchlike	58	53	36	24	Old Men (39%)
	(31)	(53)	(107)	(71)	
% High Churchlike	43	39	37	24	Old Women (33%)
	(28)	(56)	(147)	(123)	

[13] To those acquainted with the statistics relating age to religiosity, this dichotomy may seem to violate an important finding. Thus, the relationship is generally curvilinear since adolescents have a high rate of religiosity, the rate is at its nadir among young adults, and thereafter it undergoes steady increase until it reaches a zenith among persons over 65. Here, however, there are very few adolescents in the sample. Therefore, a three-way categorization is unjustified and the dichotomy itself is more warranted. Later we will resort to a three-way age-classification of a slightly different sort when considering the entire sample in relation to status discrepancy. There the objective will be slightly different and the available sample will be considerably larger.

beginning to scatter and who have generally found their occupational ceiling with retirement the next major step. In order to facilitate comparison of the age and sex groupings alone, I have given summary percentages on the far right of the table.

It is plain that the effect of status persists despite controls for age and sex. Within each age-sex category, the incidence of high churchlike involvement declines with decreasing status. The pattern is remarkably consistent and justifies further confidence in the original relationship. It is fortunate, however, that age and sex are test factors and not a major concern of the study. Here the results are more confusing. The summary percentages on the extreme right reveal no major differences, although older women are slightly less predisposed to churchlike religiosity than older men (33 per cent as opposed to 39 per cent). But note the interaction between status, age, and sex. Among the younger parishioners, high-status men are *less* churchlike than high-status women, yet low-status men are *more* churchlike than low-status women. Among the older Lutherans, there are no differences for those of low status, but high-status men are *more* churchlike than high-status women. I have no ready explanation for these complex findings. They do suggest, however, that the effects of age and sex are partially dependent upon status if not vice versa.

Table IV–13 considers sectlike commitment. Again, the primary object is to insure that the original relationship between status and involvement persists, and, again, the objective is met. Unlike churchlike commitment, sectlike *increases* with decreasing status. Although differences between upper- and middle-status and working- and lower-status young men are too slight to be meaningful and the same is true in comparing upper- and middle-status older women, the remaining comparisons satisfy the hypothesis. Moreover, unlike Table IV–12, Table IV–13 is relatively clear in comparing age and sex categories. Status is less important to the effects of age and sex on sectlike involvement than it was for churchlike. The figures on the right indicate that older women are more often sectarian than older men, and older persons are much more often sectlike than younger. Thus, the church may take on added prominence as a communal institution among those with mounting age. Alternatively, the

TABLE IV–13
Sectlike Religiosity and Objective Status
within Categories of Age and Sex

	Upper	Middle	Working	Lower	
% High					
Sectlike	10	13	19	20	Young Men (16%)
	(78)	(146)	(189)	(70)	
% High					
Sectlike	8	14	20	25	Young Women (18%)
	(90)	(225)	(387)	(109)	
% High					
Sectlike	10	26	31	39	Old Men (30%)
	(31)	(54)	(102)	(64)	
% High					
Sectlike	16	15	43	50	Old Women (38%)
	(31)	(65)	(129)	(118)	

elders may be maintaining a sectlike culture from a ghettoed youth as members of German or Scandinavian immigrant groups.

As the final step in our now standard procedure, Table IV–14 offers the ratio between pure churchlike and pure sectlike involvement. Once more, the original association obtains within all four categories of age and sex, since, in each case, the ratio increases within decreasing status. There are two minor excep-

TABLE IV–14
Ratio of Pure Sectlike to Pure Churchlike
Involvement and Objective Status
within Categories of Age and Sex

	Upper	Middle	Working	Lower	
$S\bar{C}/C\bar{S}$	.05	.21	.51	.64	Young Men (.31)
	(42)	(64)	(80)	(23)	
$S\bar{C}/C\bar{S}$	.02	.27	.74	1.50	Young Women (.54)
	(42)	(105)	(141)	(45)	
$S\bar{C}/C\bar{S}$	.14	.05	.84	1.86	Old Men (.53)
	(16)	(21)	(35)	(20)	
$S\bar{C}/C\bar{S}$	.60	.25	.96	2.90	Old Women (.98)
	(16)	(25)	(45)	(39)	

tions, in the comparison of upper- and middle-status older men and in the surprisingly high ratio of the upper-status older women. But the first reversal is too small to be meaningful, and the second is based on only 16 cases, one of the two smallest cells of the table. Note that age and sex differences are especially clear with respect to these pure types of involvement. Women and older parishioners are more apt to be pure sect types, and, in both cases, the ratio differences are substantial and hold even within categories of status. It is possible then that the church-sect distinction is applicable to age and sex as well as to the more conventional facets of stratification. But, in general, women and older parishioners tend to be more involved in both a churchlike and a sectlike fashion.

Summary

This chapter put the theory to its first empirical test. After developing a measure of objective socioeconomic status, we noted that it bore a positive relation to churchlike religiosity but a negative relation to sectarianism among Lutherans. This was also the case for pure churchlike and pure sectlike commitment.

The following sections sought added confidence in these associations. Instead of statistical tests of significance, they relied upon the procedures of elaboration by successive third variables. Although subjective class, age, and sex were likely candidates to alter the original effects, none did so. The influence of objective status persisted in each case, despite some interesting but minor interaction and despite the independent effects of these new factors. This, of course, did not prove the theory, but it did lend added assurance of its validity.[14]

[14] As Alan B. Wilson has suggested to me, it remains possible that a person's status and his religiosity can be explained by some event that precedes both of them. Thus, ethnic cultures may give rise to certain orientations and ideologies that affect an individual's status and also dictate his mode of religious involvement. While these possibilities lurk menacingly in the wings, there are no data available with which to test them here. One might predict, however, that such a possibility is less likely today than at the turn of the century. In the interim, ethnic cultures have lost much of their cohesiveness under assimilation. Status has taken on a new independence. And, finally, individual religion has become more flexible and more changeable under currents of secularization and increased geographical mobility.

In order to gain still more assurance, the next chapter considers several additional factors that could account for the original relationship. These, however, are of a different order. Whereas subjective class, age, and sex are individual characteristics, the next are contextual. It is possible that differing status among the Lutheran congregations and the differences among Lutherans, Presbyterians, Congregationalists, Baptists, and Disciples of Christ will at least localize the coexistence of churchlike and sectlike modes of commitment, if not obliterate them altogether. In any event, this possibility must be explored if the study is to apply to American Protestantism generally as the title proposes.

V

Individual Commitment and the Religious Context

The previous chapters have followed the social-psychological emphasis of previous research. The influence of status on religiosity is essentially a matter of individual characteristics affecting individual behaviors. Of course, this is sociologically relevant because the characteristics are socially defined and the behaviors are socially significant. Nevertheless, it is also important—and more in the classic vein of sociology—to consider the added impact of the context that surrounds this interplay of individual action. No individual acts in a vacuum. Most of us are nudged, driven, pushed by the groups and organizations to which we belong. Sometimes this external, contextual influence[1] even directs us againt our personal inclinations.

[1] Contextual analysis relating individual behaviors to the groups in which these behaviors occur has had a long and varied history. As early as 1897, it was used in Durkheim's classic study of suicide. Since then it has had currency in studies of voting, military behavior, welfare agencies, and universities. Recently, however, the technique has been scrutinized more systematically. See, for example, Peter M. Blau, "Structural Effects," *American Sociological Review*, XXV (1960), 178–93; James A. Davis, "Compositional Effects, Role Systems, and the Survival of Small Discussion Groups," *Public Opinion Quarterly*, XXV (1961), 574–84; James A. Davis, Joe L.

The relevant contexts for this analysis are plainly the denominational affiliation of the individual and his immediate congregation. A statement that different denominations vary in their rituals, beliefs, church government, and composition needs no support. That congregations within the same denomination may also vary considerably is less obvious. This chapter will examine the possible effects of both types of contextual variation. Beginning with the latter, it will examine the parishioners from two groups of Lutheran congregations. Proceeding to the former, it will inspect status and religiosity among Presbyterians, Congregationalists, Baptists, and Disciples of Christ.

In all of this, the chapter shares two objectives with its predecessor. For one, it seeks assurance that the relation between individual status and individual religiosity is not an artifact of other factors. It is conceivable that the findings so far are produced by congregational differences among Lutherans and that they are not really the effects of individual status or generalizable to other denominations. A second objective goes further. Instead of looking for the mere persistence of the original relationships, it explores the independent effects of the contexts themselves. Rather than simply vindicate the thesis, this tack seeks further specification.

There are essentially two ways in which a study like this one can delineate contexts. On the one hand, it can distinguish them through qualities that are irreducible to the individual data available. For example, denominations and congregations differ in dogma and this is more a matter of church history than of individual composition. On the other hand, it is also possible to distinguish between contexts precisely on the grounds of composition. Thus, denominations and congregations vary in the social status of their memberships. This latter type of analysis will be especially important in the following. Dogma and ritual do not always conform to the official statements of denominations, and congregations within the denomination may

Spaeth, and Carolyn Huson, "A Technique for Analyzing the Effects of Group Composition," *American Sociological Review*, XXVI (1961), 215–25. The present analysis is, finally, similar in structure to Alan B. Wilson, "Residential Segregation of Social Classes and Aspirations of High School Boys," *American Sociological Review*, XXIV (1959), 836–45.

differ. Not only is stratification important to the religious context, as the classic church-sect literature indicates, but a comprehensive treatment of stratification itself requires attention at the contextual level. Let us turn first, then, to status differences among the Lutheran parishes. This will conclude the case study of the Lutherans and provide a model for the wider analysis of differences among whole denominations.

Status Differences among Lutheran Congregations

I mentioned earlier that the Lutheran sample is neither nationwide nor denomination-wide. It includes only twelve urban congregations in cities such as Philadelphia, Pittsburgh, New York, Milwaukee, Chicago, and Los Angeles. The absence of probability techniques and a clearly defined population is, of course, a hindrance. But, in this case, it is also an asset. An over-all sample would have represented separate congregations so thinly that an analysis of any particular context would have been precluded. Here, however, an analysis of contexts is invited.

In this section, I will focus on only one type of difference among Lutheran congregations: their status composition. Note, however, that this difference implies others. Traditional church-sect theory, reviewed in Chapter II, indicates that low-status religious groups are more apt to be sectlike, and, hence, more apt to stress conservative dogma, the parish as a moral community, and the "priesthood of all believers." This can be extended to apply to congregations within the same denomination. Low-status Lutheran congregations should have more sectlike characteristics than high-status Lutheran congregations. These differences should have an impact on individual religiosity when this is broken into churchlike and sectlike components. Although the original effects of individual status should persist, it is reasonable to expect that the context will impart added influence of its own.[2]

[2] For evidence that local congregations are responsive to contextual status differences and establish consequent norms of their own related to church-giving, see Kenneth J. Lutterman, "Giving to Churches: A Sociological Study of the Contributions to Eight Catholic and Lutheran Churches," unpublished Ph.D. dissertation, University of Wisconsin, 1962, especially Ch. VIII, p. 38.

Three items provide for a distinction between high-status and low-status Lutheran parishes. Two of these are the familiar Index of Objective Status, formed in Chapter IV, and the respondent's own subjective estimate of his class, also discussed in Chapter IV. The third item is new. Here the respondent was to estimate the over-all class position of his congregation. Is it predominantly upper class, middle class, working class, or lower class? As with the question pertaining to the subject's own class position, few were so bold as to affix extreme upper- or extreme lower-class labels to their parishes. Nevertheless, the differences between the proportion of middle- and working-class estimates is revealing.

Table V-1 profiles the high- and low-status Lutheran parishes, using the three items mentioned. The parishes were divided so as to maximize the status differences among them. When the types are compared on the distribution of individual objective status, a majority of the members of the high-status parishes

TABLE V-1

High- and Low-Status Lutheran Congregations and Their Distributions on Individual Status, Subjective Class, and Evaluations of Parish Status

	High-Status Congregations	Low-Status Congregations
Objective Status Index		
% Upper	20	9
% Middle	32	23
% Working	37	46
% Lower	11	24
N	(586)	(1523)
Subjective Class Self-Estimates		
% Upper and Middle	57	40
% Working and Lower	43	60
N	(739)	(1902)
Parishioners' Evaluations of Parish Status		
% Upper and Middle	60	36
% Working or Lower	19	48
% Don't Know	21	17
N	(779)	(2069)

come from either upper- or middle-status brackets (52 per cent), but this is true of less than a third from low-status congregations (32 per cent). A similar difference emerges with respect to subjective self-estimates of class. Only 40 per cent of the low-status parishes think of themselves as upper or middle class; this increases to 57 per cent among the high-status congregations.

It is possible, of course, that these differences in class and status distributions are unimportant. They are not especially large; perhaps the respondents themselves are unaware of them. Apparently not. If these were merely epiphenomenal and unreflective of any "felt" reality, there would be no differences when the parishioners themselves estimated the status of their parishes. Instead, the differences are considerable and are even more pronounced than the previous comparisons would suggest. Fully 60 per cent of those in the high-status congregations think of their congregation as upper or middle class. The figure is only 36 per cent among members of the alleged low-status parishes. This difference in perception exaggerates the empirical difference, indicating that the context may indeed have effects of its own.

In order to assess the effects on religiosity, we can use the same third variable strategy used in Chapter IV. Each of the original relations between individual status and religiosity will be examined within categories of congregational status. The extent of churchlike commitment should decrease among the low-status parishes for each category of individual status. Conversely, the extent of sectlike religiosity and the ratio of pure types should increase.

Table V–2 tests the first of these propositions. Within both categories of congregational status, it gives the relation between individual status and churchlike religiosity. Clearly the contextual difference does not explain away the influence of individual status as the original relations persist strongly. Regardless of the congregational context, churchlike religiosity is highest among the upper-status parishioners and lowest among the low-status parishioners. But this is not to say that the contextual difference is irrelevant. As expected, it has an independent influence and one that is very nearly as emphatic as the effect of individual status. For each category of in-

TABLE V–2

Churchlike Religiosity and Individual Status within Categories of Parish Status

Religiosity	Individual Status				Parish Status
	Upper	Middle	Working	Lower	
% High Churchlike	56	50	39	35	High-Status Parishes
N	(109)	(171)	(202)	(55)	
% High Churchlike	47	43	28	22	Low-Status Parishes
N	(109)	(299)	(626)	(325)	

dividual status, the percentage of churchlike commitment is higher in the high-status, presumably more churchlike, parishes. As an example, only 47 per cent of the upper-status members of the low-status parishes manifest a churchlike commitment; this increases to 56 per cent among the upper-status members of the high-status congregations. Here is more evidence that congregational status is felt by the parishioner and not a fantasy of the researcher.

Now consider sectlike religiosity under contextual variation. Here the relation with individual status should be inverse, and Table V–3 gives firm support. Again, the contextual difference does not account for the influence of individual status. The percentage highly involved in a sectlike fashion increases from 8 per cent to 41 per cent in the high-status parishes, comparing from left to right, and from 9 per cent to 34 per cent in the low-status parishes. But if the contextual influence does not explain away the effect of individual status, it does retain some influence of its own. In line with the second expectation and classic church-sect theory, the low-status parishes produce a higher proportion of sectlike commitment for every individual status category save one. True, it is almost negligible among the upper-status parishioners, but it is clear-cut among the middle- and working-status Lutherans. In both cases, the increment is.

TABLE V–3

Sectlike Religiosity and Individual Status within Categories of Parish Status

Religiosity	Individual Status				Parish Status
	Upper	Middle	Working	Lower	
% High Sectlike	8	10	18	41	High-Status Parishes
N	(114)	(174)	(193)	(54)	
% High Sectlike	9	18	28	34	Low-Status Parishes
N	(116)	(313)	(619)	(311)	

10 per cent, a substantial proportion when one considers the myriad factors which affect the variance of religious commitment.

Note, however, the exception among the extreme lower-status persons. While their percentage of sectlike commitment is high within the low-status parishes, it is even *higher* within the high-status parishes: 41 per cent as compared with 34 per cent. One possible explanation for this lies in an often-noted difference between the working- and lower-status individual. Whereas the former has hopes of upward mobility and may even anticipate it sufficiently to adopt middle-class norms and concerns, the latter has little hope and hence little reason for "anticipatory socialization." The more churchlike concerns of a high-status parish, as manifest in sermons, formal ritual, and informal conversations, may drive these lower-status members back into themselves. They may band together as a means of self-defense. To test this conjecture one would have to investigate not only the number of friends, but also who these friends are. If the range of friends of the low-status parishioners is restricted to members of the lower-status group, then the speculation that the lower-status members in a high-status parish are a school of fish out of water would be partially supported. Unfortunately, the data are not available, but this is the kind of information needed in a study of institutional commitment, whether it be commitment to a church or to any other type of organization.

Predictably, the lower-status parishioners are also the exception in Table V–4 and for what should be the same reason. Here the ratios of pure churchlike to pure sectlike commitment are presented for each individual status group within both categories of parish status. Again the original relation persists in that the ratio increases with decreasing individual status within both contexts. But, also again, the lower-status Lutherans are the sole aberration when one inspects the independent contextual effect. For every other status group, the ratio is higher in the low-status parishes. For the low-status groups, there is a greater predominance of those with only sectlike commitment

TABLE V–4

Ratio of Pure Sectlike to Pure Churchlike Involvement and Individual Status within Categories of Parish Status

| Ratio | Individual Status | | | | Parish Status |
	Upper	Middle	Working	Lower	
S$\overline{C}$/C$\overline{S}$	.04	.12	.35	2.00	High-Status
	(59)	(83)	(74)	(12)	Parishes
S$\overline{C}$/C$\overline{S}$	.19	.29	.88	1.60	Low-Status
	(57)	(133)	(229)	(117)	Parishes

in the high-status congregations. Apparently, the finding in Table V–3 was no accident.

This concludes the case study of the Lutherans. It has isolated two distinct religious styles and shown them to be related to individual status in reverse ways. It then checked to insure that age, sex, subjective class, and parish status do not account for the original finding and, in the process, discovered that each of these factors carries an independent influence of its own. While all of the factors fall loosely under the rubric "stratification," they differ considerably. This is especially true of the last factor which is a group influence rather than a purely personal, social-psychological one. Although the high- and low-status Lutheran congregations do not differ greatly in their distribution of individual status or subjective class, the difference seems sufficient to create a distinct difference in religious climate. The next section turns to even wider differences of this sort. Instead of looking at subtle and constructed distinctions within a single denomination, it asks about the persistence of the original findings within altogether different Protestant denominations. If the analysis of Lutheran congregations provided an *internal replication,* this next section seeks an *external replication,* as one more step in the never-ending search for confidence in one's hypotheses.

Religiosity and Status in Other Protestant Denominations

Perhaps as a residue of the competition for members, American Protestantism has made much of its denominational differences and the lay public has made still more. In fact, Protestantism is frequently divided into three camps: the aristocratic trinity of Episcopalianism, Congregationalism, and Presbyterianism; the middle-class Methodists together with a number of denominations undergoing status changes such as the Lutherans and the Disciples of Christ; and finally the churches of the lower class or the euphemistic common man, best represented by the Baptists.

Whether the differences are myth or reality, few are apt to confuse a description of, say, a Congregationalist church with one of a Baptist church. Not only are the sermons, rituals, and dogmas different: the sheer physical setting and its appurtenances are even more so. The stereotype of a Congregationalist church graces a New England town with a sparkling whiteness from its prominent location on the most expensive lot in town. By contrast, the Baptists are often "across the tracks" in an area where fresh paint dirties quickly. More to the point is the contrast in membership. Denominations are not labeled "aristocratic" or "common man" solely because of their present composition. There are historical bases as well. Sinclair Lewis' description of the various churches in Zenith offers biting distinctions on the grounds of social composition in the 1920's. The Lynds and Lloyd Warner provide more systematic accounts of Middletown and Yankee City in the 1920's and 1930's.

Finally, H. Richard Niebuhr argued some 35 years ago that American religion is fragmented by status and doomed because of it.

Note, however, that recent observers of American religion have begun to regard these differences as decreasingly important. A case in point is Robert Lee's recent study of *The Social Sources of Church Unity*. Essentially a documentation of the trend toward institutional togetherness, the book cites instances of church mergers and numerous other compromises of denominational distinctions. The current discussions of a united Protestantism—discussions led by the Presbyterians but frustrated by the Episcopalians—offer a capstone to past steps in this direction. Not only have there been recent mergers between the Unitarians and the Universalists and between the Congregationalists and the Evangelical Reformed Church, but there are increasing councils of "comity" in which a town's several denominations agree to a single strategy and a division of labor, and there are also growing numbers of trans-denominational parishes following the Richland, Washington, ecumenical experiment. The Richland congregation includes "Advent-Christian, American Baptist, Disciples of Christ, Evangelical and Reformed, Presbyterian, U.S.A., United Presbyterian, Friends, Church of the Brethren, Evangelical United Brethren, Methodist, and Congregational-Christian."[3] All of this suggests the new possibility that status-linked denominationalism may be a blurred phenomenon of the past.

For our purposes, the debate between the denominationalists and the ecumenicists is more than academic. If denominations are still meaningfully different, it is possible that the findings for the Lutherans are unique to the Lutherans. The relations between status and religiosity should at least vary considerably within different denominational contexts. On the other hand, if denominational lines are vestiges of a competitive past, the results for Lutherans should be no different from the findings for any other denomination. The clergy aside, this would suggest that the laity are little affected by such formal distinctions.

In sum, the analysis has two aspects. First, it aims for some

---

[3] Robert Lee, *The Social Sources of Church Unity* (Nashville, Tenn.: Abingdon Press, 1960), p. 162.

partial evidence concerning the extent and significance of denominational lines in American Protestantism for the behavior of individual Protestants. The phrase "partial evidence" is perhaps a euphemism for "inadequate evidence"; nevertheless some clues may emerge. The second aspect of the analysis concerns replication. Here the object is not to provide insights into denominationalism, but rather to assess the generalizability of our original relationships. In this sense, the denominational context is a third variable, methodologically akin to subjective class, age, sex, and parish status in the foregoing. Of course both of these aims are related, although an answer to the second question may be insufficient as an answer to the first.

The available data do not cover the whole range of major Protestant groups, but they do extend to four denominations, all of which are different from the Lutherans in some way. Both the Presbyterians and the Congregationalists are higher in actual and reputed status than the Lutherans; the Baptists are somewhat lower (see Tables I–1 and V–5). Lutheranism has a relatively sophisticated European background, while the Disciples of Christ began as an indigenous American church. Finally, Lutheranism is organized in highly structured synods and governed largely from the top. By contrast, the Presbyterians are organized on a less hierarchic, regional basis, and the Congregationalists, Baptists, and Disciples of Christ all idealize the autonomy of the local parish. This is not to say that the autonomous ideal always reflects reality. As Paul Harrison has pointed out, bureaucracy is making covert but deep inroads into the Baptists, and this seems to be the case for the others as well. Nevertheless, ideals are important in themselves and often carry independent influences.

Clearly the four added denominations not only differ from the Lutherans; they also differ among themselves. Much of this can be related to the church-sect distinction, our seemingly endless theoretical thread. The Congregationalist is the highest-status church; the Baptist is the lowest; and the Presbyterians and Disciples of Christ fall somewhere in between, judging from the present sample. Accordingly, the Congregationalists have the most liberal theology—liberal enough to overlook theological differences with the Evangelical and Reformed church in their recent merger.[4] The Baptists have the most conservative dogma, a more "hell-fire and brimstone" approach, with a sectarian intolerance of other interpretations.

But not all of the differences can be located in the church-sect distinction. Local parish autonomy is presumably an eminently sectlike ideal, and yet it characterizes the high-status and otherwise churchlike Congregationalists as well as the Baptists. A relatively conservative theology should go hand in hand with a relatively low-status membership, but the Disciples of Christ are conservative with a status distribution that closely approximates that of the liberal Presbyterians, the "emancipated Calvinists."

In short, the same confusion arises for the denominations included in this study as for American Protestantism generally. Are there systematic differences between denominations? Do they cancel each other out, or do they even reach the practicing laity? Finally, can such differences as do exist be represented along the church-sect distinction as this is applied to individual religiosity and ordered in terms of status distribution?

The strategy for answering these questions is by now familiar. The relation between individual status and the various measures of religiosity will be considered for each denominational context. Two hypotheses inform the analysis. First, we should expect that the original findings are not unique to Lutherans; they should persist for all denominations despite any independent denominational influences just as they persisted within categories of class, age, sex, and parish status. The second hypothesis concerns the denominational influence per se. Although we have already seen some reasons for caution, the hypothesis is that high-status denominations will manifest more churchlike religiosity while low-status denominations will evidence more sectlike commitment.

Before moving to the data, some advance notices are necessary.

---

[4] *Ibid.*, pp. 111–18. Lee suggests that differences in dogma were minimized during discussions of the merger and that discrepancies in church government and economics received far more attention. In this connection, it was apparently important that the Congregational bastion was in the East, while the Evangelical-Reformed strength was in the West and Midwest. This allowed for a merger that was geographically mediated if not merely "token."

The measure of status is identical for each of the denominations. It uses the same income categories as well as the same occupational and educational groupings. This is not precisely the case with religiosity. The Lutheran data are slightly incomparable to the data provided by the other denominations in the measure of sectlike religiosity. One ingredient of the index for Lutherans was whether or not the minister should participate in community affairs: "no" and "don't know" answers were considered sectlike. For each of the other denominations, however, the item was slightly different. Their questionnaires asked whether the minister should preach on *controversial issues* in the community. Again "no" and "don't know" answers were sectlike, but the frequency of these answers was much greater. Hence, the proportion of sectlike respondents is higher among Congregationalists, Presbyterians, Disciples of Christ and Baptists than among the Lutherans, and this justifies excluding the Lutherans from the ensuing comparative analysis. I will check, of course, that the relations between individual religiosity and status move in the same direction as in the Lutheran case. But I will only compare the actual proportions involved among the other four denominations themselves.

Table V–5 begins the analysis by offering the relation between individual status and churchlike religiosity for all of the new denominations. The measure of churchlike commitment is identical to that for Lutherans and includes church attendance, parish activities, and outside organizational affiliations. Note first that the original relations with individual status persist. In each case, the proportion highly involved in a churchlike fashion decreases with decreasing individual status. Among the upper-status parishioners, the percentage ranges from 65 per cent among the Congregationalists to 73 per cent among the Disciples of Christ. Among the low-status members, the proportion stands at 42 per cent among the Disciples and 32 per cent among the Baptists.

Unhappily, the second hypothesis fares less well. It predicted a decrease in churchlike commitment within every category of individual status as one moved from the high-status Congregationalists to the low-status Baptists. It is true that the

TABLE V–5

Churchlike Religiosity and Individual Status among Congregationalists, Presbyterians, Disciples of Christ, and Baptists

| Religiosity | Individual Status | | | | Denomination |
	Upper	Middle	Working	Low	
% High Church-like Involved	65	62	46	34	Congre-gationalists
N	(1346)	(1185)	(535)	(91)	
% High Church-like Involved	67	55	45	36	Presbyterians
N	(670)	(624)	(423)	(124)	
% High Church-like Involved	73	63	55	42	Disciples of Christ
N	(389)	(407)	(282)	(54)	
% High Church-like Involved	67	54	37	32	Baptists
N	(171)	(232)	(220)	(71)	

extreme comparison between Congregationalists and Baptists alone is supportive; for all but the upper-class individuals, Congregationalists have higher rates of churchlike religiosity than Baptists. But it is also true that the Disciples of Christ evidence more frequent churchlike commitment than even the Congregationalists, though the Disciples are lower in over-all social status. Apparently, then, denominations are not amenable to a rank ordering that scales both status and churchlike commitment simultaneously. Nor are denominational differences large for at least this facet of religiosity.

But if the denominational context makes little difference for churchlike involvement, it is of considerable influence for sect-like religiosity (Table V–6). Again the first hypothesis is confirmed in that the original, negative relations between individual status and sectlike commitment persist within each of the new denominational contexts. The percentage difference between the upper- and low-status parishioners is as low as 14 per cent among the Baptists (56 percent–42 per cent) and as high as 20 per cent among the Disciples of Christ

TABLE V–6

Sectlike Religiosity and Individual Status among Congregationalists, Presbyterians, Disciples of Christ, and Baptists

| Religiosity | Individual Status | | | | Denomination |
	Upper	Middle	Working	Low	
% High Sect-like Involved	22	27	32	37	Congre-gationalists
N	(1386)	(1145)	(572)	(102)	
% High Sect-like Involved	33	41	51	52	Presbyterians
N	(711)	(674)	(471)	(129)	
% High Sect-like Involved	36	45	43	56	Disciples of Christ
N	(387)	(396)	(284)	(52)	
% High Sect-like Involved	42	48	50	56	Baptists
N	(171)	(233)	(218)	(75)	

(56 per cent–36 per cent). Tables V–5 and V–6 differ, how-'ever, with respect to the second hypothesis concerning independent denominational influence. Unlike Table V–5, the data in Table V–6 offer relatively strong support. With only one exception,[5] all of the differences among denominations are predicted by the given ordering in terms of status. The lower the denomination in over-all status, the higher the percentage of sectlike commitment within each category of individual status. The differences between Congregationalists and Baptists at the extremes are consistently on the order of 20 per cent. Differences between the contiguous Presbyterians and Disciples of Christ are smaller but, with one exception, in the predicted direction.

[5] The 51 per cent of the working-status Presbyterians who ranked high in sectlike religiosity is an aberration for which I have no ready explanation. While it may be an important deviant case from some other perspective, it does not vitiate the present one. In fact, it is remarkable that this is the only cell out of 16 that is out of sorts. The remainder are technically isotropic with linear relations moving both vertically and horizontally for every row and column.

Table V–7 presents the ratio between pure churchlike and sectlike behavior as a last check. The original relation with individual status persists here with no exceptions. In each denomination, the lower-status parishioners are more frequently involved in sectlike religion alone. As for independent denominational influences, there is support here as well. It is true that the Disciples of Christ are again assymetrical, owing more to their greater proclivity for churchlike involvement than to any lesser penchant for sectarianism. At the same time, the Congregationalist, Presbyterian, and Baptist scores are predictable by the over-all status ranking of the denominations.

TABLE V–7

Ratio of Pure Sectlike to Pure Churchlike Religiosity by Individual Status within Categories of Denominations

| Religiosity | Individual Status | | | | Denomination |
	Upper	Middle	Working	Low	
$S\overline{C}/C\overline{S}$	.08	.20	.48	1.12	Congregationalists
$S\overline{C}/C\overline{S}$	.16	.43	1.27	2.54	Presbyterians
$S\overline{C}/C\overline{S}$	.16	.36	.44	2.00	Disciples of Christ
$S\overline{C}/C\overline{S}$	.28	.79	1.88	3.43	Baptists

The lower the denomination's relative status, the higher the $S\overline{C}/C\overline{S}$ ratio for each category of individual status, and, hence, the greater the proportion of those who are committed in a sectlike but not in a churchlike fashion.

To review, then, each of the foregoing tables has replicated the original relations between individual status and religiosity. Each has also given some evidence that denominational differences are more than myth and are, in fact, amenable to prediction on grounds of relative status ranking. At the same time, the tables raise two additional problems. First, why are denominational differences more pronounced for sectlike religiosity than for churchlike? Second, why do the Disciples of Christ prove an exception to the rules established by the Congregationalists, Presbyterians, and Baptists?

A possible answer to the first revolves about the distinction between *formal* and *informal* aspects of the church program.

Recall that the index of churchlike religiosity included attendance at formal Sunday worship and participation in formal church organizations. Now, regardless of the actual context of the worship services or the organizations, it remains true that every Protestant group considers them to be central aspects of the religious program. At this level, we should expect little denominational difference that is irreducible to individual predilection. By contrast, however, our measure of sectlike religiosity is more informal. Items such as the number of friends in the congregation, estimated religious reward, and attitudes towards ministerial participation in controversial community issues are more vulnerable to differences in denominational climate and ideology. These go beyond the formal expectations of lay commitment; they more easily reflect a denomination's past history and present mood.

Consider now the second major problem in the preceding tables. Why should the Disciples of Christ be anomalous in bearing a higher degree of churchlike commitment than their status ranking would predict? The conventional image of the Disciples of Christ is that of a fundamentalist sect "on the make." That is, they are regarded as a once-revivalistic group taking on the mantle of churchly legitimacy, stability, and sobriety. In this light they are seen as similar to the Baptists and their departures from the Baptists are all the more surprising. But, in fact, this image may be erroneous.[6] Richard

[6] One of the most damning judgments that can be made of any theory is that it is difficult to spot its concrete referents. Unhappily the church-sect theory is a case in point. I mentioned earlier that Catholicism and indeed the whole Protestant Reformation can be seen as both churchlike and sectlike, depending upon which criteria are used. This applies to the Disciples of Christ as well. While I shall cite Niebuhr and Craig in their interpretation of the Disciples as inordinately churchly, there are opposing views. For example, Oliver Whitley, *Trumpet Call of Reformation* (St. Louis, Mo.: The Bethany Press, 1959), has argued just the reverse and has cited the Disciples as an instance of a denomination that remains very sectlike. In part, the disagreement is an impasse, and the reader may prefer an interpretation at odds with my own. It is likely, however, that Niebuhr and Whitley are discussing two quite different things. Thus, Whitley may be concerned with the internal organization of the Disciples, while Niebuhr may be more interested in their dogma and posture relative to the external society. Because the latter is more important to my present problem, I have adopted Niebuhr's interpretation as a conceivable, though far from certain, explanation of the issue at hand.

Niebuhr's account of the development of American Protestant denominations indicates that the Disciples of Christ never went through the perfervid, revivalist stage that characterized the Baptists and even the Presbyterians and Congregationalists on the expanding Western frontier.

> The church of the Disciples remained a Western, but primarily a Middle Western, church. It was not a frontier faith in quite the same way as were Methodism and the Baptist movement. Not only did it start its course later than these, achieving organization only after the frontier had passed hundreds of miles further inland, but it lacked much of the emotional fervour these other denominations possessed. It was somewhat more interested in the social principle of union than in the individual principle of the salvation of souls. Perhaps this was the reason why it was less aggressive than its rivals.[7]

In short, the Disciples do not have the same sectlike legacy that stamps the other denominations we have considered. One can speculate that the sectarianism of the other denominations lingers as succor for the present-day lower classes, but in the Disciples of Christ there was nothing along this line to begin with. That there is little now is reflected in James E. Craig's response to the question "Who Are the Disciples of Christ?" in Leo Rosten's simplistic book on the *Religions of America*.

> The Disciples are inclined to regard formal creeds and historical sects as so many milestones on the long highway of an evolving theology. As for themselves they put aside ancient speculations and dogmas. . . . The Disciples have had little trouble in discarding most of the dogmas which sprang up between the first century and the nineteenth. . . . They are not concerned about such matters as original sin or predestination. . . . To Disciples, the rising trend towards a mutual ground of faith marks a steady advance toward ultimate church unity. And in this field the Disciples have made their influence most heavily felt.[8]

[7] H. Richard Niebuhr, *The Social Sources of Denominationalism* (New York: Henry Holt & Company, Inc., 1929), pp. 180–81. By permission of Mrs. H. Richard Niebuhr.

[8] James E. Craig, "Who Are the Disciples of Christ?" in Leo Rosten (ed.), *Religions of America* (rev. ed.; New York: Simon & Schuster, Inc., 1963), from pp. 58–65. Reprinted by permission of *Look* magazine.

Craig is effectively disclaiming sectlike concerns for a special doctrine, for an intimate community of the morally elect, and for a community set apart from other confessions and the secular world. The disclaimer suggests that compromise and universality have always been inordinately stressed among the Disciples. This would account for their exceptionally strong showing on the churchlike index. The peculiarity then is not a matter of status in this case. It is a matter of denominational history and the persistence of early denominational attributes. Status is, again, only one of many important influences bearing on religiosity.

Summary

This chapter has emphasized the context of individual religiosity, especially as the context can be understood in terms of social stratification. In considering differences between Lutheran congregations and among various other American Protestant denominations, the chapter has pursued two hypotheses successfully. First, the original relations between individual status and the types of individual religiosity persist, regardless of the parish or denominational context. Whether one considers high- or low-status Lutheran parishes, whether one considers Congregationalists, Presbyterians, Disciples of Christ, or Baptists, the incidence of churchlike religiosity is positively related to individual status, and the incidence of sectlike religiosity is negatively related.

The second hypothesis has been concerned with the independent effects of parish and denominational contexts. Even though these effects are not so powerful as to engulf the influence of individual status, they are sufficient to demonstrate that stratification is potent as more than an individual factor. In general, the incidence of churchlike commitment falls and the incidence of sectlike religiosity rises with decreasing contextual status. This is true for all categories of individual status and, thus, is not reducible to the individual status composition or recruitment of these contexts. Apparently, different parishes and denominations take on a particular tone which is influenced by their over-all status. This tone has organizational reinforcement and is a generalized influence that moves beyond its source.

Finally, there are three principal exceptions to the hypotheses and to the data's general pattern. First, the extreme low-status members of the high-status Lutheran congregations show an inordinate rate of sectarianism. This may be a defensive reaction by which a sectlike island protects itself against a churchlike sea. Secondly, denominational context has more influence on variation in sectlike involvement than on variation in churchlike commitment. This may be related to the informal character of the former as compared with the formal nature of the latter. Sectlike religiosity is less ritualized and hence more vulnerable to differences in denominational climate; churchlike religiosity is almost a prescribed ingredient in all church programs and is less free to vary. The third exception involves the Disciples of Christ who display an inordinately high rate of churchlike involvement, given their over-all status ranking. This is speculatively attributed to the Disciples' early history as an indigenous American church that has largely avoided the sectlike stages of the transplanted Congregationalists, Presbyterians, and Baptists.

Part Three

VI

Status Discrepancy and Religious Commitment

All of the previous chapters have stressed a vertical dimension of stratification. Whether discussing individuals, congregations, or denominations, whether examining aggregate objective status, subjective class, age, or sex, the assumption has always been that some units rank higher than others in their fulfillment of secular values. Terms like "upper class" versus "lower class" imply nothing if not a vertical hierarchy. Yet is this vertical dimension all of stratification?

Consider three hypothetical persons who share the same, middle-status score on our Index of Objective Status. The index is, of course, an amalgam of rankings on education, income, and occupational prestige. The first person may be a clerk in a small business who has identical scores on all three status indicators. When each indicator is scored from 0 to 5, he has a score of 3 on each and a total of 9 out of a possible 15. The second person, however, may also have a total score of 9 but from a different combination. Perhaps a successful door-to-door salesman, he may score 5 on income, 2 on occupational prestige, and 2 on education. Finally, the third person may have a still different status profile. Scoring 5 on education, 4 on occupational prestige, and 0 on

income, he may be a free-lance writer with an unpopular interest or even a college instructor.

Although all of these persons have the same over-all vertical
status position, there is clearly something else at work. The
second and third cases not only share a middle-status niche, but
they also share an inconsistency in their rankings on the separate
indicators. In contrast to the first person, these two are characterized by "status discrepancy."[1] Contrasted with each other,
their profiles of discrepancy differ. Here, then, is another dimension of stratification, a non-vertical facet that is independent
of our prior focus.

Unlike conventional status, status discrepancy is not yet a
major weapon in the sociologist's "war of explanation." To date
it has nearly as many labels as it has had empirical treatments.
Although it has been called "discrepancy," "crystallization,"
"consistency," "homogeneity," "equilibrium," and "congruency,"[2] its effects have not been explored beyond the areas of
politics, secular organizational commitments, and psychosomatic
symptoms. The relation between discrepancy and religion has
so far been ignored.

Without suggesting that religion must be considered *per force*
and for its own sake, several considerations recommend an in-

[1] There are clearly many other forms of discrepancy which I have
neglected to mention. An inconsistency between the individual's status and
his father's status may be important. So may the discrepancy between an
individual's own past, present, and future status and aspirations. Then too,
some have considered the distinction between one's racial status and one's
economic standing. Finally, the disparity between objective rank and subjective evaluation has already been considered partially in Chapter IV.
All of these are important, but, unhappily, the data do not allow full
coverage. Note, too, that there is a danger in lumping all of these "pathol-
ogies" under a single rubric. While it is true that all involve discrepancy
in some form or another, the type of discrepancy may be revealingly different, and the correlates of one may be antithetical to those of another.

[2] When this research was begun, all of the terms enjoyed a somewhat
equal currency. I chose the label "status discrepancy" because it seemed
more parsimonious, less invidious, and more stylistically felicitous (compare
the phrase "highly discrepant" with "highly inconsistent," "low crystallized,"
"highly disequillibrated," or "highly heterogeneous"). Subsequently, however, the term "consistency" has begun to take the lead. While the semantic
race may be interesting to the sociologist of knowledge, I have no particular
bets to hedge and have retained "discrepancy" more out of convenience
than out of principle.

spection of its link with discrepancy. One is that this study is meant to canvass the general association between stratification and religion, and discrepancy is a new but undeniable aspect of the former. Another is that because discrepancy is underexplored, new research should be helpful for its general contributions to theory and methodology. Finally, religion is representative of a number of institutions whose ideologies differ from the secular values that inform status judgments and their consequences. In this light, it should offer special interest by carrying a special appeal for the status discrepant themselves.

The chapter comprises three major sections. First, I will consider the conceptual development of discrepancy and its empirical correlates in the literature. Second, I will speculate concerning its influence on religiosity. Third, I will subject the speculation to a first test using the data available from American Protestants. More refined analysis will follow in Chapter VII.

The Theoretical and Empirical Development of Status Discrepancy

Like so much of contemporary sociology, the concept of status discrepancy arose from Weber's[3] sympathetic critique of Marx. The Marxian[4] view of stratification was, of course, inflexible and deterministic. Classes were determined by economic forces. Depending on one's role in the productive process, and one's awareness of it, one was either for or against the prevailing system, and conflict was inevitable and inexorable. Although Marx did not deny that certain persons were either ambiguous in their class position or were falsely conscious of the consequences, these problems were seen only as arresting minutiae in the broad sweep of history.

To Weber, on the other hand, these exceptions were more important. Weber's notion of stratification derived from his

[3] See, for example, Max Weber, "Class, Status and Party," in Hans Gerth and C. Wright Mills (eds.), *From Max Weber: Essays in Sociology* (New York: Oxford Galaxy Books, 1958), pp. 180–95.

[4] For a summary and discussion of Marx's view of stratification, see Reinhard Bendix and S. M. Lipset, "Karl Marx's Theory of Social Classes," in Bendix and Lipset (eds.), *Class, Status and Power* (Glencoe, Ill.: The Free Press, 1953), pp. 26–35.

image of society and his hopes for the future.[5] Unlike Marx, he was concerned less with wholesale economic justice and more with individual freedom. Unlike Marx, he saw society as an interstice of pluralistic forces rather than an arena for polarized conflict. Finally, unlike Marx, he saw stratification as a *series* of hierarchies that crosscut each other so that individuals might occupy different positions on each and societies might give different emphases to each.

Weber described three primary types of stratification that coexist in society: class, status, and power. His conception of *class* was very nearly Marxian except that it referred more to consumption than to production. Thus, one's class position was a function of one's property, buying capacity, and position in the marketplace. *Status* referred to social honor and was theoretically independent of the market. Weber went to some length to explore the nouveaux riches who had money without honor; deposed monarchs were frequently case studies of honor without funds. Finally, *power* referred to the ability to manipulate others, and it too was conceived as independent. To use a contemporary example, the political "boss" may lack both money and honor; he is nevertheless a commanding figure who gets things done.

For all of this, Weber never used the term "status discrepancy" or any of its contemporary synonyms. In fact, he was less interested in the dilemma of the discrepant individual than in the consequences of a multifaceted stratification scheme for the social structure as a whole. Some structures were primarily built around power, some around honor, and some around class, just as some stuctures depended on charismatic leadership, some upon traditional authority, and some upon rational-legal controls.[6] Nevertheless, Weber planted the seed whose growth concerns us here.

[5] For a description of this image and a cataloguing of these hopes, see Reinhard Bendix, *Max Weber: An Intellectual Portrait* (Garden City, N.Y.: Doubleday & Company, Inc., 1960).

[6] See Max Weber, *The Theory of Social and Economic Organization* (Glencoe, Ill.: The Free Press, 1947), pp. 324–406, for a discussion of these different forms of leadership. The same concern with societies rather than individuals occurs in Emile Benoit-Smullyan, "Status, Status Types, and Status Interrelationships," *American Sociological Review*, IX (1944), 151–61. Some twenty-five years elapsed between Weber's original treatment and Benoit-Smullyan's very similar restatement. This attests to the slow development of the concept at issue.

Most of Weber's seeds found quick root; this one did not. Little attention was given to the concept initially, but after a lapse of twenty years interest in it was awakened by a second school of early German sociology led by Georg Simmel.[7] Simmel was concerned with interaction within small groups instead of whole societies. He was concerned with the instabilities of situations rather than their monolithic structures. In all of this, Simmel found an appreciative audience in the so-called Chicago School of American sociology, notably in the work of Robert Park and Ernest Burgess and their emphasis on the marginal man in society.[8] Park and Burgess were at their zenith in the 1920's, but their influence has lingered at Chicago. Among others, it has had an impact on Everett C. Hughes,[9] whose work resumes the development of status discrepancy per se.

The marginal man is one at odds with his contemporaries. Caught between worlds, he is not amenable to easy categorizations; his self-image and the image others have of him are at best ambiguous. Hughes sees much of this hinging upon "Dilemmas and Contradictions of Status." He uses examples like the Negro doctor and the female scientist to point out that role conflicts ensue, and that these, in turn, create peculiar patterns and strategies of interaction. Will patients react to the Negro or to the doctor? Which aspect will be most salient for the Negro doctor himself? In seeking answers to these questions, Hughes has restimulated concern for status discrepancy and directed it more toward the individual than toward the problems of social structure that occupied Weber.

This is not to say, however, that status discrepancy was a "hot topic" in 1944. Like Weber's, Hughes's stimulus was slow to find response. But after some ten years, Gerhard Lenski has taken up the issue and advanced the concept with empirical evidence. In 1954, Lenski published the first of two studies con-

[7] Georg Simmel, *The Sociology of Georg Simmel*, trans. and ed. Kurt H. Wolff (Glencoe, Ill.: The Free Press, 1950). Although Simmel was a contemporary and a student of Weber's his work is generally put to one side of the mainstream of early German sociology. Even the Chicago School was insufficient to bring him to real prominence. His reputation only crested with the advent of small-group research in American sociology.

[8] Cf. Robert E. Park, *Human Communities* (Glencoe, Ill.: The Free Press, 1952).

[9] Everett C. Hughes, "Dilemmas and Contradictions of Status," *American Journal of Sociology*, L (1944), 353–59.

cerned with the correlates of discrepancy, or what Lenski preferred to call "status crystallization." He begins with the simple
hypothesis that

> . . . individuals characterized by a low degree of status
> crystallization [i.e., high degree of status discrepancy] differ
> significantly in their political attitudes and behavior from
> individuals characterized by a high degree of status crystal-
> lization, when status differences in the vertical dimension
> are controlled.[10]

He goes on to show that the highly discrepant seem more apt to
vote Democratic and favor left-wing political ideologies[11] advocating social and economic changes. Lenski has speculated that the
highly discrepant contain a revolutionary spark. He goes further
to account for the bourgeois leaders of the proletariat in these
terms rather than in those of the Marxian notion of an enlight-
ened few. But the highly discrepant are not only likely to be
politically left. In 1956, Lenski published evidence that they are
also less frequently committed to secular voluntary organizations.[12] Even among those who are members, there is an inordinately low rate of interpersonal relations and a strong tendency
to token affiliation.

In all of this, Lenski has been more concerned with empirical
correlates than a theoretical accommodation of the concept as a
whole. Implicitly, however, he uses role theory very much like
Hughes. The highly discrepant are unable to define their position
and are uncomfortable under the prevailing status system. They
seek to change the system and, in the meantime, they withdraw
from voluntary organizations where status judgments are most
blatant. Lenski's empirical results as well as his implicit theory
have found subsequent support and elaboration.

Further empirical evidence of the significance of discrepancy
has come from several quarters. Irwin Goffman's[13] results on

[10] Gerhard Lenski, "Status Crystallization: A Non-Vertical Dimension of
Social Status," *American Sociological Review*, XIX (1954), 405–6.

[11] More recent speculation is that some types of discrepancy lead to political extremism on the *right*. The John Birch Society, for example, seems
overrepresented among successful small businessmen with low education.

[12] Gerhard Lenski, "Social Participation and Status Crystallization,"
American Sociological Review, XXI (1956), 458–64.

[13] Irwin W. Goffman, "Status Consistency and Preference for Change in
Power Distribution," *American Sociological Review*, XXII. (1957), 275–81.

"status consistency" and political liberalism are generally supportive of Lenski's, though he offers some qualifications according to the level of vertical status considered. Sokol and Zelditch[14]
also replicate Lenski in so far as they find that the highly discrepant are more likely to favor a change in power structure,
although they also find that the type of change depends upon the
type of discrepancy analyzed. Elton Jackson[15] has extended this
profile analysis further. He finds that political liberalism is
common among the highly discrepant whose ethnic status is low
but whose economic status is high. Among those with the reverse
pattern, however, political liberalism is supplanted by a high
rate of psychosomatic symptoms of stress. Jackson builds upon
this finding ingeniously. He invokes the broader distinction between "ascribed" and "achieved" status. He argues that a deficiency in the former is likely to be blamed against the society,
whereas a deficiency in the latter is more likely to be blamed
upon oneself. Thus, low ascribed status should conduce to political radicalism, while low achieved status should result in intra-
punitive symptoms such as psychosomatic stress. Unhappily, as
Chapter VII will indicate, Jackson's theory may lack the empirical support that is imputed to it.

While the preceding studies focus on the individual as a member of large samples in which there is presumed to be no interpersonal interaction, a number of other studies are closer to the

[14] Robert Sokol and Morris Zelditch, Jr., A Further Test of the Effects
of Gross Status Inconsistencies, a paper delivered to the American Sociological Association, St. Louis, Missouri, September, 1961. See also Werner
S. Landecker, "Class Crystallization and Class Consciousness," *American
Sociological Review*, XXVIII (1963), 219–29, for another political correlate
of an intervening sort. Class consciousness may well provide a key to the
imperfect relations noted here, since Landecker generally finds the most
discrepant to be the least class conscious. Thus, the ambiguity may frequently counteract a radical disposition.

[15] Elton F. Jackson, "Status Consistency and Symptoms of Stress,"
American Sociological Review, XXVII (1962), 469–80. Apparently unpublished research by Kleiner, Parker, and Taylor demonstrates a further relation between status incongruence and full blown mental illness, moving a
step beyond psychosomatic symptoms of stress. Here incongruence is defined
as the gap between education and occupational standing, where education is
considered a measure of aspiration and occupation is taken as an indicator
of achievement. The research is cited in Edward E. Sampson, "Status Con-
gruence and Cognitive Consistency," *Sociometry* XXVI (1963), 146–62.

Simmelian tradition in examining status discrepancy in small-group situations. These studies are primarily concerned more with group efficiency, and they find that discrepancy can be an important disruptive influence. Zaleznik[16] and his associates explore the consequences among workers in machine shops; Clark[17] has examined interactions among supermarket personnel; Exline and Ziller[18] manipulate the effects of discrepancy in an experimental laboratory; and Stuart Adams[19] has explored the phenomenon among bomber crews. Indeed Adams' work is one of the early studies in the area and provides some of the most provocative findings. Where he compares groups rather than individuals on discrepancy (a group may have members of the same general status or it may have some high- and some low-status members), he finds a beguiling curvilinearity. Too much discrepancy reduces efficiency by making cooperation difficult. Too little discrepancy also reduces efficiency by reducing the basis for authority differences and by increasing camaraderie to the point where it takes precedence over the task at hand. Note, however, that these studies are to some extent incomparable with the present concern. Although discrepancy is important to both, it makes a difference whether one is looking at discrepancy on the group or on the individual level, and whether one is examining inter- or intra-individual consequences.[20] Because this study

---

[16] A. Zaleznik *et al., The Motivation, Productivity, and Satisfaction of Workers* (Cambridge, Mass.: Harvard University Press, 1958).

[17] J. V. Clark, "A Preliminary Investigation of Some Unconscious Assumptions Affecting Labor Efficiency in Eight Supermarkets," unpublished D.B.A. thesis, Harvard Graduate School of Business Administration, 1958, cited in George C. Homans, *Social Behavior: Its Elementary Forms* (New York: Harcourt, Brace & World, Inc., 1961), pp. 256–52. This occurs in the midst of Homans' broader discussion of status discrepancy in small groups, pp. 248–64.

[18] Ralph V. Exline and Robert C. Ziller, "Status Congruency and Interpersonal Conflict in Decision-Making Groups," *Human Relations*, XII (1959), 147–62.

[19] Stuart N. Adams, "Status Congruency as a Variable in Small Group Performance," *Social Forces*, XXXII (1953), 16–22.

[20] See Robert E. Mitchell, "Methodological Notes on a Theory of Status Crystallization," and Gerhard Lenski, "Comment," *Public Opinion Quarterly*, XXVIII (1964), 315–30. This exchange illustrates the friction as well as the possibilities generated by these multiple approaches. Perhaps the logical capstone would be to examine groups with different rates of individual status discrepancy among their members. A group with a high percentage of members characterized by discrepancy should be less efficient and less

focuses primarily on the latter, I will adhere most closely to it in developing the theory to follow.

Of course, all of these studies deal with theory to some degree, and yet there are more intensive discussions outside of this empirical tradition. Frederick Bates and Roland Pellegrin[21] have charted a variety of types of "status incongruity" within organizations and have elaborated role theory as a perspective for analysis. Specifically, they introduce the concepts of *relative deprivation* and *reference group*. That is, the highly discrepant individual is torn between a high-status and a low-status reference group. On absolute grounds, he may feel that his over-all middle-status ranking is satisfactory. But relative to the high-status, non-discrepant reference group, he feels deprived and his search for a remedy takes on a certain urgency. Although Bates and Pellegrin may be suspect for assuming that discrepancy is an attribute of which the individual is fully conscious, their article is outstanding for its ingenuity.

If Bates and Pellegrin describe the illness, Leon Festinger[22] suggests the range of remedies available. Festinger is not concerned with status discrepancy as such. But his notion of *cognitive dissonance* is the genus of which discrepancy is one species, as Sampson[23] has recently suggested. Under conditions of dissonance (or status discrepancy), three general solutions are possible. First, the individual may change one or more of the dissonant elements. In the context of stratification, this can be translated into vertical mobility so that the low-status ranking is raised to a level commensurate with the high. It might also refer to a wholesale change in the status system itself, presum-

---

friendly than a group with a low percentage. Robert R. Alford is currently exploring this on a larger scale as an aid in distinguishing the local political climates of four Wisconsin cities. See also Ronald Freedman *et al.*, *Principles of Sociology* (rev. ed.; New York: Henry Holt & Company, Inc., 1956), pp. 521–40, and Werner S. Landecker, "Class Crystallization and Its Urban Pattern," *Social Research*, XXVII (1960), 308–20.

[21] Frederick L. Bates and Roland J. Pellegrin, "Congruity and Incongruity of Status Attributes," *Social Forces*, XXXVIII (1959), 23–28.

[22] Leon Festinger, *A Theory of Cognitive Dissonance* (Evanston, Ill.: Row, Peterson & Company, 1957), especially pp. 263–64.

[23] Sampson, *op. cit.* While Sampson explores the general parallel between research on status discrepancy and work on the psychological reactions to perceived imbalances, he does not utilize Festinger's work in the same way or to the same extent as in the present framework.

ably the intent of those political radicals who support programs of social change. A second remedy lies at the opposite extreme. Instead of actively changing one or all of the dissonant elements involved, one may passively withdraw from the dissonant situation so that none of the elements are salient. Here is a niche for Lenski's findings that those with high status discrepancy have a low rate of commitment to secular voluntary organizations in which status judgments are allegedly most pronounced.

In theory, these first two alternatives are not mutually exclusive. One may withdraw from secular organizations while awaiting mobility or social change. In practice, however, these active and passive responses are less complementary. One who is active is apt to belong to a large number of organizations, which serve either as aids to mobility or as political vehicles of change. Conversely, one who is passive is not likely to involve himself in struggles which necessarily involve direct confrontation with the problem at hand.

But note that the two do share a quality in common. Both are unstable positions in that they sever the individual's ties with conventional society. This is less true of those pursuing mobility, but certainly those advocating radical change and those who effect a complete withdrawal risk converting status discrepancy into alienation. Festinger's third resolution of dissonance avoids these pitfalls when it is applied to status discrepancy. It simply involves adding new elements to the situation which reinforce one or more of the disputing factors. Thus, a person who is ranked both high and low in secular status, may seek other status criteria for evaluation. He may find an alternative orientation which contributes to a more consistent self-image.

However, one does not simply pluck orientations from the clouds. Instead different types of social institutions represent different orientations and different criteria for status judgments. Of course, conventional status is tied largely to economic institutions in our society. But, it is possible to supplement conventional status with judgments drawn from other institutions. Thus, the status discrepant may put inordinate emphasis on his role in the family, the academic community, or, indeed, religion. All of these carry values that are in some measure distinct from those which frame conventional status. In each case, it is possible to reinforce a self-image of high status by adding new criteria to the range of conventional standards. If, for example, one stands high on education but low on income, he is likely to maintain the saliency of educational status, reinforce it with a notion of general intellectual worth, and then neglect his income as a frame for self-reference. He has buttressed his high-status position by adding a new criterion and reducing the significance of an older one. In addition, he has accommodated himself to the social context by becoming even more integrated into one phase of it. His position is not one of total withdrawal or radical protest. It is essentially a more stable adjustment.

None of the previously cited research explores this third alternative. In fact, some of the research may be criticized for failing to see its possibilities. Thus, Lenski's statement that the highly discrepant are less involved in voluntary organizations requires specification. It may be that they are less involved in those voluntary organizations which subscribe to the secular values that determine the conventional status system. On the other hand, the highly discrepant may be *more* involved in organizations which harbor non-economic values or values unrelated to status judgments. We might expect, for example, that they will be inordinately involved in the family, in educational groups, and in the church, while, at the same time, they will be less involved in trade unions, country clubs, and fraternal organizations.

Of course, religion and the church will be the prime focus of what follows. But here, as with vertical status, the relation with religiosity is primarily interesting because it signifies the general relation between discrepancy and institutions which advocate somewhat unconventional values and criteria of judgment. Before turning to the actual findings, let us sharpen our expectations.

First, how should the distinction between churchlike and sectlike religiosity apply to status discrepancy? A central idea behind the distinction is that the church may be seen as more or less unconventional by its parishioners. To the church type the religious experience is valuable in its reinforcement of secular values. To the sect type, religion is important as an alternative orientation. Accordingly, the sect type and church type emphasize different aspects of the religious program and are committed in qualitatively different ways. All of this should apply to discrepancy as well as vertical status. Both low status and high discrepancy involve the search for a new framework for self-evaluation, one that reduces either a critical problem of self-esteem or an equally critical problem in role confusion. Hence, both low status and high discrepancy should predispose one to sectlike religiosity. On the other hand, both the high-status parishioners and those with low status discrepancy should be more churchlike in their commitment. Whether because of high secular standing or a status that is at least consistent, these people need a complement to their secular values rather than an entirely new criterion for self-judgment.

There is, however, one special qualification. I mentioned earlier that the influences of vertical status and status discrepancy are not mutually exclusive but work together. This means, then, that they may exert conflicting pressures on the individual. Consider the person who has relatively high over-all status and a high degree of status discrepancy. The former may predispose him to churchlike religiosity; the latter may lead to a more sectlike form of commitment. How does he resolve the dilemma? One hypothesis is that he will compromise. He may reject the most extreme aspects of churchlike religiosity, those which carry him furthest into the secular arena that he wants to minimize. Thus, he will belong to few organizations outside of the church; he will be reluctant to participate in those church activities that deal with secular problems and employ status judgments in their recruitment of members. He will, however, attend church regularly. As for sectlike commitment, he may find a large number of his close friends in the church and report a high degree of general religious influence and reward in his everyday activities. He may not, however, go so far in a sectlike direction as to disapprove of the minister's participation in controversial community affairs. All of this is, of course, speculation. Nevertheless it dictates a close look at the separate items involved in the churchlike and sectlike indexes to check for internal variation in the relations with discrepancy. This will follow, after a brief detour to develop an index of discrepancy with which to work.

A Measure of Discrepancy

The status indicators available for analysis are the same that were used in the Index of (vertical) Socioeconomic Status: education, income, and occupational prestige. Note, however, that these have not been the only items used to determine status discrepancy in previous research. Lenski, for example, adds ethnic status to the present three, and Jackson uses ethnicity but not income. In both cases, the major ethnic difference is between Negroes and whites. Unhappily, the present sample includes too few Negroes to make them a significant status category. While it would be preferable to include ethnicity for comparison with previous analyses, there are several reasons for going ahead without it. First, the concept of discrepancy is interesting in itself even if, here, it does refer only to achieved and not to ascribed status. Second, following Jackson's previous logic, the predicted relation with religiosity should be strongest for the present achieved status, since deficiencies here should result in an embarrassed retreat from the system instead of an aggressive attack upon it. But third, the exclusion of ethnicity may be a blessing in another sense, since Mitchell[24] has suggested that ethnicity alone accounts for many of the findings that Lenski attributes to status discrepancy. If discrepancy has an independent influence, it is important to test this where ethnicity is not a contaminating factor. Finally, although the present secondary analysis must make do with education, income, and occupation, surely these are more generalizable status characteristics than ethnicity. It has become tragically clear that the United States is unique in the magnitude of its racial problem. To rest a case on such a sickly stigma might preclude an extension to other, perhaps saner, societies.

But given the present three status measures, how do we arrive at a summary index of status discrepancy? It is possible to consider income, education, and occupation as simple dichotomies on which a person may rank high or low. A highly discrepant person would rank high on one or two but low on the remaining factor. This would make for a simple analysis, but it is discouraged by two of Lenski's findings. First, he concludes that

[24] Mitchell, *op. cit.*, pp. 321–22.

only an extreme form of status discrepancy produces distinctive behaviors and attitudes, and it is, therefore, necessary to isolate a high discrepancy group on a finer scale than dichotomous indicators provide. Second, since the Negro-white differences which are Lenski's most powerful factor are lacking here, it may be even more important to treat the existing measures in more detail if one is to produce anything at all.

For both reasons, I have divided each of the three status indicators into five categories, ranging from high to low. The breakdown is identical with that used in the aggregate Index of (vertical) Socioeconomic Status. A person may have an income over $9,000, at one extreme, or under $2,000, at the other extreme. He may be a professional, at one end, or an unskilled laborer, at the other. He may have a college education and score extremely high, or he may not have finished grade school and score extremely low. While the distributions of the variables are not formally standardized, they are all similarly normal or bell-shaped.

A combination of all three status variables with five categories each results in a 125-cell table. It is possible to calculate relative scores of discrepancy by a rough approximation to standard deviation. First, take the mean score of each cell, when the three indicators may contribute numerical rankings from 1 to 5. Then, sum the separate absolute deviations from the mean. As an example, consider a cell with combined scores of 5–3–1. The overall mean is 3. The sum of the separate deviations from the mean is 4, which is the status discrepancy value. As another example, take a cell combining scores of 5–1–1. Here the mean is approximately 2.3, and the sum of the absolute deviations is 5.3, which is an even higher degree of status discrepancy. Using this technique, all 125 cells fall into one of nine positions on a scale of status discrepancy. A score of 0 represents the perfectly consistent profile, whether 5–5–5, 4–4–4, 3–3–3, 2–2–2, or 1–1–1. A score of 5.3 is maximum discrepancy, whether 5–5–1, 1–1–5, etc.

Instead of working with all nine points on the scale of discrepancy, three categories seemed more practical. Actually, the three were dictated by the numerical-scale scores themselves. The three highest scores were bunched at one end; the next four were also clustered; the final two were similarly set apart. The resulting groups are "high," "moderate," and "low" status discrepancy.

Table VI–1 presents the over-all distribution of respondents in these categories. Note that the distribution pools all of the denominations that were analyzed separately in the analysis of vertical status and religiosity. Presbyterians, Congregationalists, Lutherans, Baptists, and Disciples of Christ are merged to represent American Protestants generally. There are two reasons for this. First, unlike vertical status, status discrepancy should not produce systematic differences among denominations (see Chapter VII). All of the denominations have roughly the same proportions of high discrepancy; discrepancy is primarily

TABLE VI–1

Distribution of High-, Moderate-, and Low-Status Discrepancy within the Sample of Protestants

Discrepancy Categories	Percentage Distribution	
High Status Discrepancy	(308)	3.5
Moderate Status Discrepancy	(3806)	43.0
Low Status Discrepancy	(4745)	53.5
Total N	(8859)	100

an individual attribute without the contextual influence of vertical status. Secondly, there is a methodological reason. Since very few persons are highly discrepant, the number for any single denomination would be insufficient to bear elaborate analysis. By combining denominations, the number becomes larger and more workable.

Look then at the distribution of discrepancy among our five Protestant denominations. The highly descrepant do indeed comprise only a small proportion of the whole. Of the total sample, only 308 or 3.5 per cent are characterized by extremely high status discrepancy. By contrast, 43 per cent are moderately discrepant, and fully 53.5 per cent have a low degree of discrepancy.

Two questions immediately arise. Why does high discrepancy characterize so few? And is it worth our effort to analyze such a sparse minority?[25] In answer to the first, note that we are

[25] I have explored these issues at greater length in Status Discrepancy and Vertical Status: Criticisms and Suggested Remedies, a paper delivered to the American Sociological Association, Washington, D.C., September, 1962.

talking primarily of *economic* status discrepancy within a highly stable economic structure. In general, the American economy has developed to a point where occupation, income, and education are joint prerequisites for success. The lionized entrepreneur has given way to the industrial bureaucrat. Education is essential for occupational success, and occupational success and high income are tightly related in the economic structure. Thus, economic status discrepancy should be rare in the United States, just as it should be rare in underdeveloped areas with traditional non-industrial status systems. Discrepancy should have maximum impact in the societies which lie between these two types, the so-called developing areas whose status systems are undergoing sporadic change.

This reasoning also helps to answer the second question, "Why bother?" Even though discrepancy affects so few in the United States, the results have wider applicability in other contexts. In addition, it is worth observing that even a 3.5 per cent minority can be important as a source of major social movements. If Lenski is correct in assuming that many of these are potential revolutionaries, then it is possible that religion channels some of their enthusiasm in other directions. Fortunately, sociology does not define the worth of its research in terms of the number of people to which the research applies. Even in the sociology of religion, research on small religious splinter groups, who are intriguingly exotic but account for less than 5 per cent of the church-going population and less than 3 per cent of the population as a whole, is overrepresented. Like these sects, discrepancy may be important analytically if not numerically.

Discrepancy and Religiosity: A First Test

At this point we have theory, speculation, and a measure of status discrepancy. In addition, of course, we have our familiar measures of churchlike and sectlike religiosity. Table VI–2 brings all of this to first fruition. It presents the percentage in each category of status discrepancy who score high on the indices of churchlike and sectlike commitment. Here, as with vertical status, the hypotheses are supported. The table shows an inverse relation between discrepancy and churchlike commitment but a positive

TABLE VI–2
Status Discrepancy and Churchlike and Sectlike Religiosity

Type of Religiosity	Categories of Discrepancy		
	High	Moderate	Low
% High Churchlike	45	50	55
N	(277)	(3565)	(4507)
% High Sectlike	40	34	31
N	(294)	(3690)	(4633)

relation between discrepancy and sectlike religiosity. For the former, the percentage involved is only 45 per cent among the highly discrepant, and this increases to 50 per cent and 55 per cent among those with moderate and low discrepancy. For the latter, the trend is reversed; 40 per cent of the highly discrepant are sectarian, but this declines to 34 per cent and 31 per cent among those with moderate and low discrepancy.

Table VI–3 offers similar results on the basis of the pure types. When churchlike and sectlike commitment are treated as mutually exclusive, the ratio between them decreases with decreasing discrepancy. Here, as before, a higher ratio signifies a higher proportion of those who are *only* involved in a sectlike religiosity. The figure is .60 for the highly discrepant and reduces to .40 and .26 among those with moderate and low discrepancy. Again it seems that discrepancy leads to a form of religiosity that is most removed from secular life and the more worldly aspects of the parish program. In this light, the findings offer conditional rebuttal and elaboration to Lenski. It may not be that the discrepant are wholly isolated and withdrawn. Rather, they pick their involvements with care, and sectlike religion

TABLE VI–3
Status Discrepancy and the Ratio between the Pure Modes of Religiosity

	Categories of Discrepancy		
	High	Moderate	Low
$S\bar{C}/C\bar{S}$	.60	.40	.26
	(104)	(1455)	(2070)

seems to be one of the few commitments that provides salve
instead of exacerbation for their status ambiguities.

Still another elaboration of Lenski's findings concerns the
moderately discrepant. Lenski's work on political ideology and
secular affiliations used only the two categories of high and low
discrepancy, partly because of his smaller sample and partly because of a pre-inspection that showed only extreme discrepancy
to have distinctive effects. Here, however, moderate discrepancy
seems to have a distinct position in relation to religiosity. It
stands between the extremes, suggesting a linear association
which in turn implies a broader impact for discrepancy generally. Actually, however, the suggestion will later prove abortive,
as the gap between low and moderate discrepancy will narrow
to insignificance.

But while we are comparing, let us compare the effects of discrepancy to the earlier effects of vertical status. In both cases,
the hypotheses were corroborated. Yet, recalling Chapter IV, the
support was stronger for vertical status than it has been here.
That is, the percentage differences between vertical status groups
were larger than between discrepancy groups. One plausible
explanation is that vertical status differences are more obvious
and more meaningful than the degree of discrepancy. Conventional status is more salient because it is culturally reinforced
and driven into individual awareness by a spate of symbols and
social patterns. It has even been argued that sociologists themselves are to blame for much of the emphasis. In contrast to
conventional status, status discrepancy is far from a byword in
our society. It has not been the basis for movies or political
ideologies. Sociologists have not yet rammed it home through
extensive interviewing and writing.

There is, however, another possible explanation for the differential impact of vertical status and status discrepancy. Appendix
A shows that vertical status affects all of the components of the
churchlike index similarly and all of the components of the sectlike index similarly. This may not be the case for status discrepancy. Among the churchlike indicators, say, discrepancy may be
directly related to Sunday attendance but inversely related to
parish activities. Among the sectlike measures, it may be directly related to communal involvement but inversely related to

ministerial participation in community controversy. If this were the case, then the relations to the summary indexes would be composites of conflicting relations at a lower level. This would reduce the over-all percentage differences considerably.[26]

Tables VI–4 and VI–5 examine the possibility. The first of these considers the churchlike measures; the second turns to sectlike indicators. In general, of course, discrepancy should be inversely associated with the former and directly related to the latter. That is, churchlike commitment should decline with increasing discrepancy; sectlike commitment should increase. Actually the comparisons all follow this pattern, with *two* exceptions, both among the churchlike measures. For one, there is no

TABLE VI–4

Status Discrepancy and the Three Separate Measures of Churchlike Religiosity

Measures of Religiosity	Categories of Discrepancy		
	High	Moderate	Low
% High Sunday Attendance	68	59	58
	(301)	(3530)	(4398)
% High Parish Activities[a]	62	61	62
	(306)	(3826)	(4776)
% High Outside Organizations[a]	61	67	73
	(301)	(3654)	(4581)

[a] "High" signifies participation in one or more.

[26] Hortense Horwitz and Elias Smith—the latter an inseparable companion of Paul F. Lazarsfeld—have argued in *The Language of Social Research* (Glencoe, Ill.: The Free Press, 1958) that the components of indexes are interchangeable. That is, it makes no difference which items are selected from a related pool: the resulting index will bear the same relation to some third, dependent variable. Horwitz and Smith test this with various measures of status in relation to voting and political attitudes. But, while the authors may be correct in assuming that a change in indicators will *rarely* make a difference, this *can* happen. Certainly the magnitude of the relation is vulnerable; even the direction may be affected. In fact, the methodologist seeking a message in this study may find one here. The research originally began with one single six-item index of religiosity that had only a slight positive relation to status. It was only by dividing the index into two separate measures that two strong relations were uncovered in opposite directions. This occurred despite the fact that all six of the initial items were positively related to each other, although a preliminary factor analysis did suggest two distinct dimensions.

TABLE VI-5

Status Discrepancy and the Three Separate Measures of Sectlike Religiosity

Measures of Religiosity	Categories of Discrepancy		
	High	Moderate	Low
% High Communal Involvement	39 (308)	36 (3797)	34 (4742)
% High Religious Rewards	48 (308)	43 (3806)	39 (4745)
% Against Minister's Participation in Controversy[a]	40 (327)	30 (2711)	30 (3453)

[a] The results of the relation between discrepancy and the minister in community controversy are based upon Baptists, Congregationalists, Disciples of Christ, and Presbyterians alone, since the Lutherans were asked questions that are non-comparable at this close level of analysis.

relation at all between discrepancy and parish activities. For another, the relation with Sunday service attendance defies the hypothesis so that in at least this churchlike activity the highly discrepant are the *most* involved. Some 68 per cent of the highly discrepant attend every week; the percentage drops to 59 and 58 among those with moderate and low discrepancy. Apparently, then, churchlike religiosity is not all of a piece with reference to discrepancy, although sectlike commitment seems to be.

In interpreting these aberrations, it is important to note that relations with the churchlike measures do maintain a pattern, however. Certainly outside affiliations are the most secular of the three; hence, it is reasonable that they should claim the single inverse association, one that is consonant with Lenski's results. Similarly, I argued earlier that parish activities were more secular in spirit than church attendance. Thus, it is also reasonable that the direct relation should be restricted to the latter. In addition to being less painful reminders of secular status, Sunday services are more central to the religious program. Indeed, from the church's own perspective, the services may be indispensable to life in the church, and conventional life in some organization may be *de rigeur* for those who are at least partially higher-status. It is well documented that higher-status persons have an appetite for affiliations, and the hunger may be more acute when discrepancy complicates its satisfaction.

Actually the existence of a partial high-status rank is important for another reason as well. As mentioned earlier, the highly discrepant are analogous to the cross-pressured voters in that their discrepancy leads to one pattern of religiosity but their over-all status may lead to quite another. It is possible that church attendance reconciles the two tendencies. It is the most traditional of the churchlike modes and is thereby closer to the sectlike ideal. The notion of cross pressures will be especially important in Chapter VII during the analysis of discrepancy and vertical status as joint influences. This is only one of the several complexities to be dealt with later. The goal here has been to present the simple relations between discrepancy and religiosity in order to get a broad perspective and provide a basis for further study. The next chapter will look at the findings more rigorously. Do the relationships persist or do the already small percentage differences vanish altogether when other factors are controlled? The question is far from idle; it is more important here than in any of the previous sections.

Summary

After defining status discrepancy, I offered a brief recapitulation of its conceptual and empirical development. Although the concept was suggested by Weber, it has enjoyed surprisingly little prominence. Nevertheless, the few studies available in the literature have uncovered correlates of organizational withdrawal, political radicalism, and mental disorders. Still a third strategem available to the discrepant had gone unexplored. Instead of withdrawing from the system altogether or reacting against it politically, the discrepant might withdraw from some phases of society but immerse himself more deeply in others. Religion should offer one alternative commitment that does not invoke secular status standards and does not urge wholesale social change. At least, this is true of a sectlike commitment to any of the major Protestant denominations.

The first tests of this hypothesis have been successful. The highly discrepant Protestants are indeed more involved in a sectlike religiosity. They also attend Sunday services more frequently, although they are no more prone to participate in parish activities. At first glance, it seems that the discrepant are not necessarily adrift or revolutionary, and, again, we glimpse a distinctive function of religion in a secular context. Yet, Chapter VIII will seek to undermine this preliminary conclusion—and with some success.

VII

Status Discrepancy under Harsher Light

New concepts are like new employees; after a round of sympathetic introductions, they are expected to prove their worth under sterner scrutiny. Although status discrepancy persisted through the initial pleasantries, it must now face more rigorous tests. What happens when one controls for separate denominations, age, sex, subjective class, vertical status, and different combinations of discrepancy? Does its influence disappear entirely? Is it restricted to certain subgroups of parishioners only? Or is it perhaps maintained only for certain types of religiosity and not for others?

Much of this analysis is similar to the earlier elaboration of conventional vertical status. There are, however, two important departures. For one, status discrepancy will indeed be trimmed in its effects, while vertical status remains virtually intact. Another departure is more technical. It is relatively simple to control for denomination, age, sex, and subjective class. To control for vertical status is both more difficult and more important. It is plausible indeed to hold that discrepancy is an artifact of conventional status since both are measured by the same indicators. But precisely because both discrepancy and vertical status are measured by identical items, there is a problem in isolating them for simultaneous inspection. After critically exploring several previous attempts to deal with the dilemma, the chapter will conclude with a strategy of its own. The strategy is designed to examine different combinations or profiles of discrepancy as well. Does it make a difference, for example, whether one scores high on education and low on income or vice versa? Do education, income, and occupation contribute equally to discrepancy or does one seem to be more strategic than another?

All of this shows a secondary concern commanding temporary prominence. If my interests were exclusively in the sociology of religion, the chapter would be an unjustified digression. We have already seen that high discrepancy is rare and that its influence is comparatively slight. It could hardly be a major force in American religion, even if no further limitations were introduced. But I am also concerned with stratification itself. As a new and underexplored facet of the domain, discrepancy deserves critical attention. Valid concepts are often abandoned for lack of research interest. Faulty concepts are sometimes perpetuated for the same reason.

Discrepancy and Religiosity within Categories of Denomination, Age, Sex, and Subjective Class

A key difference between the previous analysis of vertical status and the present inspection of status discrepancy lies in the treatment of the separate denominations in the Protestant sample. Whereas the former considered each denomination separately, so far the latter has used a pooled sample that brings all of the denominations together. The advantage of the aggregate is its ability to meet the problem of small numbers in the high-discrepancy category. No single denomination has sufficient persons in this group to sustain the kind of elaboration that this chapter requires. By combining denominations the analysis is more feasible and more reliable.

Yet there remains the nagging possibility that the pooled sample is illegitimate. It is conceivable that status discrepancy exerts no influence at all on religiosity within any separate denomination and that its seeming impact is due to combining different denominations with different rates of discrepancy and different levels of religious involvement. Or it may be that the influence of discrepancy is restricted to one denomination where the differences are large enough to emerge even when other denominations are included.

Table VII–1 examines these possibilities. Before looking at the actual results, note the departure in the religiosity items considered. The Index of Sectlike Involvement is included here as before, but the Index of Churchlike Religiosity has been decomposed and one of its constituents has been eliminated. This is due to the findings of Chapter VI. There we saw that discrepancy bore opposite relations to church attendance and outside affiliations, and that it seemed to have no influence at all on activities within the parish. Accordingly, the last item has been dropped, while church attendance and outside affiliations are included separately to preserve their differences.

TABLE VII–1

Status Discrepancy and Religiosity within Categories of Denominations

Religiosity			Status Discrepancy				Denomination
	High		Moderate		Low		
	29%	(104)	28%	(1317)	23%	(1784)	Congregational
% High	54	(76)	42	(848)	40	(993)	Presbyterian
Sectlike	56	(52)	42	(757)	41	(876)	Lutheran
Involvement	37	(41)	43	(506)	36	(631)	Disciples of Christ
	58	(24)	47	(295)	48	(378)	Baptist
	58%	(104)	53%	(1326)	52%	(1790)	Congregational
% High	74	(78)	70	(861)	68	(1009)	Presbyterian
Church	78	(60)	57	(837)	58	(968)	Lutheran
Attendance	59	(41)	66	(506)	60	(631)	Disciples of Christ
	56	(25)	41	(299)	40	(381)	Baptist
	74%	(99)	81%	(1264)	90%	(1725)	Congregational
% High	69	(67)	66	(826)	75	(964)	Presbyterian
Outside	40	(55)	47	(765)	52	(891)	Lutheran
Affiliations	74	(39)	78	(500)	79	(623)	Disciples of Christ
	68	(25)	71	(299)	72	(378)	Baptist

Returning to the denominational distinctions and their impact, there are clearly differences in the level of religiosity for each denomination. But these were explored in Chapter IV and do not concern us here. Instead, the important thing is the relationship between discrepancy and religiosity. On this point, the table is more uniform. With the exception of the Disciples of Christ, every denomination maintains the original relationships uncovered in the previous chapter. Status discrepancy is positively related to sectlike commitment and church attendance, but it is negatively related to outside affiliations. Some of these differences are extremely small as, for example, the relation with sectlike religiosity among the Congregationalists and with outside affiliations among the Baptists and Presbyterians. Nevertheless, it is clear that status discrepancy has an impact in the predicted direction for four of the five denominations and this is enough to justify the pooling. In fact, even the Disciples of Christ conform on the last item.

But why should the Disciples be so insensitive to discrepancy where attendance and sectlike involvement are concerned? The finding should come as no surprise for the denomination was similarly deviant with respect to vertical status in Chapter V. There I speculated, on the strength of Richard Niebuhr's assertion,[1] that this may be because the Disciples of Christ never went through a sectarian, developmental phase. Thus, the denomination may be too churchlike to hold a special niche for either the highly discrepant or the low-status parishioners. But I also noted that this interpretation has been questioned. Oliver Whitley[2] argues the reverse in suggesting that the Disciples of Christ have never transcended a sectlike state. Apparently, Niebuhr and Whitley are defining sectarianism in slightly different ways. Whitley's conception is more organizational; Niebuhr's definition is more theological.[3] The latter is the more

[1] H. Richard Niebuhr, *The Social Sources of Denominationalism* (New York: Henry Holt & Company, Inc., 1929).

[2] Oliver Whitley, *Trumpet Call of Reformation* (St. Louis, Mo.: The Bethany Press, 1959).

[3] Actually there has been a good deal of dispute among church-sect theorists over this point. Some argue that the distinction should be exclusively theological without reference to organizational characteristics. Others argue the reverse. The issue remains and accounts for many disagreements in addition to the present one between Niebuhr and Whitley.

relevant to the particular issue in question, but the Disciples of Christ remain an enigma for which I have no certain solution.

Because the Disciples provide the only major exception in Table VII–1, let us retain the pooled sample and go on to consider age and sex. Earlier we saw that both had independent influences on religiosity, although neither affected the impact of vertical status. Status discrepancy may be more vulnerable. This is especially likely since women and older people are more likely to be discrepant and more likely to be religiously involved.

In testing this, the pooled sample allows consideration of three age groups instead of the two used in Chapter IV. Here the young are defined as those under 35; the middle-aged are between 35 and 55; the older parishioners are those over 55. Table VII–2 presents the results. It is divided into three layers representing sectlike involvement, church attendance, and outside affiliations. For each layer or for each measure of religiosity, the relation with discrepancy is given within categories of age and sex.

The findings for sectlike involvement provide the first major qualification of the results in the previous chapter. Apparently, the influence of discrepancy is indeed an artifact of age and sex distributions. The original pattern persists only among middle-aged women, and even there somewhat inconsistently. Middle-aged and older men provide relations that move in the opposite direction. The remaining age-sex categories show little or no relationship at all between sectlike religiosity and status discrepancy. All of this suggests that sectlike religiosity is too extreme an escape for the highly discrepant who are both high- and low-status by definition. These people may retain some hope of equilibrating their over-all status by shoring up the lower ranks. In this case, pure sectlike involvement may seem too severe and premature as a form of low-status resignation and identification.

A similar pattern—or lack of it—obtains for discrepancy and outside affiliations. The hypothesis and original finding was that persons of high discrepancy have fewer secular memberships. This persists only among middle-aged men. For all other age-sex categories, there is no consistent relation, suggesting that the impact of discrepancy on such affiliations is spurious and super-

TABLE VII–2

Status Discrepancy and Religiosity within Categories of Age and Sex

Religiosity Items	Status Discrepancy						Age and Sex
	High		Moderate		Low		
	22%	(37)	22%	(262)	20%	(147)	Young Men
	26	(23)	31	(514)	30	(530)	Middle-Aged
% High							Men
Sectlike	31	(45)	42	(242)	47	(106)	Older Men
Involvement	23	(44)	26	(389)	21	(266)	Young Women
	49	(65)	32	(1130)	34	(903)	Middle-Aged
							Women
	47	(94)	47	(338)	47	(177)	Older Women
	65%	(37)	68%	(262)	45%	(147)	Young Men
	61	(23)	73	(514)	71	(530)	Middle-Aged
% High							Men
Outside	76	(45)	72	(242)	76	(106)	Older Men
Affiliations	50	(44)	66	(389)	52	(266)	Young Women
	55	(65)	66	(1130)	59	(903)	Middle-Aged
							Women
	63	(94)	60	(338)	57	(177)	Older Women
	62%	(37)	57%	(262)	48%	(147)	Young Men
	65	(23)	58	(514)	57	(530)	Middle-Aged
% High							Men
Church	60	(45)	62	(242)	65	(106)	Older Men
Attendance	64	(44)	58	(389)	51	(266)	Young Women
	66	(65)	59	(1130)	58	(903)	Middle-Aged
							Women
	76	(94)	66	(338)	66	(177)	Older Women

ficial. Again, the explanation may lie in the cliché, "hope springs eternal."

Now one of the operating axioms of elaboration is that when a relation disappears it disappears for good.[4] Since the seeming associations between discrepancy, sectlike involvement, and out-

[4] Note that this is an operating axiom and not a logical truth, however. Actually there are no ultimate limits to the elaboration procedure as it is abstractly defined. Any zero relationship may be brought back to life if the proper controls are exerted. Thus, if age and sex are further supplemented by eye color, it is logically possible that discrepancy retains its effect for men and women of blue eyes, if for no others. But while this is possible, it is hardly probable, and one must put limits on the procedure that are determined by practical sense and diminishing cell sizes.

side affiliations are accountable through age and sex, they are revealed as fictions and need no more attention. It is simply that women and older people are more likely to be *both* highly discrepant and sectarian as well as *both* highly discrepant and less involved in outside affiliations. Discrepancy itself has no influence on these matters, and I will omit them in the rest of the analysis.

But now consider the controlled relation between discrepancy and church attendance. Although age and sex take a heavy toll from discrepancy, they do leave one pattern fundamentally intact. Those with high discrepancy continue to have higher rates of attendance at Sunday services. Except among older men, the difference is consistent and on the order of ten percentage points or better.

Why should the impact of discrepancy on church attendance persist? What is there about the Sunday service that makes it peculiarly attractive to the highly discrepant, regardless of their age or their sex? Much of the answer may lie in some earlier speculation in Chapter VI. There I noted that Sunday services are more compatible with sectlike religiosity than either parish activities or outside affiliations. The service may be formal and ritualistic with a sermon that addresses secular problems from a frequently secular perspective. Nevertheless, the hymns, the prayers, the Biblical text, and the traditional overtones of the meeting are in keeping with sectarianism. Then too, the services form the core of most Protestant church programs. If one has any allegiance to the church, service attendance may seem a minimal obligation. And, finally, since attendance is both churchlike and sectlike, it may offer an inviting niche to the discrepant who are both high-status and low-status. The services combine two religious worlds, and the highly discrepant are people who have a vested interest in both of them. In any event, and for whatever reason, church attendance is the only measure of religiosity that remains meaningfully associated with discrepancy. Chapter VI disposed of parish activities, and Table VII–2 eliminated the explicitly sectlike measures as well as outside affiliations. Accordingly, church attendance will be our sole interest in what follows. It too may disappear as the analysis proceeds.

In considering the person's denomination, age, and sex, we

have not yet moved into the more traditional realm of status factors. Here, however, we make that step in turning to the respondent's self-estimated, *subjective* social class position. The shibboleths concerning the hyper-status-consciousness of the American middle class suggest that those who see themselves as middle class may be the most vulnerable to the effects of discrepancy. On the other hand, one can argue that the self-styled working class should be the most affected. They have not yet made it to the middle-class level, and their ambition may be the more frustrated by the tantalizations of status discrepancy.

Table VII–3 presents the results. Here the relation between discrepancy and church attendance is offered within categories

TABLE VII–3

Status Discrepancy and Religiosity within Categories of Subjective Class[a]

| Religiosity | Status Discrepancy | | | | | Subjective |
	High		Moderate		Low	Class
% High Church Attendance	76	(53)	56	(434)	55	(313)	Middle
	72	(28)	54	(366)	53	(484)	Working

[a] Subjective class data were available only for Lutherans and Baptists. This accounts for both the low percentage bases.

of subjective class. For once, the original findings persist with no exceptions. Within both the middle and the working class, high discrepancy is associated with high church attendance. In fact, the differences are not only consistent, but relatively large and on the order of twenty percentage points. Apparently subjective class does not affect the influence of discrepancy. The effect remains, and, moreover, it seems to be about the same for both class categories. This suggests that neither of the two possibilities mentioned above are correct. Although it remains conceivable that discrepancy is influential for different reasons in the middle- and working-class groups,[5] the important point is

[5] In Chapter IV we saw that combinations of class and status were meaningful since a person could be high in status but low in subjective class or vice versa. Unfortunately, there are insufficient cases to test the relevance of the combination to discrepancy. While it can be shown that the self-deprecators (high objective status but low subjective class) are the only group for whom discrepancy does not lead to high attendance, the

that the relation between discrepancy and attendance lingers. Let us move on to another and more heralded candidate for upsetting the relation: vertical *objective* status.

Vertical Status and Status Discrepancy: Criticisms and Rebuttals

Critics of discrepancy may argue that the preceding elaborations both beg and postpone the ultimate issue. This issue is the problematic independence of discrepancy and vertical objective status. There is continuing suspicion that the effects of the former are reducible to the latter. The influence of high discrepancy may be the camouflaged artifact of low status. Perhaps the concept of discrepancy is itself the fabrication of unduly ingenious theorists. Since, in methodological justice, the suspect is guilty until proven innocent, the burden of absolution is on the researcher.

Actually neither the suspicions nor the charges are baseless. The correlates of high discrepancy and low status are closely similar. For example, both groups are prone to political radicalism. Both belong to relatively few voluntary organizations. Both seem to have high rates of psychosomatic symptoms. It is hardly far-fetched to suppose that identical effects may have only one instead of two causes.

In the face of these allegations, assertions of independence must be buttressed by data. Unfortunately, the data are peculiarly hard to come by. The problems are essentially two. First, since vertical status and status discrepancy are measured by the same items—in this case, occupation, education, and income—one cannot simply control one while allowing the other to vary. Ideally one would look at each of the particular combinations of these three status variables, gauging both its vertical status and its status discrepancy in comparison with all of the other combinations. This, however, would involve an inspection of 125 different cells in the present instance, and it leads directly to the second major difficulty. Since high status discrepancy characterizes a very small minority in our society, by the time one sepa-

---

demonstration is unreliable. There are only seven cases in the crucial high-discrepancy category, and this makes any relationship precarious.

rates *them* into their various cells, the numbers become precari-ously small and the conclusions may be fortuitous.

I am not suggesting, however, that previous researchers have been oblivious or unresponsive to the problem. All have grappled with it. While most end with a plea for help from future investi-gators, three particular attempts stand out. Let us consider each in order to gain a further understanding of the difficulties and the pitfalls.

Gerhard Lenski,[6] the empirical pioneer of research on discrep-ancy, found the issue to be a major obstacle. Lenski knew that political radicalism and withdrawal from conventional secular organizations marked those with low status as well as those with high discrepancy. In order to show that the two effects are inde-pendent, he devised a method that deals with the mean scores of each of the discrepancy categories on each of his status indi-cators. He reasoned as follows: if a group is manifestly higher in status, it would be absurd to attribute its effects to low status. If the high discrepancy group has a *higher* mean score on all of the status indicators, then it cannot be true that its influence is reducible to its *lower* status. Lenski applied this line of reasoning to the data. He manipulated the discrepancy groups so that their mean scores conformed to the pattern.[7] He found that the origi-nal results persisted even under these controlled conditions. He then concluded that discrepancy is, in fact, independent of vertical status.

But Lenski's technique has found its critics. Kenkel[8] has ques-tioned the replicability of the results. Roderick Frederickson[9] has pointed out that identical means can be produced by quite

[6] Gerhard Lenski, "Status Crystallization: A Non-Vertical Dimension of Social Status," *American Sociological Review*, XIX (1954), 405–13.

[7] Actually, Lenski has been faulted for his delineation of the discrepancy categories themselves. Instead of deciding upon the categorization *before* looking at the relations with political radicalism, he devised his cutting-points on the discrepancy scale so as to maximize that relationship.

[8] William F. Kenkel, "The Relationship Between Status Consistency and Politico-Economic Attitudes," *American Sociological Review*, XXI (1956), 365–68. See also Lenski's rejoinder in the same issue, arguing that the Kenkel items are incomparable and therefore unsuitable for a replication.

[9] Roderick M. Frederickson, "The Utility of the Status Equilibrium Index As a Methodological Tool in Predicting Social Participation," unpublished M.A. thesis, Department of Sociology, University of California, Berkeley, 1955.

dissimilar distributions, and that this raises some disturbing possibilities that Lenski fails to preclude. Consider that the highly discrepant are defined by their juxtaposed extreme status rankings. Since these extremes counteract each other when more than one indicator is considered, the aggregate status of the highly discrepant necessarily falls into the middle range of the over-all vertical status scale. On the other hand, the less discrepant are defined by their more consistent rankings on the separate indicators. Here any extreme rankings that do occur are not offset by equal extremes in the opposite direction. Hence, low discrepancy includes a higher percentage with extreme over-all status, whether extreme upper or extreme lower.

The point then is that mean scores not only *may* reflect different distributions here; they *must*. Lenski was concerned to show that the effects of high discrepancy are not due to low status. In this he was successful, for all of the aggregate low-status types are in the low discrepancy group by definition. But so are the aggregate high-status types, and this may be an equally strong contamination. It is well known that those of high status are particularly averse to political radicalism and particularly drawn to voluntary organizations. In contrast with these people, the middle-status high discrepants may seem radical and withdrawn indeed. This is a matter of vertical status rather than discrepancy. Hence the bias remains and the skeptics retain grounds for suspicion.

If Lenski's procedure appears to be unsatisfactory, let us turn to the method advanced by Irwin Goffman.[10] As in the present study, Goffman uses occupation, education, and income as status factors. His control technique is distinctive in that it focuses on only one of these items as the baseline for his analysis. Occupation is Goffman's primary variable. If a person's income and/or education departs from his occupational rank by more than 20 per cent in the sample distribution, he qualifies as highly discrepant. To control for vertical status, Goffman simply compares his high- and low-discrepancy groups within categories of occupation.

Now in all of this, Goffman assumes that occupation alone is

[10] Irwin W. Goffman, "Status Consistency and Preference for Change in Power Distribution," *American Sociological Review*, XXII (1957), 275–81.

the core of social status. But this is no matter for fiat. Unless it can be shown that occupation is central to the respondents themselves, the assumption remains dubious. To some persons, education may be the most salient status factor; to others; income. Perhaps simply the highest-ranking factor will be the most persuasive in self-judgment. Finally, Goffman's assumption is even less plausible under conditions of discrepancy. Certainly occupation should not be the core status measure if both education and income rank the individual higher. It is even unlikely that occupation will be the focus if both education and income produce much lower rankings. In short, Goffman's control technique rests on a premise concerning the individual's status perceptions. The more the discrepancy, the less tenable the premise, and, hence, the more vulnerable the research.

A third technique was originally used in Elton Jackson's work on status discrepancy and psychosomatic symptoms of stress.[11] It appears more recently in Gerhard Lenski's reply to Robert Mitchell,[12] and it is to Lenski's great credit that he has abandoned his earlier method to seek a more satisfactory alternative. I have already mentioned the dangers in using only one status indicator as a control. I have also suggested the difficulty of dwindling cell sizes in the simultaneous inspection of three or more status factors. The present technique offers a compromise, since it examines two status variables at a time, including all combinations.

Table VII–4 presents some fictitious data for illustration.[13] Imagine a sample of academicians. Here each inner cell represents the percentage who are sociologists within the various categories of income and education; the row and column totals present the marginal relations between the percentage of sociologists and education and income respectively. In inspecting the table, Lenski would reason as follows: If we compare the upper-left and lower-right inner cells with the upper-right and lower-left inner cells, we are comparing the two maximally consistent

[11] Elton Jackson, "Status Consistency, Vertical Mobility, and Symptoms of Stress," unpublished Ph.D. dissertation, University of Michigan, 1960.

[12] Gerhard Lenski, "Comment," *Public Opinion Quarterly*, XXVIII (1964), 326–30. It is worth noting that Lenski's data satisfy the conditions of the technique better than Jackson's. The conditions will be specified below.

[13] I am indebted to Alan Orenstein for this illustration.

TABLE VII–4

Fictitious Data on the Percentage of Sociologists among Academicians within Categories of Income and Education

% SOCIOLOGISTS WITHIN					
			Income		
		(1)	(2)	(3)	*Row*
		High	*Medium*	*Low*	*Total*
	(1) *High*	24%	30%	48%	34%
Education	(2) *Medium*	20	25	30	25
	(3) *Low*	18	20	24	21
	Column Total	21	25	34	

cells with the two maximally discrepant cells. Moreover, since each pair includes two ranks of (1) and two ranks of (3), the average vertical status is identical. Thus, any difference between the two percentage sums cannot be due to vertical status and must be due to status discrepancy.

Let us then apply the logic. A sum of the percentages for the two consistent cells yields 48 (24 + 24); a sum for the two discrepant cells yields 66 (48 + 18). Clearly discrepancy makes a difference. Even if we subtract the effect of vertical status by subtracting 48 from 66, we still have a bulge of 18 per cent that can only be explained by discrepancy. Sociologists are indeed less consistent, a finding that should surprise no one. Discrepancy is independently effective with vertical status held constant.

But is it in fact held constant? For a sobering second thought, look closely at the marginal relations in the row and column totals. Note that these relations move in opposite directions since the percentage of sociologists mounts with increasing education but declines with increasing income. This suggests an alternative explanation of the inner cells. Thus, the two consistent cells have equal percentages of sociologists (24), since both combine one of the most predisposed status categories with one of the least predisposed status categories. The lower left-hand cell has the lowest percentage of sociologists (18), since it combines the two least predisposed status categories. Finally, the upper right-hand cell has the highest percentage of sociologists (48), because it includes the two most predisposed categories. In short, the interpretation is quite plausible on the sole grounds of additive vertical-status effects. To introduce the concept of discrepancy is to violate the scientific canon of parsimony.

It is true, of course, that I have stacked the data against the advocates of discrepancy in this table. Contradictory marginal relations are unusual. And yet they are hardly nonexistent, since they do occur in two of Jackson's three tables and leave his conclusions in considerable doubt. Jackson is well aware of this, however, and is preparing a research note on the topic for future publication.[14] In the meantime, it is important to indicate that the fault does not lie with the technique but rather with the failure to meet one of its assumptions. Since my own status indicators do not run in opposite directions, I will later return to the procedure with minor variations for the present anlysis.

A Two-Stage Exploration of Vertical Status, Status Discrepancy, and Church Attendance

As mentioned earlier, there are at least two basic objects in the process of elaboration. The first is to try and specify the original relationship to see if it works for some types of persons

---

[14] After several long discussions, Jackson and I are now independently pursuing the same technique for a broader, more rigorous, and more elegant control for vertical status where the direction of the marginal relationships is not a possible disqualification. Both of us arrived quite separately at a technique used by Otis Dudley Duncan in the analysis of residential and status mobility related to fertility. Essentially the strategy invokes analysis of variance to compute expected values for each cell on the basis of sheer additivity. One then compares the expected values with the actual values and any departure is due to statistical interaction, in this case, status discrepancy. It is possible to use an F-test of significance to find out whether these departures are worth taking seriously. Unfortunately, this technique is not yet developed enough to apply to the present data. Nonetheless, it is to be hoped that either Jackson or myself (with the collaboration of Alan Orenstein) will register it in the literature soon. For Duncan's technique, see "Residential Areas and Differential Fertility," unpublished paper, University of Michigan, Ann Arbor.

but not for others. The second is to see whether or not the original relation is spurious and can be accounted for by additional factors that were originally neglected. Now in most cases, these twin goals can be realized simultaneously. It is one of the peculiarities of vertical status and status discrepancy, however, that they must be realized separately. In order to get a reliable picture of the respondent's over-all vertical status position, one must work with all three status indicators at once as in our familiar Index of Objective Socioeconomic Status. But these over-all categories are not precise enough to examine the proposition that vertical status may account for status discrepancy. To get a rigorous test of this, one must pull apart the index and inspect the status measures separately.[15] Accordingly, the first stage of this exploration seeks specifications and considers the relation between discrepancy and attendance within the conventional categories of upper, middle, working, and low status. The second stage seeks more detailed information and will consider the indicators of education, income, and occupation separately. By analyzing them in pairs, we will not only test for the possible spuriousness of discrepancy, but we will also examine the differences among various discrepancy profiles and assess the relative importance of each status measure for discrepancy and religiosity.

Table VII–5 is similar to numerous other tables in this chapter and the preceding. The closest parallel is to Table VII–3 where the association between discrepancy and attendance was examined within categories of subjective class. There we saw that class added little. Yet it is still conceivable that vertical status will have an impact. After all, the possibility of one factor being influenced by another is greater when both are measured by the same particular indicators. There may have been a contamination in the measurement itself.

For whatever reason, the results suggest that objective status does make a difference. Although the extreme upper- and low-status categories show no real distinctions in attendance, this is because there are no highly discrepant persons in these extreme and necessarily more consistent groups, and we have already seen

---

[15] This is because of the possibility that only one status factor produces the seeming effects of discrepancy and this single factor may be lost in the over-all index.

TABLE VII–5

Status Discrepancy and Church Attendance
within Categories of Aggregate Vertical Status

Religiosity	High	Discrepancy Moderate		Low		Vertical Status
	........[a]	60	(576)	58	(2318)	Upper
% High Church	62 (180)	60	(1803)	57	(962)	Middle
Attendance	76 (128)	58	(1072)	57	(1167)	Working
	....	41	(391)	44	(347)	Low

[a] Because extreme upper and low status demand consistently high or low rankings on all three status measures, they preclude any high discrepancy.

that differences are negligible between moderate and low discrepancy. Consider the middle- and working-status groups where all three levels of discrepancy are included, and the differences are more arresting. In both cases, the predicted relation persists. But note that the persistence is very slight among the middle-status respondents, while it approaches a 20 per cent difference among those of working status. Church attendance seems to have a greater appeal for the highly discrepant who are working status in their over-all vertical rank. This may be a kind of overcompensation. Their high discrepancy defines them as persons with some claim to high status. Their church attendance may be a way of staking this claim deeper. On the other hand, the highly discrepant of over-all middle status may be more secure in the first place. If the working-status discrepants combine one high rank with two lows, the middle-status discrepants have two highs with one low. The single dissenting rank may not be enough to threaten their generally high-status image of themselves.

It would seem from Table VII–5 that vertical status specifies the relation between discrepancy and attendance without accounting for it. Yet I have already noted that the table does not test for the latter in a rigorous fashion. Skeptics may still argue that discrepancy is an artifact, and demand the coup de grâce. Let us attempt to find one more systematically.

Consider again Elton Jackson's procedure. Earlier I pointed out that it provides inconclusive evidence on the independence of vertical status and status discrepancy since the results can be explained by vertical status alone on the simple assumption of additivity. And yet the baby should not be thrown out with the bathwater. I also suggested that the fault lies not with the procedure itself, but rather with the failure of the data to meet one of the procedure's preconditions. Thus, Jackson's two status indicators—occupation and racial-ethnic rank—had *opposite* relations to symptom occurrence when, in fact, the relations should be identical for the technique to work. In contrast to Jackson's work with psychosomatic symptoms, the present analysis of religiosity conforms to the need. Here all three status measures—occupation, education, and income—have the same general relation with church attendance. The technique is therefore appropriate. The real advantage of Jackson's procedure is that, in considering only two variables at a time, one can look closely at their combinations with sufficient numbers to sustain analysis. Figure VII–1 presents the model for the current application. Because none of our three status variables provides as extreme a distinction as Negro versus white, it was necessary to break them down into five categories instead of the three that Jackson

FIGURE VII–1

A Two-Variable Model for the Simultaneous Inspection of Vertical Status and Discrepancy

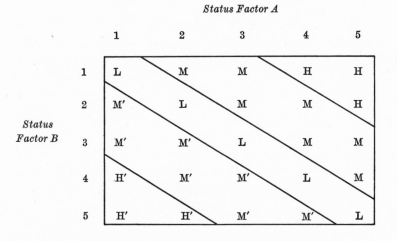

Status Factor A

	1	2	3	4	5
1	L	M	M	H	H
2	M′	L	M	M	H
3	M′	M′	L	M	M
4	H′	M′	M′	L	M
5	H′	H′	M′	M′	L

Status Factor B

(% RELIGIOUSLY INVOLVED TO BE GIVEN FOR EACH CELL)

TABLE VII–6

Church Attendance within All Cells of the Two-Variable Combinations of Income, Occupation, and Education

	(High) 1	2	3	4	(Low) 5
INCOME AND OCCUPATION % High Attendance		*Income*			
Occupation (High) 1	60 (1187)	62 (633)	60 (710)	55 (384)	66 (141)
2	54 (983)	63 (367)	53 (476)	56 (237)	68 (80)
3	55 (220)	55 (336)	55 (892)	59 (929)	57 (218)
4	66 (35)	57 (49)	53 (160)	58 (238)	62 (96)
(Low) 5	63 (30)	58 (55)	56 (131)	52 (165)	58 (74)
INCOME AND EDUCATION % High Attendance		*Income*			
Education (High) 1	57 (1170)	61 (516)	58 (612)	60 (343)	68 (93)
2	59 (661)	60 (389)	56 (630)	57 (514)	59 (121)
3	59 (376)	63 (297)	54 (656)	54 (501)	60 (114)
4	63 (194)	59 (179)	58 (341)	56 (407)	57 (152)
(Low) 5	66 (56)	54 (59)	52 (130)	64 (193)	84 (128)
OCCUPATION AND EDUCATION % High Attendance		*Occupation*			
Education (High) 1	59 (1758)	52 (627)	64 (266)	58 (43)	57 (40)
2	59 (765)	54 (677)	60 (721)	56 (94)	61 (57)
3	59 (321)	60 (494)	54 (826)	55 (168)	54 (134)
4	66 (166)	63 (259)	56 (546)	55 (175)	53 (127)
(Low) 5	76 (45)	57 (86)	58 (240)	66 (98)	57 (97)

used. This allows for a more precise isolation of high status discrepancy, and, as we saw in Chapter VI, only very high status discrepancy produces appreciable effects.

The twenty-five cells divide into three basic groups. Those marked with an *H* are those of high discrepancy; those marked *M* are characterized by moderate discrepancy; and those with an *L* have low discrepancy. Further, two of these three groups are subdivided again. Those with prime marks score higher on status factor *A* than on status factor *B*. Those without primes have the reverse pattern with higher scores on *B* than on *A*. Of course, there are no primes among the low-discrepancy cells because here the two status ranks are identical.

Now the point in all of this is that one can compare groups of high, moderate, and low discrepancy by taking the mean percentage of involvement within each of the five divisions set off by diagonal lines. Unlike Lenski's use of the mean, we are assured here that vertical status is controlled since the present means represent cells with the same average vertical-status rank. Regardless of whether one considers the high-, moderate-, or low-status groups and regardless of whether one considers those with or without primes, the average status rank of the cells combined is six.

Finally, the technique not only allows us to control for vertical status, but it also provides for an inspection of different profiles of discrepancy. It is possible that a discrepancy profile that involves a higher score on *A* than *B* will lead to increased religiosity but that a discrepancy profile with the reverse pattern will not.

Table VII–6 contains the raw data with which to fill in the dummy in Figure VII–1. The three layers correspond to each of the possible two-variable combinations of education, income, and occupation. Each cell has two numbers; the first is the percentage who attend church services regularly, and the second is the total number of persons in the percentage base.

Without conducting a cell-by-cell tour through these figures, one can discern two things at a glance. First, the relation between vertical status itself and church attendance (along the upper left to lower right diagonals) is small to the point of insignificance. Appendix A considers this at greater length and

offers an explanation in terms of the disproportionate numbers of
the highly churchlike Congregationalists and Presbyterians in
the sample. Secondly, however, note that this disproportion is
reflected in the percentage bases for each cell. Whereas only 97
parishioners fall into the lowest category for occupation and
education (extreme lower right), fully 1758 are in the highest
category (extreme upper left). The two other subtables are
similarly skewed.

Now this has ramifications for summarizing Table VII–6 in
the form suggested by Figure VII–1. There I mentioned that
one could compute the average percentage of high attendance for
several strategic subgroups of cells, whether L, M, H, M', or H'.
A key process in averaging percentages is "standardization." In
general, this means that one should take the percentage bases
into account so as to allow the largest absolute cell to have more
weight in the over-all average for several cells. Here, however,
standardization is less desirable. Precisely because the vertical
status distributions are so skewed, they should not be allowed
to affect summaries that are intended to measure the separate
factor of status discrepancy. If one were to standardize here, it
would mean that those with low discrepancy (in the middle
diagonal from upper left to lower right) would have a higher
loading on upper vertical status than those of high discrepancy
(in the lower left and upper right corners). In short, vertical
status would not be controlled.[16] The best procedure is simply to
average the percentages themselves within each of the groups
in Figure VII–1. Where no allowance is made for different percentage bases, this is tantamount to assuming that vertical status
is evenly distributed instead of skewed. The assumption is an
important though artificial one. Jackson makes it as well.

So much for the methodological rationale. Now for the findings. Within each of the three layers of Table VII–6, I com-
pued simple mean percentages for each of the subgroups in
Figure VII–1. The results are in Table VII–7, a considerable

[16] In fact, standardization is not empirically important here because the
relation between vertical status and church attendance is so slight. The
results do not differ appreciably whether one standardizes or not. Nevertheless, the point is important for other instances where vertical status is
more strongly aligned with the dependent variable. The present instance is
an exception to the rule.

TABLE VII–7

Summary Comparisons of Discrepancy Groups and Profiles with Vertical Status Constant

Religiosity	Discrepancy				
	High		Moderate		Low
	63	$(O\overline{I})$	58	$(O\overline{I})$	59
	62	$(I\overline{O})$	55	$(I\overline{O})$	59
% High Church	61	$(I\overline{E})$	59	$(I\overline{E})$	59
Attendance	62	$(E\overline{I})$	58	$(E\overline{I})$	59
	66	$(O\overline{E})$	60	$(O\overline{E})$	56
	59	$(E\overline{O})$	56	$(E\overline{O})$	56

distillation of the previous data but perhaps confusing in its organization and labeling. Here, as before, the focus is on the relation between discrepancy (high, moderate, and low) and church attendance. The table comprises three layers that correspond to the larger layers of its predecessor. The first concerns income (I) and occupation (O) as these are held constant. The second layer examines the control for income (I) and education (E). The third layer inspects the data within occupation (O) and education (E). Another bit of shorthand concerns opposite combinations of each of these pairs of status measures. Thus, O refers to a relatively high score on occupation, but $\overline{O}$ refers to a relatively low score on occupation. Whereas $O\overline{I}$ indicates a discrepancy profile that involves a higher score on occupation than on income, $I\overline{O}$ signifies a discrepancy profile with the reverse characteristic: a higher score on income than on occupation. Of course, these differences in profiles only apply to those with high or moderate discrepancy. Those with low discrepancy have consistent rankings on both of the two status measures involved; here I have simply repeated the single mean percentage for the low discrepant in both rows of each layer to facilitate comparisons.

First, then, consider the problems of whether different profiles of discrepancy produce different results and whether different status indicators have different degrees of importance. The answer to both questions seems to be "yes." Contrast the results for those who have high occupation and low education ($O\overline{E}$)

with the results for those with high education but low occupation $(E\overline{O})$. The former offer firm support to the thesis that discrepancy leads to increased attendance; the latter are at best weak and at worst equivocal. In general, the three status indicators can be ranked for their importance in discrepancy if one judges by the difference between profiles in which they score high and profiles in which they score low. Income is clearly the least influential factor as it makes little difference whether one scores high or low here in combinations with occupation and education.[17] On the other hand education and occupation themselves are about equal in influence. On both it makes a measurable difference whether one scores high or low. This accounts for the above disparity between the $(O\overline{E})$ profiles and the $(E\overline{O})$ profiles, the largest difference within any layer of the table. Apparently, high occupational prestige without a college education leads to greater anxiety (or at least greater church attendance) than the reverse. Those people who do have college educations without comparably high occupations are seemingly less vulnerable to discrepancy. It may be that education leads to a set of values that is less sensitive to status judgments. It is also possible that many of these persons have such low-status jobs as high school and elementary teaching, where the school itself provides a retreat from, and reorientation for, discrepancy. Or, finally, it is conceivable that these people are drawn to political radicalism rather than the church as an extracurricular outlet.

But as interesting as these results may be, they skirt the primary issue of whether or not status discrepancy and vertical status are empirically independent. Clearly vertical status does account for some of the effect of discrepancy. Previous differences in the rates of high attendance for the three discrepancy categories approached 20 per cent. Here the differences are less than 4 per cent in some cases, and they reach 10 per cent in only one of the six comparisons. These are inviting grounds for reject-

---

[17] Many persons have argued that the American status system is dominated more by how much one earns rather than how one earns it or what background one has. This emphasis on income and consumption is not reflected here and may give pause for thought to theorists of American stratification generally. It is worth noting, too, that Lenski also finds income to be of relatively little importance for status discrepancy, and Jackson omits it altogether on the strength of Lenski's results.

ing discrepancy altogether. Yet a more systematic assessment would be preferable.

One of the best formulas for evaluating tables of this sort is provided by Hanan Selvin.[18] Selvin suggests that where the percentage base of the smallest cell is greater than 15, as it is here, then the percentage differences must be greater than 3 per cent to be meaningful. He goes on to discuss three possibilities for any comparison. First, the difference may be greater than 3 per cent and *agree* with the hypothesis and original relation. Secondly, the difference may be less than 3 per cent in which case it is considered a *tie*. Third, the difference may exceed 3 per cent but in the opposite direction from the predicted; it may *disagree* with the theory and previous results. Selvin then sets up two criteria which any set of comparisons must meet in order to vindicate the hypotheses over-all. For one, the number of agreements must be greater than double the number of disagreements $(A > 2D)$. For another, the number of ties must be equal to or less than the sum of agreements and disagreements divided by two $(T \leqq A + D/2)$. Since Selvin referred specifically to dichotomous comparisons, the technique requires a slight adjustment for the present three categories of high, moderate, and low discrepancy. Thus, I have compared the highly discrepant, on the one hand, and the average percentage for the moderate and low discrepant, on the other. As an example, the first row of Table VII–7 compares 63 per cent high attendance among the highly discrepant with 58.5 per cent high attendance among those of moderate and low discrepancy taken together.

Using this procedure, Table VII–7 yields four agreements $(O\overline{I}, I\overline{O}, E\overline{I}, O\overline{E})$, two ties $(I\overline{E}, E\overline{O})$, and no disagreements. It happens that the combination does satisfy the requisite equations, although by a slim margin. Thus, the number of agreements is indeed greater than twice the number of disagreements, since there are two agreements but no disagreements. Further, the number of ties is equal to, though not less than, the sum of agreements and disagreements divided by two $(2 = 4/2 = 2)$.

Now all of this does not mean that status discrepancy has passed the ultimate test with flying colors. In fact, the colors are

[18] Hanan C. Selvin, *The Effects of Leadership* (Glencoe, Ill.: The Free Press, 1960), especially Appendix C, pp. 192–98.

somewhat limp and the skeptics retain more than token vindication. Not only does discrepancy pass this particular test by the barest of possible margins, but there are other tests[19] and other variables that may be insuperable. The final verdict on discrepancy must rest with the reader and with future research. However, the research must be as careful to explore possible spuriousness as it is vigorous in turning up new correlates. Certainly, this analysis has been far more convincing in the former respect than in the latter.

Summary

During the early stages of this analysis, three warnings were issued. First, in failing to include ethnicity, the present study may have deprived itself of the most potent element of status discrepancy. Second, the United States should be the least fertile field for socioeconomic discrepancy because there is a tendency for status to become standardized and stabilized in a highly industrialized and bureaucratized society. Third, discrepancy may be a chimeric artifact of more conventional status.

All of these warnings have received support. Whether because of the omission of ethnicity or not, the present measure of dis-

[19] The test briefly discussed in footnote 14 should be more accurate and more stringent. Another recent test is offered in David R. Schmitt, "Effects of the Status Congruency of Married Women," unpublished paper, University of Wisconsin, Madison. Schmitt replicates Lenski's finding that incongruency or discrepancy is related to left-wing politics, where discrepancy is measured by status indicators that the respondents themselves rate for their relative importance on a floating scale. The control for vertical status, however, uses the technique of partial correlation. After subtracting the variance in political behavior accountable through vertical status, it is assumed that vertical status is held constant in determining the variance accounted for by various profiles of discrepancy. All of this is done algebraically. But note that this has its drawbacks. The essential problem is to test for the independence of vertical status and status discrepancy, but the method of partial correlation takes such independence as an article of faith. Thus, the algebra does not preclude later contamination. Moreover, the technique does not allow one to inspect cell-by-cell interaction since it produces only correlation coefficients for the larger relationships. Finally, in producing correlation coefficients for a relationship where one discrepant cell may produce the reverse effect of another, it is possible that the correlation will seem zero when, in fact, it is composed of two strong but opposite effects that cancel each other in the computation. Schmitt is aware of these pitfalls, however, and his methodology should get a more sympathetic hearing than this brief mention provides.

crepancy is far from overpowering. High discrepancy characterizes less than 3 per cent of the sample when education, occupation, and income are the status ingredients in question. Moreover, even the effects of high discrepancy are severely limited.
Of all of the various measures of religious involvement, high
discrepancy is meaningfully related only to church attendance
when other factors are controlled. Attendance may have a special
appeal as a compromise between churchlike and sectlike religiosity for people who are both high and low in status. But not
only is the impact of discrepancy restricted to one type of
religiosity; it is also limited to only a few particular profiles
of discrepancy and it is considerably reduced when vertical
status is taken rigorously into account. Thus, high discrepancy
does lead to high attendance when it involves high occupational
prestige but low education. It does not lead to much greater
attendance when it involves high education but low occupation.
As for the over-all impact of vertical status, it reduces the impact of discrepancy even on attendance to the point where it
only barely passes a test for independence.

In a very real sense, then, this and the preceding chapter form
a *cul de sac*. Although near-zero relationships are commonly
uncovered, they are rarely reported, and the reader may wonder
why the present case is an exception. Actually it is a mistake to
consider the lack of relationship to be an empirical still-birth.
It is, of course, a finding in its own right and deserves attention,
if only as a caution to others. This caution is perhaps particularly appropriate with regard to status discrepancy. Partly because it is new, and partly because it is not a rehearsal of "mere
common sense," discrepancy has caught the fancy of a good
many, and embellishments on it have already marched far in
advance of substantiation. And yet this is not to deny all hope
of substantiation. It may be that religiosity is not related to
discrepancy but that other phenomena are; it is possible that
discrepancy is influential only under certain conditions that have
so far gone unspecified. The point is, however, that empirical
treatments of status discrepancy must be especially rigorous to
offset the beguiling qualities of the theory. To this end, results
like the above may be more than just a contribution to a hypothetical "Journal of Uncorroborated and Negative Knowledge."

Part Four

VIII

Conclusions and Implications

Empirical standards are only one criterion for assessing research. A study's theoretical import and its provocativeness for future research are equally important, and these are the focus in this last chapter. Rather than catalogue the findings with a full list of exceptions and specifications,[1] the chapter will risk a bit of *hubris* by addressing the broad pattern of results to larger issues. It is directed to the question, "so what?" instead of "to what extent?"

The Introduction mentioned three particular issues to which the study is oriented. First, what is the role of religion and the church in the contemporary United States? Second, to what extent does the study bear on the problem of institutional commitment in general? Third, what suggestions can be inferred for the broader issues of social stratification? Let us consider the results from each of these perspectives in turn.

[1] Some readers may have skipped the technical analysis in the foregoing chapters in hopes of finding a general summary here. This is understandable. But since each chapter ends with a summary of its own to serve this purpose, I have decided to avoid yet another recapitulation.

177

Religion and the Church in Society

Two extreme positions emerge in the debate over the role of religion in society. The first is represented by the volatile combination of Karl Marx[2] and Sigmund Freud.[3] Both argued—for different reasons—that religion is an illusion that distracts its adherents from their real selves and situations. For Marx, it was an "opiate" that converted economic oppression into a "false consciousness" of well-being. For Freud, it was a sexual sublimation that merely tightened constraints on the natural impulses.

The contrasting second position is more firmly sociological. Although neither Emile Durkheim nor Max Weber were religious themselves, each described religion s importance to society. For Durkheim,[4] religion supported basic values; indeed, it was society itself that was being worshipped. For Weber,[5] religion gave the stamp of legitimacy which an activity required for full development. If religion was a "moon for the misbegotten" in the eyes of Marx and Freud, it could be a source of light for society as a whole in the judgment of Durkheim and Weber.

Now one rapprochement for this divergence inheres in the classic church-sect distinction. The distinction suggests that Western societies at least confirm both views. On the one hand, the *church* caters to those who are firmly integrated into society by providing justifications for secular values and pursuits. On the other hand, the *sect* serves the disenfranchised by providing an escape to a community that is set apart from the secular world. If the church is evidence for Durkheim and Weber, the sect is a buttress for Marx and Freud.

Yet the foregoing research presents a complication. The division of labor may not be so segregated. A single church may perform *both* churchlike and sectlike functions for different types

[2] See, for example, T. B. Bottomore and M. Rubel, *Karl Marx: Selected Writings in Sociology and Social Philosophy* (London: C. A. Watts and Co., Ltd., 1956), especially pp. 26–27.

[3] Sigmund Freud, *Civilization and Its Discontents* (London: Hogarth Press, Ltd., 1930).

[4] Emile Durkheim, *The Elementary Forms of the Religious Life* (Glencoe, Ill.: The Free Press, 1957).

[5] Max Weber, *The Protestant Ethic and the Spirit of Capitalism* (New York: Charles Scribner's Sons, 1958), and *The Sociology of Religion*, trans. by Ephraim Fischoff (Boston: Beacon Press, 1963).

of parishioners. Specifically, the middle- and upper-status parishioners stress churchlike aspects of the program such as Sunday services and parish activities, while, at the same time, they participate highly in other organizations. Conversely, the working- and lower-status adherents are more sectlike in their emphasis on the communal features of the church, in the greater influence religion exerts upon their everyday lives, and in their disapproval of the minister's participation in secular affairs.

Now this is not to say that social class explains *all* of the variance in religious commitment, or that the churchlike and sectlike parishioners divide into distinct camps, or even that religious organizations serve two explicit menus in a religious *table d'hôte*. Social class is only one of many influential factors. The distinction is between two tendencies rather than between two explicit factions. Finally, most religious groups are likely to be unaware of the two functions, and the program of the church may be a *tabula rasa* on which the parishioner places his own interpretation. He may allocate his commitment selectively. He may invest a common activity like the Sunday worship service with his own peculiar meaning.

Nevertheless, I am suggesting an *undercover* tension, and tensions may be the more pronounced for being undercover. The typical denomination or parish is not a seamless whole. The two religious functions pose a conflict with ramifications for the structure and continuation of the organization. On the one hand, there is a pressure to accommodate the secular world and to formalize the church program. On the other hand, there is a competing demand for an insulated community that maximizes the intimate rather than the impersonal, the spontaneous rather than the ritualized. Should the church turn to society and accept its values? Or should the church resist these values as conflicting with traditional doctrine?[6]

It is possible that the two functions are mutually defeating. One may inhibit the other, and any attempt to fulfill both may result in fulfilling neither. Of course, the most dramatic evidence

---

[6] In some cases, the conflict may be more fabricated than real. Sects often manufacture points of difference with the secular environment in order to insure their continued existence. Sectlike parishioners may do much the same in their interpretations of church dogma.

of disruption is the breaking off of splinter groups. Here the conflict has become so great that separate houses are required for the separate functions. The dissident minority cuts itself apart and begins anew. Specialization may seem an inviting avenue to success and stability. This, for example, is Richard Niebuhr's[7] explanation for denominationalism within American Protestantism; it is hard for any single structure to minister to the needs of different classes, ethnic groups, and geographical areas.

Less spectacular evidence of friction falls short of fragmentation but is nonetheless revealing. Milton Yinger[8] points to a church-sect dilemma that has led to alternating phases in the development of Christian theology and formal church structure. In his eyes, the dilemma is ineluctable. In his phrase, it has inhibited religion's "struggle for power." As a specific example, consider R. H. Tawney's remarks on the development of Puritanism. Although Tawney's psychological rhapsody may explain too much, his sociology is very much to the point:

> In every human soul there is a socialist and an individualist, an authoritarian and a fanatic for liberty as in each there is a Catholic and a Protestant. The same is true of mass movements in which men marshal themselves for common action. There was in Puritanism an element which was conservative and traditionalist, and an element which was revolutionary; a collectivism which grasped at an iron discipline, and an individualism which spurned the savorless mess of human ordinances; a sober prudence which would garner the fruits of this world and a divine recklessness which would make all things new.[9]

Both Yinger and Tawney echo earlier insights of Ernst Troeltsch,[10] who saw a church-sect duality that extends from "primitive Christianity" through the fullest flowering of the Catholic monolith.

[7] H. Richard Niebuhr, *The Social Sources of Denominationalism* (New York: Henry Holt & Company, Inc., 1929).

[8] J. Milton Yinger, *Religion in the Struggle for Power* (Durham, N.C.: Duke University Press, 1946).

[9] R. H. Tawney, *Religion and the Rise of Capitalism* (New York: Penguin Books, Inc., 1946), p. 176. Reprinted by permission of Harcourt, Brace & World, Inc. and John Murray (Publishers) Ltd.

[10] Ernst Troeltsch, *The Social Teachings of the Christian Churches* (New York: The Macmillan Company, 1932).

Still more symptoms of tension can be inferred from the contemporary scene. For example, Charles Glock and Benjamin Ringer comment on the political postures of the Episcopal church in this way:

> The church's social policy, then, depends on the nature of the issue and the state of sentiment among parishioners. On issues where parishioner sentiment is relatively homogeneous and self-interest considerable, the church's ability to deviate from the views of its parishioners is severely limited.[11]

By itself, this is evidence for conflict between the clergy and the laity rather than for conflict between churchlike and sectlike parishioners. At the same time, an inference to the latter is invited. Many political issues are aligned with social class, and social class, in turn, is aligned with the church-sect distinction among the laity. Hence, the clergy's hesitancy may be traceable to their position as moderator between churchlike and sectlike adherents. On many economic issues, we can expect the ministers and the lower-status sect types to find accord in traditional doctrine. The difficulty is that the higher-status church types offer an opposition that is strengthened by their position in the church structure. These are the people who contribute most to the organization's efficiency and strength. It is precisely these people, then, who cannot be alienated.

It should come as no revelation that the clergy are in a delicate position in the parish. Several studies have commented on the discrepancy between the ideal world of the seminary and the realities of parish responsibility.[12] The problem may be even more salient when the ideals of the seminary are reinforced by the sectlike parishioners who thereby insure that the discrepancy will persist. It is true that these sectarians are less visible than the church types in the formal rounds of congregational life.

[11] Charles Y. Glock and Benjamin B. Ringer, "Church Policy and the Attitudes of Ministers and Parishioners on Social Issues," *American Sociological Review*, XXI (1956), 155.

[12] See, for example, James M. Gustafson, "An Analysis of the Problem of the Role of the Minister," *Journal of Religion*, XXXIV (1954), 187–91. For a similar analysis of the Conservative Rabbi, see Marshall Sklare, *Conservative Judaism* (Glencoe, Ill.: The Free Press, 1955), pp. 159–98. And for a more general treatment of the clergy of all faiths, see James M. Gustafson, "The Clergy in the United States," *Daedalus*, XCII (1963), 724–44.

Nevertheless, even a fringe minority may feed the tension expressed in reports like these:

> The modern ministry is in no easy position; for it is committed to the espousal of ideals which are in direct conflict with the dominant interests and prejudices of contemporary civilization. This conflict is nowhere more apparent than in America, where neither ancient sanctities nor new social insights tend to qualify, as they do in Europe, the heedless economic forces of an industrial era. Inevitably a compromise must be made, or is made, between the rigor of the ideal and the necessities of the day.[13]

> Anyone looking over my sermons for the last few years would probably regard me as schizophrenic. I'm strongly for biblical religion. I do believe God stands in judgment upon man. But I can't be so much against popular religious stuff as some of the other ministers I know. I think a man's religion should be of real help to him, give him comfort and relieve his mind.[14]

While literature on the minister has repeatedly pointed out the anxieties inherent in his "role conflict," the concept may be inadequate to account for all of his quandary. Another concept is that of "role set," which refers to the various audiences which the performer must address.[15] If the audience is heterogeneous, as I am suggesting for the churches, then still more of the confusion is understandable. In this case, anxiety would occur even if the minister had one and only one role to play, since he enacts it before different groups with different needs. Robert Mitchell amplifies the point in his forthcoming analysis of "minister-parishioner relations."[16]

A final example of denominational conflict that can be inter-

---

[13] Reinhold Niebuhr, *Leaves From the Notebook of a Tamed Cynic* (New York: Living Age Books, 1957), p. 13. Reprinted by permission of Meridian Books, Inc.

[14] Quoted in Louis Schneider and Sanford M. Dornbusch, *Popular Religion: Inspirational Books in America* (Chicago: University of Chicago Press, 1958), p. 135.

[15] See R. K. Merton, "The Role-Set: Problems in Sociological Theory," *British Journal of Sociology*, VIII (1957), 106–20, and Erving Goffman, *Encounters: Two Studies in the Sociology of Interaction* (Indianapolis: The Bobbs-Merrill Company, 1961), pp. 85–86.

[16] Robert E. Mitchell, "Minister-Parishioner Relations," unpublished Ph.D. dissertation, Department of Sociology, Columbia University, 1962.

preted in terms of the coexistence of churchlike and sectlike parishioners stems from Paul Harrison's analysis of the American Baptist Convention.[17] Harrison notes a distinction between those who honor the tradition of local parish autonomy and those who press for efficiency through bureaucratization. The former can be seen as sectlike—Harrison himself calls them "fundamentalists"; the latter are plainly more churchlike. The interesting point here, however, is that the conflict is covert. Harrison indicates that this covertness is a stimulant, for conflict must be recognized to be controlled.

In brief, each of these instances carries a common suggestion. The church is indeed a point of friction. The concomitance of churchlike and sectlike functions carries a tension which often leads to conflict and may go to actual dissolution. There seems little doubt that the coexistence is a liability. Separate movements representing separate functions would avoid the conflict and find less qualified fulfillments. Not only has this been an actual pattern in American Protestantism, but it has been a major theme in scholarly writings on the subject.[18]

And yet there is an opposite possibility as well. The church-sect distinction has broader parallels in sociological theory. It is related to Tönnies'[19] dichotomy between *Gesellschaft* (association) and *Gemeinschaft* (community), Durkheim's[20] delineation of organic and mechanical solidarity, Cooley's[21] distinction between secondary and primary relations, and even the Mayo school's[22] line between formal and informal relations. In each

[17] Paul M. Harrison, *Authority and Power in the Free Church Tradition* (Princeton, N.J.: Princeton University Press, 1959).

[18] In addition to the authors already cited, Talcott Parsons argues similarly in his theoretical work on American "religious pluralism." Unlike Niebuhr, Parsons does not deplore denominationalism. Instead he sees it as the only path to religion's continued effect in a heterogeneous society. Talcott Parsons, *Structure and Process in Modern Societies* (Glencoe, Ill.: The Free Press, 1960), pp. 295–322.

[19] Ferdinand Tönnies, *Community and Society*, trans. and ed. Charles P. Loomis (East Lansing: Michigan State University Press, 1957).

[20] Emile Durkheim, *The Division of Labor in Society* (Glencoe, Ill.: The Free Press, 1960).

[21] Charles H. Cooley, *Social Organization and Human Nature and the Social Order* (Glencoe, Ill.: The Free Press, 1956).

[22] Elton Mayo, *The Human Problems of an Industrial Civilization* (New York: The Viking Press, 1960).

case, the first of the pair signifies impersonal ties for specific tasks with an emphasis on efficiency. The second of the pair connotes affective ties where the whole person is involved and the emphasis is on the group rather than the task. Clearly, the first suggests the church; the second is akin to the sect. But one of the contributions of sociological research is to point out that the polarities are unreal. One pole without the other is precarious. Efficiency without affect is no more viable than affect without some measure of efficiency.

In this light, it may be that the churchlike function requires a simultaneous sectlike function and vice versa. Not only is there a division of labor among religious groups but also within them. There may indeed be short-run friction and even rare cases of dissolution. But, in the long run, the coexistence is an asset for the organization's endurance, and this may be true even of the friction generated.

Consider the outcome if churchlike tendencies were to be given their unbridled head. It is possible that the church would lose its distinctive identity as a religious organization. The pressure to accommodate secular society; the tendency to treat the church as any other organization maximizing formal efficiency; the inability to accept otherworldly goals; and the tendency to lend only partial commitment would all contribute to this demise. The church would blur with a host of other voluntary associations. In fact, there is some evidence that this has already occurred to a limited extent within American Protestantism. The ultimate end of Christian salvation is often upstaged by the proximate goals of regular Sunday attendance, increased church membership, and growing parish affluence. The latter are more "real," hence more discernible, as organizational objectives. As another example, many groups have begun to pursue these goals through eminently secular means. Church-sponsored recreation leagues, businessmen's luncheons, therapy circles, and nursery schools are all competing with their secular counterparts. One of the most blatant forms of competition has only recently taken root. In Detroit, the Crossroads Supper Club offers liquorless evenings with gospel singing as entertainment. Even so, a local pastor commented:

Why stop here? Why not create a religious key club, the "Prayboy club," in which each member has a key to a private chapel?[23]

Here, then, is an extreme emphasis upon the individualism of churchlike religion and an extreme example of religion's willingness to meet its parishioners more than halfway.

On the other hand, what about an unfettered sectarianism? Here, of course, the best evidence comes from the sects themselves. The world of religion becomes withdrawn and insular. It may lose contact with secular reality altogether. It certainly neglects the mundane but important exigencies of religious organization. The consequences, then, are twofold. First, the sect takes its members farther away from society instead of helping them to relate to it in a new and more constructive fashion. Second, the sect becomes unstable, and churchlike innovations must be introduced if it is to attain any permanence. These innovations have occurred within American Protestantism as the examples of the Quakers, Mormons, and Jehovah's Witnesses attest. From the organization's own standpoint, there is a danger of converting a desperate innovation into a tragic emasculation.

Now, however, let us consider the advantages of coexistence. The most obvious of these is that each tendency curbs the other. The churchlike prevents the sectlike from leaving the pale altogether. The sectlike prevents the churchlike from a total merger with secular society. A second advantage refers to the division of labor mentioned earlier. Thus, the sectlike reinforces a concern with traditional doctrine and spirituality. The churchlike is best fitted to meeting the church's extrareligious needs as these involve finances, formal organization, community representation, and interfaith relations. Still a third advantage is that successful functions in one direction complement successful functions in the other. The churchlike parishioner may use membership in a coldly calculated fashion to win social respect and upward mobility; nevertheless, he may also need a nonsecular reinforcement for his values. Since the church must have a distinctive basis from which to provide this reinforce-

[23] Marc Raizman, " 'Night Club' Succeeds Without Liquor, Sexy Waitresses, Jokes," *Milwaukee Journal*, February 28, 1963.

ment, and since the sect type helps to insure this distinctiveness, it follows that the sectlike parishioner is an asset. Conversely, the sectarian risks total alienation and a cure that is worse than the illness unless his religion has some relation to reality. His churchlike fellows insure that the experience will not convert an alternative orientation into a catatonic escape.

A final advantage of the coexisting functions concerns their conflict through time. I have already mentioned the short-run effects of friction and the possibility of fragmentation. But conflict is not always contrary to the persistence of an organization.[24] For one thing, conflict may clarify competing demands and sharpen objectives. For another, it produces a force for change as the conflicting parties spur and check each other in seeking resolution and rapprochement. All of this is especially important for a traditional organization in a changing, secular context. It supplies a dialectic that insures a continued process of dynamic adaptation. Without it, the organization may stagnate and become meaningless for both the churchlike and the sectlike adherents. While specialization may provide short-run advantages, it may be deleterious to long-range success.

Of course, specialization has been deplored before by theologians and ''religious sociologists''[25] who deplore the splinter movement as a breach in a divinely ordained, Christian unity. The present analysis, however, is more theoretical than theological and is meant to apply to non-religious institutions as well.

[24] The literature on conflict harbors two distinctive positions. Marx, of course, held that conflict leads to ultimate dissolution and the production of new forms in a dialectical synthesis. For at least the early Marx, conflict inevitably led to revolution. Against this position, however, stands Georg Simmel. Simmel argued that revolution is only one of many forms of conflict resolution. In fact, conflict may be salutary as well as disruptive. For the best statement of this position see Lewis Coser, *The Functions of Social Conflict* (Glencoe, Ill.: The Free Press, 1956).

[25] Both Richard and Reinhold Niebuhr as well as Will Herberg are prominent examples here. While their theology is sometimes irrelevant to their analysis, it intrudes sufficiently to warrant a distinction between *religious sociology*, on the one hand, and the *sociology of religion*, on the other. In the former, the end is religion with sociology as a means. In the latter, religion is only a neutral case study with which to develop the discipline and learn more about society. The conflict between these postures has been vocal and digressive. It has been a major inhibition to the growth of sociological research in religion.

Furthermore, there is actual evidence that to embrace both churchlike and sectlike functions is salutary.

Although this study is primarily concerned with American Protestantism, Catholicism provides a first case in point. Few institutions—religious or otherwise—can rival the stability and persistence of the Catholic church following the Reformation. This has confounded those who have noted its peculiar mixture of churchlike and sectlike qualities and have identified conceptual purity with actual strength. It can be argued that the Catholic church occupies a mid-point on the scale between church and sect; hence it must be in a process of transition according to the assumptions of the church-sect dynamic. But if the present thesis has merit, it is precisely because the Catholic church combines these qualities that it resists this transition. The combination provides a division of labor and a needed flexibility. Since one can distinguish between churchlike and sectlike priests as well as parishioners among the Catholics, this adds further strength through diversity.

Another example returns us to the Protestants. If denominationalism was the byword of the first half of the twentieth century, there is mounting evidence that ecumenicism will be the mood of the second half. Bishop Bromley Oxnam has strongly endorsed this step for Protestantism as a whole. To date, the most spectacular merger has joined the higher-status Congregational church with the lower-status Evangelical and Reformed church. Implicit here is a confrontation of relatively more churchlike predispositions with relatively more sectlike affinities. Although the two denominators are geographically removed (the Congregationalists are stronger in the East while the Evangelical and Reformed are concentrated in the Midwest) and actual religious issues were strangely dormant during negotiations,[26] it is possible that here too is a sign of the contribution of diversity. This is not to say that the church leaders themselves anticipate fewer problems; they may well expect more. Nevertheless, there could well be "latent" advantages, in the language of the functionalist faith.

Finally consider the church-sect dynamic itself. A common

[26] Robert Lee, *The Social Sources of Church Unity* (Nashville, Tenn.: Abingdon Press, 1960), p. 103.

theme in research here is that the lower-status sect can only attain stability by becoming a high-status church. Thus, low status is associated with organizational evanescence; high status is related to permanence. Of course, there is some justification for this in the theory that high-status organizations are more socially legitimate, more affluent, and more able to call on experienced leadership. At the same time, there is a sense in which we are jousting with windmills. Few sects are exclusively lower-status. No church is exclusively high-status, since one of the defining qualities of the church is its lax membership criteria. As a graphic illustration, the Christian Science *sect* has one of the highest-status compositions among American Protestant groups, while the southern Baptist *church* has one of the lowest. Instead, a more viable distinction between sects and churches relates to *status heterogeneity*. As the sect matures, it takes on more heterogeneity; hence it is apt to combine both sectlike and churchlike parishioners and functions. This, rather than wholesale upward mobility, may account for its greater stability.

In summary, I have suggested that religion may serve two functions in a complex and prevailing secular society. Moreover, these functions will often coexist within the same denomination and parish. If this provides short-run tension and possibilities for fragmentation, it also has long-run advantages. There is a certain strength through coexistence. Even the conflict between parishioners and functions may be important for the organization's stability and adaptiveness.

To some, this may seem a violation of the spirit of the church-sect distinction. The two were intended as ideal types. It may appear rude to confront them with reality by pointing out that both contain aspects of the other. And yet the ideal types were designed to encourage precisely this rudeness, as was pointed out in Chapter III.[27] Weber meant them to be

[27] The methodology of ideal types is best expressed by Max Weber, *The Methodology of the Social Sciences* (Glencoe, Ill.: The Free Press, 1949). J. W. N. Watkins has pointed out, however, that Weber later compromised his position by reverting to *individualistic* types that were more induced than intuited, more empirical than unreal. ("Ideal Types and Historical Explanation," in Herbert Feigl and May Brodbeck (eds.), *Readings in the Philosophy of Science* [New York: Appleton-Century-Crofts, Inc., 1953], pp. 723–43.) In my opinion, the church-sect distinction belongs to Weber's early period.

self-defeating, for the goal of analysis was precisely to show how they did *not* reflect actuality. Presumably, then, this section is well within the tradition and a modest step in the direction of Weber's giant strides. This is no claim to excellence by association, but rather a comment on critical standards that may be applicable to the study.

Some Suggestions for Institutional Commitment Generally[28]

One of the consequences of secularization is that religious institutions grow more similar to institutions of other sorts. Analyses in the sociology of religion have increasing relevance for non-religious phenomena. Of course, the church is still distinctive from the standpoint of the church-goer or the theologian. It is even distinctive from the view of sociology in, for example, its premise of supernatural authority, its voluntary membership, and its position outside of the secular mainstream. But, while these qualities make the church especially interesting, they do not preclude generalizations beyond it. Such generalizations are the burden of the present section, though it seeks to generalize questions rather than answers.

The study of organizations and institutions owes its modern

[28] Throughout this section (and indeed throughout the study as a whole) I have burdened the reader with several terminological ambiguities. Two of these are especially important, the interchangeable use of "institution" and "organization," on the one hand, and of "commitment" and "involvement," on the other. To clarify the first, I am most concerned with those organizations which carry specific values and a distinctive identity. In Philip Selznick's terms, these are "institutions," organizations that had passed through a process of "institutionalization" that is discussed most thoroughly in Talcott Parsons' various works on the social system. A clarification of the second ambiguity is more difficult. Because this area is relatively underdeveloped in the literature, my own ambiguity reflects the state of the discipline. For example, the term "commitment" has been used in three quite different senses: first, to refer to a legal action such as committing an individual to a mental hospital; second, to refer to a public pledge which the individual is obligated to fulfill; and, third, to refer to an inner allegiance to a particular idea, activity, or organization. I am concerned primarily with the last of these, and it is only in this sense that the terms "commitment" and "involvement" can be interchanged. Nevertheless, I have used "commitment" because it is the more general concept of the two and because I hope that its present usage may be systematically related to others both empirically and conceptually.

inception to Max Weber.[29] At the same time, it seems to have been peculiarly invested with the axioms of another sociological pioneer, Emile Durkheim. It was Durkheim who proclaimed the importance of social facts irreducible to individuals. It was Durkheim, too, who argued that a social fact could only be explained by a social fact.[30] Both points have been important to the study of institutions. An emphasis on the effects of structural arrangements and the extent of hierarchy and bureaucracy have dominated the field. There has been a tendency to see the individual member as either irrelevant to these issues or the unwitting victim of such higher-level forces.

A major result of this analytic one-sidedness has been the neglect of individual commitment as it may bear on organizational studies. With all of the concern for properties of leadership, there has been minimal concern for properties of followers. Because one has confidence in the impact of the organization itself, there has been little attention paid to the influence of outside factors.[31] There are studies that have stressed the informal groups of, say, industrial workers.[32] There are also studies that have examined rates of participation.[33] But the problem with the former studies is their assumption that only life within the organization is influential and that all workers are equally vulnerable. The problem with the latter studies is that distinctions in commitment are primarily quantitative rather than qualitative. Moreover, these studies have been interested in individuals rather than organizations so that the coexistence of different types of commitment within a single organization is beyond their concern.

[29] Max Weber, *The Theory of Social and Economic Organization* (New York: Oxford University Press, 1947).

[30] Emile Durkheim, *The Rules of the Sociological Method* (Glencoe, Ill.: The Free Press, 1950).

[31] For an elaboration of this point, see Daniel J. Levinson, "Role, Personality, and Social Structure in the Organizational Setting," *Journal of Abnormal and Social Psychology*, LVIII (1959), 170–80.

[32] Mayo, *op. cit.*

[33] See Chapter II, pp. 8–9, for a discussion of the literature on participation in voluntary organizations, including the work of Komarovsky, Wright and Hyman, and Mather. The references are not exhaustive, but then this has been a prominent interest of empirical sociology, and participation has been related to sundry factors in addition to status.

Now none of this should suggest that the study of organizations or individuals has been irreparably damaged by the neglect. Sciences have a way of concentrating their concerns, and the interests of one period do not dictate the concerns of another. Then too, there are some exceptions to the general omission as several recent contributions have begun to focus on commitment. While they seldom discuss the issues head-on, they nevertheless contribute important, if understated, information.

A number of such studies are summarized in Peter Blau and Richard Scott's excellent review of the literature on *Formal Organizations*.[34] Under the rubric of "Professional and Bureaucratic Orientation," Blau and Scott consider several indications that academic and business organizations typically embrace two types of members. The first type—the professional—is oriented not to the organization but to his broader discipline. The second type—the bureaucrat—assigns the reverse priorities. Both types have been reported in one form or another within various contexts. Blau and Scott[35] and Reissman[36] have noted their coexistence in governmental agencies and bureaucracies. Wilensky points to their presence among intellectuals in the trade unions.[37] Janowitz notes two different career motivations in the military.[38] And Gouldner draws a firm distinction between "cosmopolitans" and "locals" in academia,[39] using terminology that Merton devised for describing community leaders.[40]

Nor are these the only studies that are relevant. Others have included similar findings as peripheral to their main interests.

[34] Peter M. Blau and W. Richard Scott, *Formal Organizations* (San Francisco: The Chandler Publishing Co., 1962), pp. 60–66.

[35] *Ibid.*, pp. 66–74.

[36] Leonard Reissman, "A Study of Role Conception in Bureaucracy," *Social Forces*, XXVII (1949), 305–10.

[37] Harold L. Wilensky, *Intellectuals in Labor Unions* (Glencoe, Ill.: The Free Press, 1956).

[38] Morris Janowitz, *The Professional Soldier* (Glencoe, Ill.: The Free Press, 1960), especially pp. 104–25.

[39] Alvin W. Gouldner, "Cosmopolitans and Locals," *Administrative Science Quarterly*, II (1957–58), 281–306, 444–80. See also Theodore Caplow and Reece J. McGee, *The Academic Marketplace* (New York: Basic Books, Inc., 1958).

[40] Robert K. Merton, *Social Theory and Social Structure* (2nd ed.; Glencoe, Ill.: The Free Press, 1957), pp. 387–420.

While Wilensky observes contrasting orientations among intellectuals in the unions, Lipset, Trow, and Coleman find them among union politicos generally. In fact, one infers that it is a distinction in commitment that provides much of the political friction within the single union of the International Typographers:

> The Independents hold their weekly meetings in a tavern near union headquarters, making their meeting a social gathering as well as a political club meeting. Characteristically, the Progressives meet under more austere circumstances, in a midtown hotel, with sociability taking a decided back seat to the business of politics. . . . [The] very different backgrounds of the two groups . . . seem to be responsible in great measure for the quite different ways in which the Progressives and Independents view the aims and purposes of the union. In keeping with their printing and craft-union backgrounds, the Independents seem most concerned about "conserving our sound, craft unionism," while the Progressives are most restless, with an image of "militant, progressive unionism."[41]

Note the echo of the church-sect distinction. It appears that religious groups are not the only groups composed of members who hold notions of sectlike communality and traditionalism, on the one hand, and members who value churchlike impersonality in the name of efficiency and progress, on the other. As for the political repercussions of the division, the two types are isolable within political organizations per se. Thus, Howe and Coser report that the "internal political life" of the American Communist Party showed similar divisions:

> Two kinds of political orientation could be distinguished among the members at this point—and in turning to this fact we leave behind the petty squabbles of Communist factionalism and approach one of the most persistent and difficult problems of radical (as perhaps any other kind of) political action: the relationship between doctrine and conduct, between eventual ends and immediate methods, between the pressure for ideological exclusivism and the pressure of political actuality. In the Workers Party, which by 1922 was still far from being a Leninist organization,

[41] S. M. Lipset, M. A. Trow, J. S. Coleman, *Union Democracy* (Glencoe, Ill.: The Free Press, 1956), from pp. 320–24.

there were first the confirmed Communists and second those radicals who had recently come from the Socialist Party and whom the Communists sneeringly called "centrists." Between these two tendencies, whose ultimate incompatibility lay equally in politics and temperament, there was at best an uneasy alliance.[42]

As if to support the assertion that this characterizes non-extremist political groups as well, Wilson's study of *The Amateur Democrat*[43] and Lane's general review of the literature on political participation[44] point out similar contrasts in commitment within the mainstream of American politics.

In sum, the coexistence of different types of commitment within a single organization is not unique to American Protestantism or religious groups in general. But although this is a finding in several studies, few have explored the consequences beyond brief assertions of resulting tension. Earlier I speculated that it may be disturbing in the short run but an asset in the longer run. Even if this is accurate for religious groups, is it true of organizations generally? It may be true of some but not others.

This last point suggests another vein of research, one highlighted by Amitai Etzioni's recent *A Comparative Analysis of Complex Organizations*.[45] Here Etzioni is concerned with

[42] Irving Howe and Lewis Coser, *The American Communist Party: A Critical History* (New York: Frederick A. Praeger, Inc., 1962), pp. 104–5. By permission of the Beacon Press.

[43] James Q. Wilson, *The Amateur Democrat* (Chicago: University of Chicago Press, 1962). Wilson distinguishes between the professional and the amateur politician in a way that crosscuts our church-sect distinction. Thus, the professional is more sectlike in the exclusiveness of his commitment to politics generally. But he is more churchlike in that the political club is perceived as a means to an end.

[44] Robert E. Lane, *Political Life: Why People Get Involved in Politics* (Glencoe, Ill.: The Free Press, 1959).

[45] Amitai Etzioni, *A Comparative Analysis of Complex Organizations* (Glencoe, Ill.: The Free Press, 1961). Another instance of the tendency to regard organizational commitment as a single, quantitative dimension is in David Mechanic, "The Power to Resist Change Among Low-Ranking Personnel," *Personnel Administration*, XXVI (1963), 5–11. At one point, Mechanic asserts: "When commitment from personnel is obtained, surveillance can be relaxed; and there is not explicit need for the exercise of power" (p. 6). But is this true of all *kinds* of commitment? Might not a church type of commitment differ considerably from a sect type in this regard?

"compliance"—the relation between types of leadership and types of followers. On this basis, he distinguishes three organizational species: the "normative" (e.g., the church), the "utilitarian" (e.g., the business firm), and the "coercive" (e.g., the prison). Because of this comparative bent, Etzioni does not look for differences in commitment *within* these forms; instead, he focuses on the differences *among* them, using each as a pure type. Nevertheless, it is possible that coexisting modes of participation are most likely in normative organizations but are least likely in the coercive. It is also possible that the effects are more deleterious in the utilitarian and most salutary in the normative.

But so far we have looked at commitment from the standpoint of the institution rather than the member. Another issue which can be raised is the pattern of commitments which a single individual holds to several institutions. If he is a sectlike member of a religious group, is he apt to be a churchlike member of his business or trade union? Are sectlike orientations to two or more institutions compatible? Is it necessary to have a sectlike commitment to at least one organization? Does this perhaps provide a basic orientation for segmental participation in others?

One of the basic premises of sociology is that institutions carry values of particular sorts. The kind of values that a church pursues will differ from the kind that a business firm upholds. Thus, the problem of the individual and his values— one that bulks large in sociological theory especially of the Parsonian social-action type—may be operationalized through an inspection of commitment patterns. It is easier to measure objective participation than subjective attitudes. Where the ideologies and values of institutions are discernible, the route to individual values may be through the study of participation profiles.

Of course, the individual's relation to social institutions has always occupied sociology to some degree. Marx saw commitment to work and the economic institutions as crucial.[46] In so far as he sketched his communist utopia, it was partially an increment in commitment through the reduction of alienation. Durkheim had a similar view of the pathology of undercommit-

[46] Bottomore and Rubel, *op. cit.*, pp. 167–77.

CONCLUSIONS AND IMPLICATIONS

ment.[47] Without allegiances of some sort, the individual was vulnerable to "egoism" and to "anomie," both of which could lead to suicide as one particular means of coping. Unlike Marx, however, Durkheim did not specify any particular type of institution as paramount. Moreover, he saw overcommitment as equally dangerous, since either "altruism" or "fatalism" could lead to suicide as well. Finally, Georg Simmel was another early sociologist concerned with the problem. His classic statement concerning the "web of group-affiliations" was among the first which noted the advantages of multiple affiliations and argued the individualizing benefits rather than the fragmenting liabilities of the pluralistic urban society.[48]

Yet none of these early students looked at different *kinds* of commitment, since they confined their insights to quantitative issues of presence or absence. Recently, however, the question of styles of commitment has been raised in several quarters. In fact, it is an important element in the debate over the ramifications of pluralism and the mass society. One of the features of this society is that the individual member has a range of affiliations spread thinly. He participates *segmentally* in a host of institutions and organizations. No one of them claims dominant loyalty; in each, commitment is more compulsory than compelling.

Debate here is largely concerned with the consequences of multiple segmental participation for ideological extremism. At the risk of profound oversimplification, one can isolate four positions which differ as much in their evaluations as in their analyses. First, there are those who applaud extremism and who see segmentalism as conducive to it. These strategists of revolution reason that segmentalism leaves the individual without a highly developed defensive mechanism. Because he has no strong existing commitments, he is apt to be insecure and he is also apt to be vulnerable to a new ideology which promises quick and simple solutions. A second and more common position, however, agrees that segmentalism leads to extremism but deplores extremism itself. This, for example, is the position of

[47] Emile Durkheim, *Suicide* (Glencoe, Ill.: The Free Press, 1951), pp. 241–77.

[48] Georg Simmel, *Conflict and the Web of Group-Affiliations*, trans. Kurt H. Wolff and Reinhard Bendix (Glencoe, Ill.: The Free Press, 1955), especially pp. 125–95.

Philip Selznick who argues that the contemporary "Stalinoid" or "mass man" is ripe for totalitarian movements like Communism or the John Birch Society.[49] A third position is represented by C. Wright Mills.[50] Here ideological passion is approved but segmentalism is seen as a barrier rather than a stimulus. In this view, the individual's many allegiances preclude mobilization of any one of them. He becomes a man of parts, and, since each part is led in a different direction, the individual becomes both unorganized and unorganizable. Finally, then, a fourth position agrees that segmentalism militates against extremism but challenges Mills's premise that this is undesirable. Lipset,[51] Bell,[52] and Gusfield[53] all seem to applaud the "end of ideology," in some sense. Lipset notes approvingly, for example, that American religion has blunted the force of American political extremism. Religion offers a passive adaptation to the world and thereby funnels off the fervor of the disenfranchised which would otherwise lead them to revolutionary extremism. Gusfield points out that multiple segmental affiliations provide training in the problem of consensus and, thus, strengthen democracy by attuning its members to one of its vital processes.

Clearly there is confusion in this speculation. While all of this is proper fodder for philosophy as well as sociology, more empirical study of patterns of involvement and their consequences is needed. Unhappily, such study has so far been rare. Yet I am not criticizing research simply for its failure to consider *my* problems. Instead I am arguing that the problems

[49] Philip Selznick, *The Organizational Weapon: A Study of Bolshevik Strategy and Tactics* (Glencoe, Ill.: The Free Press, 1960), especially pp. 275–314.

[50] C. Wright Mills, *The Power Elite* (New York: Oxford University Press, 1959), especially pp. 298–325.

[51] S. M. Lipset, *Political Man* (Garden City, N.Y.: Doubleday & Company, Inc., 1960), pp. 107–8. Actually Lipset's argument, as it is given below, is based upon religious sects rather than religion in general. Yet if the reasoning is valid, it should extend to the latter as well, since sects in America account for less than 10 per cent of the religiously inclined public and, thereby, have too little currency to drain off all political extremism from the lower classes.

[52] Daniel Bell, *The End of Ideology: On the Exhaustion of Political Ideas in the Fifties* (New York: Collier Books, 1961), especially pp. 21–38.

[53] Joseph R. Gusfield, "Mass Society and Extremist Politics," *American Sociological Review*, XXVII (1962), 19–30.

are larger than personal puzzlements and that their solution would offer more than idle pleasures. The individual's pattern of institutional commitments—distinguished in kind and degree —is important to analyses of institutional behavior, individual personality, and social order. A study of religious participation is only a beginning in its suggestion that there are indeed different modes of commitment, and that these are related to such factors as social class. The study leaves unanswered the question of how these modes are related in other institutions, although the following section hazards several guesses. Among other things, it suggests that few persons have exclusively segmental allegiances and that much of the debate over the mass society is founded on an imprecision. The issue may be more one of locating where the individual's primary allegiances fall than one of tracing the consequences of no primary allegiances at all.

Implications for Social Stratification

Robert Nisbet has commented that the treatment of stratification in American sociology is an example of "cultural lag."[54] The concept was little attended in the first part of the twentieth century when class lines were sharply drawn and influential. Now that the lines have blurred and the differences have narrowed, social class is given special prominence. From this point of view, the most revealing findings of the study may be the extent to which stratification does *not* affect religiosity. At no point were the results such that 100 per cent of the upper classes had an attribute which 0 per cent of the lower classes shared. The percentage differences in religiosity were infrequently as high as 30 per cent and often as low as 10 per cent.

And yet the influence of stratification has not wholly disappeared. Lower-class parishioners *are* more often sectlike; higher-status adherents *are* more frequently churchlike; and even status discrepancy may still relate to heightened religiosity. Although status factors do not account for *all* of the variance in religious involvement, to prove this was not the goal of the analysis. Instead we focused only on status and religiosity as

[54] Robert A. Nisbet, "The Decline and Fall of Social Class," *Pacific Sociological Review*, II (1959), 11–17.

they are representative of the general relation between secular rewards and commitment to traditional institutions that may be at odds with a secular society. Because this concerns more than religion and the church, some comments on its broader implications may be useful.

One of the premises at the outset was that churches are not the only institutions that fulfill a religious function. If a religious function is defined as one that reinforces and promotes distinctive values, then any number of institutions may qualify. Military groups, political parties, trade unions, universities, even an institution as simple as the family may serve religious functions in that all of them urge values on their members and seek to sustain them. Furthermore, each of these institutions may be seen as unique to some extent. While all of them share the secular ethos, each of them emphasizes some of its aspects while de-emphasizing others. In this respect, each has the potential to serve churchlike or sectlike purposes. If they emphasize what they hold in common with the mainstream of social values they are more churchlike. If they emphasize what they alone represent, they are more sectlike. Here again, status should determine much of the choice. Institutions are flexible, including both possibilities within themselves.

In all of this, there is a series of propositions of wider import. First, the lower one's secular status, the more he is apt to seek out institutions with unique values as a framework for interaction and self-judgment. Second, within any institution, those lower in status are more likely to seek out the least secular facets as the loci of their commitment. Third, it is possible to gain a suitably distinctive orientation in organizations other than the church. The church is not the only recourse for the disenfranchised; the lower classes may find succor in other groups and institutions as well. In each of these propositions, there is slight evidence that "status discrepant" may be cautiously substituted for "lower class," if one remembers that the status discrepants are subject to cross pressures. They may be led to one type of commitment by their status discrepancy but their over-all vertical status may dictate another. The ambivalence is deep-seated, and this may be one reason why many seek to change the system altogether rather than participate in institutions which only partially withdraw from it.

Here, as earlier, the speculations outstrip the data, since they take us beyond the analysis of religion alone. Nevertheless, it is possible to propose more concrete elaboration on a tentative basis. Consider the first proposition that the lower classes will seek out the less secular institutions. The question emerges as to what institutions are less secular than others. We have already seen that the church is traditionally non-secular in so far as it stresses a doctrine that is at odds with the rational-economic ethic. In these terms, the military is also a traditionalist enterprise that substitutes discipline for rationality and organizational security for economic success. Academia is another institution that may offer non-economic incentives, and its goal is one of pure rather than applied rationality. A further instance would be extremist political groups which seek sweeping changes in the secular order. A final example might be the extended family where members are accepted not because of their achievement but because of the fact of membership alone.

In each of these instances, then, one can predict an inordinate predilection on the part of the lower classes. The lower a person's status, the more he is likely to pursue the military as a career, the more he may value teaching,[55] the more he should be drawn to extremist political groups whether they advocate radical new values or a radical reversion to older ones, and the more he will prefer an extended family that provides

[55] These are intended as provisional hypotheses rather than statements of fact. While there is support for speculation concerning extremist political groups, the extended family, and the attractiveness of an enlisted career within the military, the university raises more complex issues. There is relatively little data available on recruitment into teaching. There is some evidence that the academic career appeals especially to ethnic groups such as the Jews. There is also evidence to show that academicians are drawn disproportionately from middle-class and professional stock. But the latter may be taken to show merely that these are the class backgrounds which enable an individual to get the requisite training. Given this training and given the opportunity to choose the ends of, say, a postgraduate education, it is still possible that the lower classes will choose teaching more frequently. And yet there is another complexity to be introduced. Recently, the university has undergone a "professionalization" under which it has come to resemble any other technological institution in the mainstream of society. Hence its attractiveness as a lower-class alternative may have diminished. The university differs from the military, political extremism, and the extended family in that success within it may also lead to success in the secular world at large. Given an education, then, those with lower-class backgrounds may no longer require a retreat for they can move into new middle- and upper-class niches within secular society itself.

withdrawal from his workaday rounds. As an illustration consider the research of Robert Dubin[56] and Louis Orzack.[57] Dubin found the "central life interests" of industrial workers did not involve the factory but revolved instead about leisure pursuits or the family. Orzack attempted a replication for professionals and found that, in contrast to the workers, the professionals did center their life interests on their jobs. Note that both Dubin and Orzack explain their findings largely in terms of the inherent properties of the job itself: its boredom, its repetitiveness, and so on. And yet another factor is the amount of reward that the job confers in terms of broader social status. This is the factor that is at issue here.

The second proposition can also be specified more closely. We have already seen that, within the church, the lower-class members focus on the least secular aspects of the church program. This should obtain in other contexts as well. A classic example is the distinction between formal and informal groups within the industrial plant. Roethlisberger and Dickson have pointed out that informal contacts provide an important respite from the straining for efficiency and help to maintain morale.[58] Elton Mayo has suggested their significance in combating absenteeism.[59] Yet informal groups are more likely to develop among blue-collar than white-collar workers. Presumably, the former are more in need of relief from an invidious status system. The informal groups are important precisely because they depart from the rational-economic standards of the enterprise. Because the white-collar employees are judged more successful by these standards, they need departures from them less.

The same should be true of relative status differences in other contexts. Those of relatively low status should be the bureaucrats rather than the professionals within governmental agencies, the

---

[56] Robert Dubin, "Industrial Workers' Worlds: A Study of the 'Central Life Interests' of Industrial Workers," *Social Problems*, III (1956), 131–42.

[57] Louis H. Orzack, "Work as a 'Central Life Interest' of Professionals," in Erwin O. Smigel (ed.), *Work and Leisure* (New Haven, Conn.: College and University Press, 1963), pp. 73–84.

[58] F. J. Roethlisberger and W. J. Dickson, *Management and the Worker* (Cambridge, Mass.: Harvard University Press, 1939).

[59] Mayo, *op. cit.*

localites rather than the cosmopolitans in the academic world, the independents rather than the progressives in the unions, and so on. In short, the lower classes are not only prone to institutions which are themselves beyond the secular pale. Even within eminently secular contexts, they will seek out distinctive niches that are, in religious terms,[60] more sectlike than churchlike.

The third proposition draws out the religious implications of the first two. Because institutions other than the church may provide withdrawal for the lower classes, there is further support for the contention that the church is not the only organization that may serve religious functions. There was a time when this was considered heretical. By now, however, it is implicit in many statements that are very nearly clichés. It is a commonplace, for example, that "Communism is a religion." Indeed, an inherent religious quality may help to explain the lower-class penchant for extremist politics in general. Extremism may not signify mere self-interest politics, as studies of the leftist vote alone conclude, or the effects of an authoritarian-personality syndrome, as Lipset has suggested after inspecting the lower-class vote on both the right and the left.[61] Instead, the more extreme the party, the more divorced it is from prevailing values and status standards. Hence the more extreme the party, the more it can serve a sectlike religious function of the type we have been discussing.

But not only political groups have religious overtones. All kinds of organizations carry distinctive values and harbor distinctive points of secular withdrawal—even those that are not explicitly ideological or action-oriented. This may help to illumine a finding reported in Chapter I: although lower-class

[60] For a rare and excellent treatment of this general area, see the recent work of Harold L. Wilensky: for example, "Work, Careers, and Social Integration," *International Social Science Journal*, XII (1960), 543–60; "Orderly Careers and Social Participation: The Impact of Work History on Social Integration in the Middle Mass," *American Sociological Review*, XXVI (1961), 521–39; and "Life Cycle, Work Situation, and Participation in Formal Associations," in Robert W. Kleemeier (ed.), *Aging and Leisure: Research Perspectives on the Meaningful Use of Time* (New York: Oxford University Press, 1961), pp. 214–42.

[61] S. M. Lipset, "Working Class Authoritarianism," in Lipset, *Political Man, op. cit.*, pp. 97–130.

church members seem to be more deeply involved in their religion, the lower-class in general does not have a disproportionately higher rate of church membership per se. Those who opt for conventional religion do so strongly, but there are many who seem to bypass it altogether. It is likely that the latter have "religious affiliations" with institutions other than the churches themselves. This is especially plausible in a society that is unrivalled in the range of voluntary associations it offers.

Throughout, however, there is one assumption that should be qualified. I have identified low status with a tendency to seek withdrawal from secularism instead of taking the system and its values as a primary orientation. But this is problematic. We have seen that a person's subjective-class estimation may be at odds with his objective ranking. We have also explored the effects of age, sex, and status discrepancy as mitigating factors. Clearly, this is an important area for research. How do people interpret their status? What influences the interpretation? One can predict that low status will lead to withdrawal in closed societies with little mobility more often than in the so-called open societies. Regardless of the facts, mythology has it that the United States is now more open than it has ever been. This may be one reason why social class has declined in influence generally and why the lower classes have less need for fringe religious cults that exist on the societal periphery. If such cults and sects offer an extreme palliative, then a more moderate one may appeal to those who are less sensitive and more hopeful. Sectlike involvement in a conventional church may move in this more moderate direction.

Summary

Research in sociology is torn between two maxims. One is to stay close to the data. The other is to address the research to larger theoretical issues that give it broader meaning. The bulk of this study follows the first of these admonitions. This chapter has turned to the second. Here I have explored several ramifications of the results as they apply to religion and the church, the wider problems of institutional commitment, and social stratification in general.

The coexistence of churchlike and sectlike parishioners within Protestant churches was interpreted as evidence that a single religious group may serve two functions: one in reinforcing secular values and pursuits, the other in providing a withdrawal from them. This suggests, in turn, a source of friction for most denominations and congregations. Occasionally the friction will lead to splinter movements and actual disruption. In the short run its consequences will be adverse to inner church harmony. In the longer run, however, the friction may be salutary, since it insures a kind of dynamic adaptation of the church to society. It provides a division of labor and source of flexibility. One may even speculate that the presence of one function may be necessary for the fulfillment of the other.

All of this seems applicable to institutions other than the conventional church. Coexisting modes of commitment have been isolated in groups as diverse as universities, labor unions, business firms, civil service bureaucracies, the military, and political parties. The consequence of variations in commitment is a problem that extends beyond the sociology of religion. And the area is important for more than organizational analysis per se. From a social-psychological standpoint, the individual's pattern of commitment to several organizations offers important clues to his values and his general social position. For those concerned with the traditional problems of social order, commitment provides a bridge between the individual and the society as a whole.

Turning to stratification, it seems that those of low status and those of high status discrepancy are likely to seek respites from the secular world that judges them. Yet the church is not the only institution that can provide this. The military, the university, extremist political groups, and even the extended family can provide withdrawal. Each offers distinctive values which depart from secular standards. Moreover, even the most conventional organizations such as the industrial enterprise have niches within them which should appeal especially to those with status deprivations.

Finally, it has become a commonplace for American students of religion to end their studies with a supplication for religious revitalization. It is appropriate, however, that this volume should end on a different note. For all its emphasis on the church, it has also stressed the similarities between the church and other institutions in society. For all its concern with religious involvement, it has tried to indicate that involvement in other institutions may be equally functional for many individuals. The object has been to raise issues rather than hopes or fears. The approach has been theoretical rather than theological in an attempt to bring the study of religion into a less inhibited intellectual cross-fire. In the eloquence of Gilbert Murray, a sociologist of religion who masqueraded as a classicist:

> As far as knowledge and conscious reason will go, we should follow resolutely their austere guidance. When they cease, as cease they must, we must use as best we can those fainter powers of apprehension and surmise and sensitiveness by which, after all, most high truth has been reached as well as most high art and poetry: careful always really to seek for truth and not for our own emotional satisfaction, careful not to neglect the real needs of men and women through basing our life on dreams; and remembering above all to walk gently in a world where the lights are dim and the very stars wander.[62]

[62] Gilbert Murray, *Five Stages of Greek Religion* (Garden City: Doubleday Anchor Books, 1955), p. 164. By permission of the Beacon Press.

Appendix A

Social Status and the Separate Indicators of Religiosity

In constructing the Indexes of Sectlike and Churchlike Religiosity in Chapter III, I relied more upon theory than actual data. While the indexes later confirmed this theory, there remains the problem of the component indicators. In each case, it is conceivable that only one indicator supports the status hypothesis and alone accounts for the association between status and the index as a whole. Indexes cultivate parsimony at the expense of detail. But the detail is important for future researchers who are planning their own measures of religiosity.

Table A–1 presents the familiar socioeconomic status categories and all six measures of involvement. The first three measures are, of course, sectlike. Each was hypothesized as having a negative relation to status: the lower one's status, the higher one's score. The next three items are, by contrast, churchlike. Here the expectation was for a positive association with status; involvement should mount with increasing status.

Clearly all three of the sectlike measures confirm the hypothesis, just as their aggregate index did earlier. The upper-status group has the lowest score on each; the low-status parishioners have by far the highest. Turning to churchlike religiosity, we find similar confirmation for two of the items. High-status adherents are indeed more likely to participate in parish activities and outside organizations. And yet church attendance poses an exception. In so far as there is any relation at all, it moves in the predicted direction. Unhappily, the relation is negligible, for a maximum difference of 2 per cent is far from reliable or church-shaking.

There are a number of possible explanations for the failure

205

TABLE A-1

Socioeconomic Status by the Separate Measures of Religiosity

Measures of Religiosity	Categories of Status			
	Upper	Middle	Working	Low
% High Communality (at least 3 of 5 closest friends in parish)	29 (2854)	32 (2903)	35 (2316)	44 (717)
% High Religious Reward ("much help" response in 6 or more of 8 areas)	34 (2326)	38 (2588)	44 (2096)	50 (611)
% Negative or Uncertain about Minister's role in Community Controversy	34 (2893)	50 (2945)	69 (2367)	84 (734)
% High Church Attendance (attend 4 or more times per month)	58 (2864)	59 (2914)	57 (2328)	57 (718)
% High Parish Activities (at least one)	68 (2844)	66 (2918)	56 (2315)	47 (718)
% High Outside Organizations (at least one)	90 (2792)	75 (2810)	59 (2232)	44 (694)

of the hypothesis for attendance, and they are not mutually exclusive. First, the results are in keeping with previous research in that class differences in religiosity are generally lower among church members than among the general population. Here the entire sample are church members; presumably they are disposed to religion generally, and vulnerable to pressures placed upon them by the church as an organization. Second, the sample is exclusively drawn from large metropolitan areas, and we saw in Chapter I that upper-class church participation is reduced in these contexts and the middle classes inherit the front pews. A third possibility originally emerged in the analysis of discrepancy. There we saw that attendance tends to straddle the church-sect distinction and appeals to the discrepant quite as much as to the purely sectlike member. This is understandable in that Sunday services are the central ritual of every Protestant denomination. Almost a requisite for the member in good standing, the Sunday service may attract lower-class adherents despite its uncomfortably secular tone.

Fourth, because the present finding falls short of the results of previous research, one cannot dismiss the possibility of bias. Given (a) the importance of attendance in the church program, (b) a questionnaire that asks cooperation in the name of church authorities as "part of God's work," and (c) the postulate that lower-class members will feel ill at ease in middle-class Protestant circles, it is conceivable that many working- and lower-status parishioners inflated their attendance in an effort to impress both themselves and their leaders. This is speculative, and yet the problem of response bias is probably greater in the sociology of religion than in any other area of sociological research. In fact, Appendix B takes up the problem of bias more directly in inspecting the characteristics of those who did not answer all of the status items.

Fifth and finally, it is important to recall the nature of the sample and the fact that it is vastly overrepresentative of the very church-like Congregationalists and Presbyterians. Within both of these denominations, Sunday services receive a high emphasis and one that should be salient to their low-status members as well as their high-status adherents. This possibility has added merit, since the predicted positive relation is indeed much stronger among the Lutherans, Baptists, and Disciples of Christ. Where the services are less stressed, there is greater latitude for individual variance and greater vulnerability to factors such as status.

Appendix B

Non-Respondents on the Measures of Social Status

Out of a total sample of 12,116 Protestants, some 3,175 failed to answer at least one of the three status items: education, occupation, and income. It would have been utopian to hope for no rejects at all; however, the rate here far exceeds the normal and is, in its own right, a problem for analysis. What characterizes the people who failed to answer these crucial items? Do their omissions invalidate the study as a whole?

The status rejects divide into three groups. First, there are those few who failed to answer any of the three status questions. Presumably these 169 respondents were *principled* rather than *accidental* rejects. The second group of 618, however, did answer one of the status items, and it is difficult to ascertain their reasons for rejecting the other two. Finally, the third group, a majority of the 2,388, failed to answer only one item, and this could well have been an accident. The following analyses will consider each of these groups in turn. For all three, it will seek clues to their objective status and subjective class. In addition, their age, sex, denomination, and, above all, their responses to the sectlike and churchlike religiosity indexes will be analyzed. The relevant comparison throughout will be with the non-rejects who were the larger part of the sample.

Table B–1 gives a summary portrait of the first group on all items except objective status where, of course, no information at all was available. Not surprisingly the response rate to every question was inordinately low, and, therefore, the data provide suggestions rather than certainties. Nevertheless, a composite picture emerges in comparison with the non-rejects. The rejects on all three status items are disproportionately older women who think of themselves as working (or lower) class.

TABLE B–1

Rejects on All Three Status Items Versus Non-Rejects on Age, Sex, Subjective Class, Churchlike and Sectlike Religiosity[a]

Measures for Comparison	Rejects on All Three Items	Non-Rejects		
Age				
Young	10%	18%		
Middle-aged	9	63		
Old	81	18		
N	(57)	(8935)		
Sex				
Men	14%	40%		
Women	86	60		
N	(49)	(8935)		
Subjective Class				
Middle (and Upper)	25%	51%		
Working (and Lower)	75	49		
	(8)[b]	(2497)		
% High Churchlike	32%	Upper	66%	(2794)[c]
N	(47)	Middle	57	(2918)
		Working	41	(2288)
		Low	30	(719)
% High Sectlike	44%	Upper	27%	(2886)
N	(54)	Middle	32	(2934)
		Working	36	(2355)
		Low	45	(723)

[a] Technically, this table should be percentaged in the opposite direction since the row variables are considered "cause" and the column variables "effect." Nevertheless, because of the gross discrepancy in totals between the rejects and the non-rejects, this was considered awkward.
[b] Here subjective data are available for the Baptists and Lutherans only, and this accounts for the unusually and unreliably low number of rejects in the cell.
[c] Since part of the objective here is to locate the status of the rejects, the non-rejects are split into status groups for comparison on the religiosity measures.

This class judgment is reinforced by their scores on the religiosity measures. Note that their levels of both churchlike and sectlike involvement are almost identical with the levels of the extremely low-status non-rejects. Thus, the rejects are disproportionately high on sectlike religiosity and disproportionately low on churchlike.

All of this makes sense. Women in our society are often forced to accept a status that is of their husbands' making and not their own. Older persons may very well feel that they have been bypassed as the status system changes. Low status may make a status admission even more difficult. Finally, the rejects' penchant for sectlike religiosity suggests a view of the church as a kind of haven into which questions of status are illegitimate intrusions. But as sensible as this is, these persons account for only a small percentage of the total number of rejects. Let us proceed to the next category: those who were rejects on only two of the status items.

Table B–2 presents data comparable to Table B–1, but it is somewhat more complex. Here, as before, it compares rejects with non-rejects. But because these rejects did respond to one status measure, this provides a better clue to their objective rank than the subjective class measure that applies only to Baptists and Lutherans. Accordingly, I have broken both groups into the three status categories of upper, moderate, and low, where moderate combines middle and working status for the non-rejects. These status categories are also used in the data for religiosity. Here the levels of involvement should be compared for status categories and not for rejects versus non-rejects as a whole.

Once again we find that the rejects are disproportionately older women. Whereas only 18 per cent of the non-rejects are older, this is true of fully 76 per cent of the rejects. Whereas 60 per cent of the non-rejects are women, this increases to 84 per cent of the rejects. But it is particularly instructive to look at the proportions of rejects and non-rejects who fall into the three status categories. Only 9 per cent of the non-rejects are low status, but this characterizes fully 50 per cent of the rejects. Again it seems that the rejects may suffer a loss of self-esteem in answering a status item. Although Protestantism is not the exclusive lair of the middle and upper classes, it has this reputation, particularly for Presbyterians and Congregationalists, and this may contribute to the inhibitions of the low-

TABLE B–2

Rejects on Two Status Items Versus Non-Rejects on Age, Sex, Objective Status, and Churchlike and Sectlike Religiosity

Measures for Comparison	Rejects on Two Items		Non-Rejects	
Age				
Young	10%		18%	
Middle-aged	14		63	
Old	76		18	
N	(588)		(8935)	
Sex				
Men	16%		40%	
Women	84		60	
N	(543)		(8935)	
Objective Status				
Upper	13%		33%	
Moderate	37		58	
Low	50		9	
N	(618)		(8941)	
High Churchlike				
Upper	67%	(52)	66%	(2794)
Moderate	51	(158)	50	(5206)
Low	44	(200)	30	(719)
High Sectlike				
Upper	49%	(61)	27%	(2886)
Moderate	50	(178)	34	(5289)
Low	59	(200)	45	(723)

status members. Later we will explore this denominational factor more empirically.

Meanwhile consider the religiosity measures in Table B–2. Although the levels of churchlike involvement are nearly identical for upper- and moderate-status rejects and non-rejects, this is not true of the low-status respondents, nor is it true for a comparison of the respondents on sectlike religiosity generally. The low-status rejects include 44 per cent who score high on churchlike involvement, but the low-status non-rejects only 30 per cent. As for sectlike religiosity, the rejects are more involved within every status category. Again, then, the rejects seem more sectarian, with a religious style which would regard questions of status as unhappy encroachments and reminders.

Finally, Table B–2 allows a preliminary answer to the important question of how serious the loss of the rejects was to the main body of the study. Although the loss deflated the number of sect types in our Protestant denominations, estimates of absolute numbers were not an important part of the research. Instead the relationship between status and religiosity was central, and here the rejects caused little damage. Regardless of the number of sectlike and churchlike respondents, the fact remains that, for the rejects as well as the non-rejects, sectlike religiosity increases with decreasing status, and churchlike involvement increases with increasing status. In short, even if the rejects were added to the main sample, the key relationships would not be altered. This, at least, is the message of Table B–2.

Table B–3 turns to the majority of the rejects, those who failed to answer only one of the three status items. I mentioned earlier that these people may be accidental rather than principled rejects; that is, they may have simply erred rather than purposely skipped the item. If this were the case, there should be little difference between these rejects and the non-rejects. Apparently it is not the case, for the same differences as occurred earlier persist. Again the rejects are disproportionately old and female. Again they tend to recruit heavily from the working- and low-status ranks (here it is possible, with two status items available, to resort to the familiar status categories of upper, middle, working, and low). Again the working- and low-status rejects have higher rates of churchlike religiosity, but also again the rejects have much higher rates of sectlike religiosity too. It is true that some of the differences here are not as large as in the previous tables, indicating that some of the present rejects are accidental. Nevertheless, the relationships between status and religiosity are identical for rejects and non-rejects, indicating that the former's absence does not distort the central analysis.

Last, for Table B–3, it is possible to compute rough measures of status discrepancy, using the two status items that

TABLE B-3

Rejects on Only One Status Item Versus Non-Rejects on Age, Sex, Objective Status, Status Discrepancy, and Churchlike and Sectlike Religiosity

Measures for Comparison	Rejects on One Item		Non-Rejects	
Age				
Young	15%		18%	
Middle-aged	29		63	
Old	56		18	
N	(2365)		(8935)	
Sex				
Men	23%		40%	
Women	77		60	
N	(2285)		(8935)	
Objective Status				
Upper	10%		33%	
Middle	28		32	
Working	40		26	
Low	22		9	
N	(2388)		(8941)	
High Churchlike				
Upper	52%	(205)	66%	(2794)
Middle	55	(583)	57	(2918)
Working	48	(855)	41	(2288)
Low	39	(435)	30	(719)
High Sectlike				
Upper	33%	(230)	27%	(2886)
Middle	40	(617)	32	(2934)
Working	45	(836)	36	(2355)
Low	59	(445)	45	(723)
Status Discrepancy				
High	10%		3.5%	
Low	42		43	
Moderate	48		53.5	
N	(2388)		(8941)	

were answered. Note that 10 per cent of the rejects are highly discrepant but only 3.5 per cent of the non-rejects. This suggests one particular way in which the high number of rejects did disadvantage the analysis. The chapters on discrepancy

lost at least 233 cases of high discrepancy. They may have lost
many others whose discrepancy kept them from responding to
any status items at all. It is certainly reasonable to expect
a high status-reject rate for those with high discrepancy. One
of our premises throughout has been that discrepancy leads
to attempts to escape the issues of stratification altogether.

We have seen so far that the rejects are a distinctive lot with
inordinately high rates of old age, femininity, low status, high
discrepancy, and high religiosity, particularly of the sectlike
variety. Two other matters require consideration before closing.
First, to what extent do the rejects represent all denominations
equally? Second, which of the status items were most likely to
be neglected?

Table B–4 compares the total rejects and non-rejects on their
denominational distributions. One might predict that the more
sectlike lower-status denominations will be overrepresented
among the rejects. On the other hand, because of the inordinately high number of low-status rejects, one could also
predict that these will be most inhibited when they belong
to high-status denominations such as the Presbyterians and
the Congregationalists. Actually neither of these predictions is
supportable. Considering the relatively low-status Lutherans,
Disciples of Christ, and Baptists, none are overrepresented
among the rejects. Considering the Presbyterians and Congregationalists as relatively high-status, there is no consistent pattern between them. It is true that the Presbyterians have a
higher-than-average rate of rejects; it is also true that the

TABLE B–4

**Rejects Versus Non-Rejects in Their Denominational
Distributions**

Denomination	Rejects	Non-Rejects
Congregational	27%	36%
Presbyterian	31	22
Lutheran	19	21
Disciples of Christ	15	13
Baptist	8	8
N	(3175)	(8941)

Congregationalists reverse this finding with a lower-than-average rate. Apparently the Presbyterians and the Congregationalists differ among themselves. This may be due to different verbal instructions accompanying the questionnaire or to different receptions given the study by the local pastors. Unfortunately this is a secondary analysis for which this kind of data is not available.

Finally, it is useful to know which status items were most commonly rejected. Table B–5 shows the percentage of rejects that failed to respond to each of the three measures. Note that the sum of the percentages exceeds 100 because many people omitted more than one answer. Clearly education is the least intimidating of the three. Since only 8 per cent of the rejects failed to respond, one can assume that low education is still not a badge of inferiority despite the heralded schooling of the United States. This is especially the case for older persons

TABLE B–5

Percentages Rejecting Education, Income, and Occupation

Status Measure	Percentage Rejecting
Education	8%
Income	48
Occupation	74

since education has made its spurt only recently. By contrast, income is a more sensitive subject, and occupation took a toll of some 74 per cent. On the last point, however, there may be a latent contributing factor. The occupational categories stem from the classification of job titles provided by the Bureau of the Census. The categories themselves are frequently vague, and there may have been many respondents who despaired of placing themselves accurately. On the other hand, there was a residual category marked ''other'' which gave the respondent an opportunity to describe his own occupation. Less than 5 per cent availed themselves of that category despite what may have been their puzzlement. Even if one allows for the 5 per cent, and even if one supposes that some 20 per cent rejected the item because of difficulties of placement, occupation is still a sore spot that is at least as painful as income and considerably more so than education. This is an arresting commentary on the American stratification system. The data run contrary to those who assert that the money one makes is more important than how one makes it. Note, however, that income seems more important and education less important here than in the analysis of status discrepancy (pp. 169–70). Such are the vagaries and risks of generalization from any single table.

301.446
D 37

73993

Date Due

73993

FE 14 '68				
MR 29 '68				
AP 28 '69				